THE RATIONAL AS REASONABLE

LAW AND PHILOSOPHY LIBRARY

AULIS AARNIO
Department of Civil Law, University of Helsinki,

THE RATIONAL AS REASONABLE

A Treatise on Legal Justification

D. REIDEL PUBLISHING COMPANY
A MEMBER OF THE KLUWER ACADEMIC PUBLISHERS GROUP
DORDRECHT / BOSTON / LANCASTER / TOKYO

Library of Congress Cataloging-in-Publication Data

Aarnio, Aulis.
The rational as reasonable

(Law and philosophy library)
Bibliography: p.
Includes index.
1. Law—Interpretation and construction. 2. Law—Methodology. I. Title. II. Series.
K290.A25 1986 340'.11 86-24876
ISBN 90-277-2276-5

Published by D. Reidel Publishing Company,
P.O. Box 17, 3300 AA Dordrecht, Holland.

Sold and distributed in the U.S.A. and Canada
by Kluwer Academic Publishers,
101 Philip Drive, Assinippi Park, Norwell, MA 02061, U.S.A.

In all other countries, sold and distributed
by Kluwer Academic Publishers Group,
P.O. Box 322, 3300 AH Dordrecht, Holland.

Printed in The Netherlands

To my dear Aira

TABLE OF CONTENTS

EDITORIAL PREFACE

During the last half of the twentieth century, legal philosophy (or legal theory or jurisprudence) has grown significantly. It is no longer the domain of a few isolated scholars in law and philosophy. Hundreds of scholars from diverse fields attend international meetings on the subject. In some universities, large lecture courses of five hundred students or more study it.

The primary aim of the Law and Philosophy Library is to present some of the best original work on legal philosophy from both the Anglo-American and European traditions. Not only does it help make some of the best work available to an international audience, but it also encourages increased awareness of, and interaction between, the two major traditions. The primary focus is on full-length scholarly monographs, although some edited volumes of original papers are also included. The Library editors are assisted by an Editorial Advisory Board of internationally renowned scholars.

Legal philosophy should not be considered a narrowly circumscribed field. Insights into law and legal institutions can come from diverse disciplines on a wide range of topics. Among the relevant disciplines or perspectives contributing to legal philosophy, besides law and philosophy, are anthropology, economics, political science, and sociology. Among the topics included in legal philosophy are theories of law; the concepts of law and legal institutions; legal reasoning and adjudication; epistemological issues of evidence and procedure; law and justice, economics, politics, or morality; legal ethics; and theories of legal fields such as criminal law, contracts, and property.

ALAN MABE
MICHAEL BAYLES

FOREWORD

> To convince someone of the truth it is not adequate to establish the truth. One has to find the *way* from error to truth.
>
> LUDWIG WITTGENSTEIN

For a long time I have been troubled by the question of whether or not interpretations of legal norms can be right in some essential meaning of this word, and whether or not we are justified in speaking of knowledge in connection with legal interpretation. The certainty with which researchers can state their views on the legal order is not at all unimportant. Are these views mere guesses, or are they somewhat stronger beliefs? Can they be regarded in some way as probable, or would it be possible to assign them even the property of truth? An even more important matter is the consideration of in what sense those who apply the law, the judge and the administrative official, can "know the law". As citizens, we would not easily submit to the notion that our matters are decided in court without the decision-maker having a clear picture of what the legal order commands, prohibits or permits. We demand that our case be decided in a lawful manner.

It is equally clear that legal norms are not theoretical propositions which describe reality. A person who interprets the law does not therefore look for theoretical truth in it. The law is not merely a cognition. The adjudication is, from a societal point of view, power wielding. The role of the law is to give support to the decisions made in this power wielding procedure. It is precisely here that the problem lies. The law is not only good advice that the interpreter (e.g. the judge) can either follow or ignore on the basis of his own judgement. It is the authoritative basis for the decision.

In many cases the basis is, however, ambiguous, full of gaps or fuzzy in some other sense. Therefore the interpreter moves around like in a "circle": The law binds the interpreter → not every interpretation accords with the law → clarification of the contents of the law thus calls for a choice between different interpretation alternatives → the choice can only deal with valid law, and so on.

When written in this special way, the circle contains a veritable tangle of questions. What is validity, how does the law differ from a legal norm, what does it mean that something "accords with the law", and above all, how should we characterize interpretation of law? In legal theory, there have been many attempts to break out of this circle by giving a normative answer to these questions: in interpreting the law, one should proceed in such-and-such a fashion. For instance, one should follow the letter of the law, or its purpose etc. Normative answers have many weaknesses. One of these seems to be paramount. Real life has not followed a single normative doctrine of interpretation as such. These doctrines have not been adequate for guiding legal thought. Another approach which is not a conceptual consequence of a normative attitude, but which often has been connected with it, is concentrated on technical aspects. The theory of legal interpretation is regarded as a collection of technical instructions ("canons", patterns). Sometimes the problems of legal philosophy have even been reduced merely to logical (analytical) questions. The idea is to explicate the formal structure of the interpretation procedure. In its extreme, this way of thinking is inclined to claim that a legal philosophical problem has sense if and only if it can be put in a logical form.

In all these answers and in answers related to them we are faced with a number of "how" questions. The answers primarily bring up the methodological structure. In this, the questions of "why" are easily left aside; these questions, in turn, are often connected with the question of the institutional goal of the interpretation of law, of the idea of interpretation.

The more I have considered the matter, the more apparent it seems to me that in the theory of the interpretation of law one must combine the "how" and the "why". This, in turn, would seem to be tied to a matter that has rarely been mentioned in the theory of the interpretation of law. This matter has been called many things. In this connection, I shall call it the social responsibility of the interpreter of law.

It would be taking the easy way out to say that the consideration of responsibility is merely a fashionable trend in the discussion of the philosophy of law and society. Furthermore, the matter cannot be considered solely from the point of view of the moral outlook, even though the moral responsibility of a judge or a scholar has its effects on the interpretation of law. It is a question of something even more. The problem of responsibility is connected with global tendencies which at this moment are shaking all of humanity. In these tendencies, a central question is the re-evaluation of the position of man. Man finds himself in a crisis both in his relation with other human beings and in his relation with nature. Since the relations among men are regulated in an important way by legal norms, neither a science that studies legal norms nor the adjudication can become merely a bystander. This is so because, especially in Western legal cultures the belief in authorities has suffered greatly over the past decades. This phenomenon is true of both secular and religious authorities. There are many different social reasons for the change in attitudes. As examples we could give the explosive increase in scientific knowledge, the increase in the level of education and the general secularization resulting from the societal development. People simply do not believe anything at all. From the point of view of our theme, the details of and reasons for this development are of secondary importance. What is essential is that we remember what has replaced the belief in authorities: the requirement that opinions be justified. The requirement of factual justification has bypassed the belief in power itself.

However, the law as such is not always a sufficient reason, although the law, especially in the statutory law system, has a special role as the justificatory basis for legal interpretation. Very often the justification refers and has to refer to different types of substantial reasons, either goal reasons or rightness reasons. In practice this means, among other things, that the law has to be connected with values and evaluations. Shortly speaking: there is a combination between the law and morals. This very feature puts special preconditions for the modern theory of legal interpretation.

The problem of societal responsibility is, however, indirectly linked also to the very concept of democracy. In modern societies most people do not have any real influence on the wielding of power. They live in a democracy but without effective means to take part in decision-making. This can be called an alienation. A parallel phenomenon is the strengthening of the bureaucratic machinery. A great deal of the administration is in the hands of specialists. The network of the administrative rules is so complicated and it presupposes such a specialized knowledge that laymen have no possibilities to control the administrative activities. The same holds true as far as the adjudication is concerned. If the system of the administration and adjudication is closed so that the decision-makers have – from a formal point of view – a very authoritative position, the whole system becomes self-sufficient. It is "reflexive", i.e. the only one that controls the system is the system itself. In this situation one possibility to open the control and to make it public is to demand a proper justification for decisions. The reasoning behind the conclusion of the decision must be opened to public inspection. As an opposite to a closed and undemocratic system we can then speak of "an open society".

In order to meet these kinds of challenges the scholarly interpretation and the adjudication must have a theoretical understanding of itself. Here also lies one kernel of this treatise. The primary goal of the work has not been to give methodological instructions for the practical legal interpretation. More important has been to try to increase the consciousness of legal scholars, judges and lawyers in general. "Know Thyself" has been my guideline especially in those parts where the basic assumptions of legal thinking have been analysed.

For these reasons, an attempt has been made in many connections to make this study more philosophical than often is the case in the theory of legal interpretation. Emphasis of this feature is of great importance because of the well-known fact that also quite recently there has been a tendency to say that the value of philosophy to legal thought is slight or, at best, problematic. The proponents of this view say that interpretation is a technical matter calling for professional skill, while philosophy is good only for providing a general educational background. Such views are not only misleading but also very damaging. They are damaging specifically because of the societal aspects referred to above. Those who are not aware of their responsibility, those who blindly practice their profession of the interpretation of the law are a threat to the sound development of society. This threat cannot be overemphasized. It has been the besetting sin of these persons to find refuge in the strict letter of the law when the problem before them would have demanded a courageous and, in a positive sense, creative approach. G. H. von Wright describes the characteristics of those who disregard theory in his recently published collection of essays entitled *Humanismi elämänasenteena* (translated: Humanism as an attitude towards life; 1981) as follows: "among intellectuals, a new type of human is spreading more and more; a researcher in a specialist field who can be quite intelligent, but who has a Philistine distain of philosophy, art and everything else which remains outside of his narrow perspective." I would add that such a person completely lacks the capacity for development, since a prerequisite for development is an understanding of the self.

Everyone who truly and seriously is anxious for the fate of such a specialist field as legal science must be strongly opposed to such an anti-philosophical attitude. For this reason, I have self-consciously directed my study against the person described above – not so much in order to sway him, but in order to lessen the danger that he presents to culture.

It would be best to characterize this study as a synthesis of ideas which have gradually been formulated over the past ten years. The original idea for the synthesis was intended only for myself after I completed the manuscript for *Denkweisen der Rechtswissenschaft* (1979). Various comments formulated by my Finnish colleagues demanded, in my view, both a sharpening of the answer and a return to some questions that I had previously – in the beginning of the 1970's – left in the background. Another argument for a redirection of focus was the fact that e.g. in European legal theory, the theory of interpretation (justification) and also the above mentioned problem of societal responsibility have been receiving increasing attention. This treatise is my own contribution to that discussion.

In the present work, I have attempted to combine especially three points of view, i.e. the so-called new rhetoric, the linguistic philosophy of the later Wittgenstein and the rationalist approach represented by Jürgen Habermas. At different stages in my scholarly work, from around 1969 on, these points of view have received somewhat different weights. Generally speaking, however, it can be said that my interest in the later philosophy of Wittgenstein has clearly dominated over the other points of view, although the rationalist aspect has got an increasing importance especially as far as the theory of legal discourse is concerned. On the other hand, it is not my purpose to enter into a discussion on what Wittgenstein or Habermas "really meant". I shall leave such considerations for professional philosophers. My own goal is much more modest. I have tried to find profitable points of contact in Wittgenstein's linguistic philosophy as well as in the Habermasian way of thinking for the theory of legal interpretation. A certain "philosophy" or a theory cannot be applied as such to the legal context. In this very respect, for instance, the Wittgensteinian linguistic philosophy gives only certain general frameworks or "touching points" in one's search for an adequate theory of legal thinking.

It was on this foundation that a construction of ideas has been erected, containing the understanding of interpretation as the sum of language games, the emphasis of the connection between language and form of life, the interpretation of the concept of the audience with the help of the concept of the form of life, the examination of coherence and consensus theories as measuring sticks of interpretative propositions, moderate value-relativism, and an attempt at locating the rationalist features of interpretation. In fact it is in connection with the last feature that a basic trend in the present study is to be found.

It is well known that in different connections Chaim Perelman has examined the relation between the terms "rational" and "reasonable". Perelman has emphasized their difference as well as the fact that the interpretation of law is closer to the domain of reason. The matter, however, is not quite unproblematic and simple. On the contrary, it is my belief that the theory of the interpretation of law requires a precisely analyzed insight into the connection between these two concepts. This connection is also helpful in understanding that in addition to the rational features, value theory, especially the theory of justice is accorded a central position in legal interpretation. It is not possible to speak about right ("sound") interpretations without taking a position on the theory of values.

In my respects, it has been possible for my ideas to germinate and develop under happy auspices. This is true both of the spiritual and of the material working conditions. Over the past years, I have had the opportunity of discussions in various connections with researchers who have left their permanent mark on the development in these fields. Neglecting none, in connection with this study I would like to single out especially my close friend and collaborator for many years, Aleksander Peczenik as well as Robert Alexy, Neil MacCormick, Hannu Tapani Klami, Werner Krawietz, Ilkka Niiniluoto, Enrico Pattaro, Robert S. Summers, Juha Tolonen, Ota Weinberger, Jerzy Wróblewski and Enrique Zuleta Puceiro. The mark of their ideas, especially their justified criticism, can be seen in many places throughout the text. I remain, however, solely responsible for whether or not the criticism is understood correctly, as well as for the fact that despite well-meaning advice I have in many respects remained true to my original ideas even though these ideas may at times have been reformulated and new justification may have been presented.

Twice (in 1978 and 1982) I have had the extraordinary privilege to be invited to give a lecture in a seminar arranged monthly by Academician Professor G. H. von Wright at the University of Helsinki. These opportunities and several private discussions concerning my topics have been of special significance for the present work. They have given a philosophical insight and deepness, so I dare to think, to the problems at issue and – at the same time – increased my courage to publish this special version of work.

In August 1984 I gave a series of seminars at the University of Buenos Aires and single lectures at the Universities of Cordoba and Rosario in Argentina. I am indebted especially to professors Carlos Alchourrón, Eugenio Bulygin and Roberto J. Vernengo not only for the opportunity to give these seminars and lectures, but also for the valuable criticism I received in the discussions following my presentations.

Kangasala, January 1986 AULIS AARNIO

CHAPTER I

INTRODUCTION

1. THE POINT OF DEPARTURE

1.1. *The Routine Cases and the Hard Cases*

A police patrol stops a driver who has exceeded the speed limit. The driver is fined. The case is part of the normal routine of traffic control. In all its simplicity, it is at the same time an example of the application of a legal norm in an individual case. It is a routine decision like so many other cases of the application of the law in practical life, cases such as the withholding of taxes from a pay check, the determination of the size of a pension, the granting of a passport and so on.

There are two reasons why we call such decisions routine. First, these cases come up repeatedly. One could speak of mass decisions. From the point of view of our theme, however, the structure of these cases is more important than the number of times that they occur. The fact that must be determined, for example whether or not a car has been driven at a certain speed, is doubtless subject to the legal norm that is being applied. In other words, the decision-maker is aware of the details of both the legal norm that is to be applied and the fact which has occurred. The decision is literally the application of the law. In referring to such cases, Kaarle Makkonen has used the term "isomorphic decisions".[1] The relation between the norm and the fact is similar to that of an object and its reflection.

I do not wish to disparage routine decisions. On the contrary, they are part of everyday life. Without them, living together in society would simply be impossible. From the point of view of the theory of legal interpretation, however, routine decisions are rather lacking in interest. As a matter of fact, they do not exhibit at all the features that are generally regarded as characteristic of legal decision-making. Routine decisions are mechanical. They do not allow for discretion among alternatives.[2] For this reason, routine decisions present their own dangers from the point of view of theory. Their quantitative preponderance may lead to the false notion that all cases of the application of the law are the same as the observance of the letter of the law. This is not true.

It can be demonstrated with two opposing examples.

The supporters of a certain ecological movement handcuff themselves to bulldozers in order to prevent them from being used in the draining of a lake that is an internationally significant bird preserve. Legally, this fact can be interpreted in different ways. Some would determine it as mutiny which, according to Finnish law, carries a very severe penalty. Another would say that it is a case of violent resistance to an official performing his duties, since the demonstrators refused to open their handcuffs voluntarily. A third observer would say that it is a case of obstruction of an official performing his duties. A more liberal interpretation would be that the demonstrators were engaged in "malicious mischief". The demonstrators themselves interpret their activity as either self-defence or as acting under duress, both of which rule out punishment for their actions. Regardless of the actual view taken in valid criminal law, the possibility of different interpretations reveals an essential feature. It is not a question of the application of an unambiguous norm to a clear fact. More than one legal provision can be applied to the same activity. The legal typification of the event is itself a problem.[3]

The second example is taken from civil law. Chapter 17, Section 3 of the Finnish Decedent's Estate Act regulates that the transfer of the share that the heir has in the estate of the deceased must be done in writing. The text of the Act does not provide any greater detail on what is meant by "in writing". There are several possibilities: it may be a document, a signed document, a document signed at the same time by the parties to the transaction, a document that is signed and witnessed, and so on. It would be quite simple to list more than a dozen alternatives. In this connection, it makes no difference which alternative is regarded as the correct one.[4] For us it is enough to note that the text can be interpreted in different ways. The text refers to more than one distinctive combination.

In order to distinguish it from routine decisions, the above type of decision can be termed a decision of discretion.[5] A typical feature is that either more than one legal norm can be applied to the same set of facts, or the same legal norm permits more than one interpretation. If we use the letter *L* to denote the law text, and the letter *F* to denote the facts (or correspondingly, the essential elements), we can draw the depiction of two decisions of discretion as shown in Diagram 1.

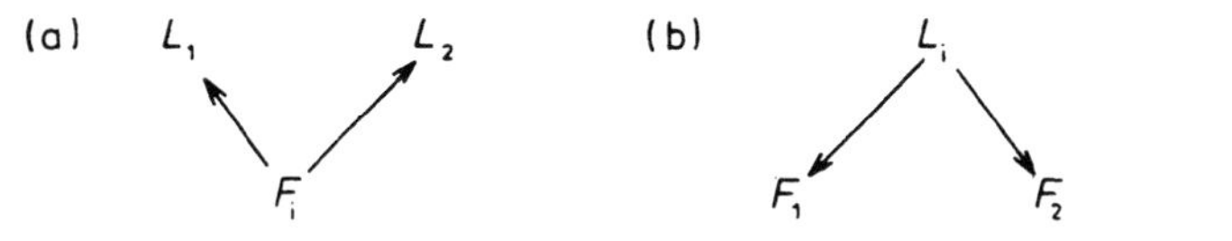

Example: The case of the ecologists

Example: Chapter 17, section 3 of the Decedent's Estate Act

Diagram 1

1.2. *The Dilemma of the Decision-Maker*

The decision-maker, no matter what his formal position may be, is assumed to act in accordance with the legal order. Literally, it is a case of applying the *law*. This places many types of pressure on the decision-maker. Let us imagine, for example, a judge who is faced with a case in which *X* demands compensation from *Y*. It is part of the duty of the judge to give a decision on every matter that comes before him. It has been said that a judge has the obligation to reach a decision.[6] On the other hand, the position of the judge also gives him the power to make decisions.[7] In accordance with the generally accepted ideology of law based on Western democracy, not every use of legal power is acceptable. We assume that the decision-maker does not reach decisions on impulse, at random or so that the pattern of decisions falters in unexpected ways. The decision-maker is expected to adhere as far as possible to legal certainty.

The concept of legal certainty occupies a key position in the following exposition. For this reason we should tentatively give a more detailed explication of this very concept. The expectation of legal certainty *sensu stricto* means that every citizen has the right to wait for legal protection, in other words, the court or another adjudicative organ has a legal obligation to give an answer when the citizen asks for legal protection.[8] This is a (legal) basic right of every citizen in society. However, the expectation of legal certainty can also be understood in a *broader sense* (*sensu largo*). It covers two substantial elements, i.e. the demands (a) that arbitrariness be avoided and (b) that the decision be "proper". Neither of these very elements alone fulfills the expectation of legal certainty. Decisions may be nonarbitrary and yet deliberately and systematically (substantially) wrong. In this case the decisions do not fulfill the criteria of just decision making. One could also easily imagine that a decision is just even though it came about at random. Both elements of legal certainty have been examined in depth by Otto Brusiin in his studies on discretion by the judge.[9]

Brusiin observes that traditionally in the Finnish-Swedish concept of law, avoidance of arbitrariness has been regarded as a basic norm for the judge. Already during the 1500's, such a norm was to be found in the so-called "Judge's Rules". Olaus Petri, the author of those rules, refers to an old saying when he says that arbitrariness or violence is not the law of the land. In this, arbitrariness is the same as randomness and the resulting unpredictability.

In other words, courts have to behave so that the citizens are able to plan their own activity on a rational basis. In many cases legal decisions are the only proper reason for the future planning. Rational planning, in turn, is a necessary condition for the continuity of society. It is one requirement for the cohesion of society. If there is no scope for predictability, society will dissolve into anarchy, which in turn is at odds a just and legal foundation.

Avoidance of arbitrariness has often been understood, *per definitionem*, as the genuine content of legal certainty. This is, however, only one side of the coin. Let us recall what people expect when they ask for legal certainty (*sensu largo*). They presuppose that the decisions are not only nonarbitrary but also substantially proper. It is not enough that the decisions are (very) predictable. For instance in a dictatorship the court practice may be nonarbitrary, i.e. the degree of the predictability may be really high and, at the same time, every single decision can heavily violate even the elementary demands of justice.

The substantial side of legal certainty consists of two elements. First of all, every genuine legal decision must be in accordance with the valid law. This is a minimum precondition for a *legal* decision. Even so, legal norms are not completely autonomous in respect of the other norms of society. They receive, at least in part, their proper content from moral and other social norms. In a way, law and other norms, e.g. moral norms work in an interlinking way. Let us take an example: in a certain sector, law demands that all individuals be treated on an equal basis. As such, the text of law does not provide an answer to the question, what is equality? The contents of the law is thus depending on interpretation and the interpretation presupposes, in turn, that also nonlegal norms concerning equality are taken into account. In this case legal certainty contains, in addition to avoiding the nonarbitrariness, two aspects: the decision must be lawful and it must be in accordance with morals and with other social norms than the law.

With this in mind, it may clarify matters to point out that the expectation of legal certainty referred to above is not an empirical concept in the sense that such an expectation either is or is not contingently in society. The expectation of legal certainty is a *cultural* phenomenon. It is deeply rooted, for instance, in the Scandinavian form of life. The above mentioned analysis of this concept can therefore be understood as a reconstruction of such elements that are "hidden" in the normal ways of Western thinking. This reconstruction makes explicit something that is only implicit in our linguistic practice. In this sense, the expectation of legal certainty is not mere conceptual, semantic or a stipulative suggestion for definition, either. It is a matter that is related to our language-games and thus to our ways of thought – and ultimately to our social existence. In this regard, the deep justification of legal certainty is of the same type as the justification of the concepts "rationality" and "rational discourse". – See pp. 195.

There are, however, also pressures that work from an entirely different direction. A judge faced with the obligation to reach legally adequate decisions and who must adhere as far as possible to legal certainty is, in an important sense, in a strange situation. The judge may often be *uncertain* as to how the case must be decided. By definition, this is always the case in decisions of discretion. The letter of the law does not provide an unambiguous answer. The situation may be depicted as shown in Diagram 2.

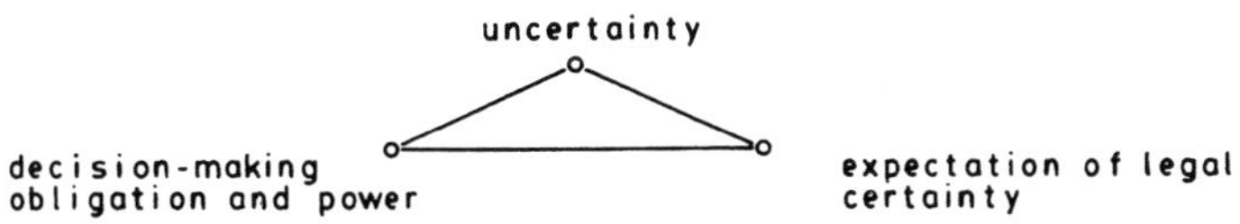

Diagram 2

1.3. *On the Responsibility to Justify the Decisions*

In such a situation the judge has the responsibility of seeing that the expectation of legal certainty is realized or at least sufficiently satisfied. The responsibililty may be met in different ways. One way of assuming the responsibility is to lean on one's authoritative position. The use of refined authority reduces the content of the decision to a position of less importance.[10] The decision-maker justifies his decision by referring to his authority. This idea may be stated as follows: the decision is the correct one, since it is the court's interpretation of valid law.

The ideology of authority has not been developed this far in, for example, Finland. Even so, hints of such development can be found in the way court decisions are justified today. It is possible that the facts of the case are set out in great detail, but the court's position on the legal question involved may be written out in a rather laconic fashion.[11] For example: "as it must be seen to have been demonstrated that . . ., X is sentenced in accordance with section . . . of the penal code. . . ." Justification for the choice of the alternative contents of the legal norm is not given even when it is taken as self-evident that the text of the law can be interpreted in many ways.

As was mentioned before, the decision-maker cannot trust anymore on a mere formal authority. In a modern society people do not ask only for authoritative decisions but they ask for reasons.[12] This also applies to the administration of justice. The responsibility of the judge has become more and more the responsibility for justifying decisions. The basis for the judge's use of power lies in the acceptability of his decisions, not in the formal position of power that he may have. The responsibility for giving justification in this sense is specifically a responsibility to maximize the public control of the decision. In this respect, the presentation of justification is always also a means of ensuring legal certainty on a rational basis in society.

The justification of decisions has special bearing in at least two dimensions. Since more than one interpretation is possible at the outset in decisions of discretion, the justification is important from the point of view of appeal. First of all, the appellant can expect to receive sufficient information on the legal arguments that were seen to affect the matter. Only if this is the case will he have the possibility of bringing forth factors that would weigh in the opposite direction. The authority to whom the appeal is directed, in turn, can effectively fulfill its supervisory role only if there is, so to speak, a dialogue between the decision-makers. This factor is of special significance in Finland, since the present limits on the possibility of appeal to the Supreme Court mean that only those decisions with precedental value may be brought before the Supreme Court.

On the other hand, it is specifically through the justification that the decision-maker himself, no matter if he is a judge or an administrative official, creates the credibility on which the confidence the citizens have in him rests. It would scarcely be wrong to state that e.g. the Finnish people have not doubted the laws themselves. On the other hand, at times the confidence that the citizens have in those applying the law has faltered.[13] This is due in part to the fact that it has not always been possible to know why the matter was decided in the way it was. It seems to be true to say that the decision can only be completely understandable on the basis of justificatory reasons and – what is most important – the result will be acceptable also by the losing party if the decision is based on proper grounds. Against this background it is not surprising that one central topic in the theory of legal thought is the theory of the justification of the legal interpretative decision. The matter cannot be examined solely from the point of view of the individual demanding legal certainty. In a larger sense, the attitude towards the justification of a decision reflects in general beliefs about law and the administration of justice.

1.4. *Legalism Contra Anti-Legalism*

One of the most important functions of legal norms is the creation of stability in legal relations. The prevailing constellations of interest and power are, so to speak, frozen in the legal norms. In the application of law, in turn, predictability is conducive towards maintaining the stability of legal relations. Real life, however, is such a many-faceted matter that it cannot be pictured in full in a network of rigid legal norms. Normally, legislation is constructed on the basis of typical examples.[14] These typical examples always leave open the question of the applicability of the typical situation to the individual situation involved. Furthermore, the typical examples do not cover all possible situations. For this reason, *flexibility* is demanded of the application of law. The decision-making activity must adapt the rigid rules to the cases which could not be anticipated. On the other hand, as was mentioned, the legal decision must remain predictable. In other words, there should be as little sway as possible in the trend of decisions. In this way a certain tension is created between stability and flexibility. To use Otto Brusiin's words, there is tension between the letter of the law and the demands that change life in society. In referring to the same matter, Aleksander Peczenik has dealt with the application of law as a compromise between predictability and justice.[15]

The legislative machinery is so slow-moving that it cannot react very quickly to problematic situations arising in society, unless these problems have particular weight in society. For this reason, the main responsibility for the fulfilment of flexibility rests on those applying the law. Much depends on the attitude assumed by the decision-making authorities; this will determine how the tension between stability and flexibility is released. A rigid legalistic tendency emphasizes the power and the authority of the legislator. The valid law in itself is sufficient justification. A more moderate view of the omnipotence of the letter of the law, in turn, forces the decision-maker to justify his decisions on a factual basis. If the law does not determine everything, support must be sought elsewhere. Also in this respect there is the danger of excess. If the significance of the law as the basis for decisions is watered down greatly or even denied, the road towards arbitrariness is opened.[16] It must be remembered that legislation – even with its defects – has been shown to be an effective and useful method of guiding behaviour on the general level. Other bases for legal justification do not have the same official nature or the same general applicability. The authority typical of law is lacking, for example, in evaluations or in considerations of goals, which themselves are important in legal decision-making activity. There is no universal method of controlling such a basis as the mere reasonableness of a decision. For this reason, it is in a statutory system not possible, without endangering stability, to make or justify a decision regardless of the law, with reference solely to reasonableness, justice or some goals which are seen to be valuable.[17] A legal decision in a statutory (or codified) legal system is always a balance between the letter of the law and other grounds having significance in the decision-making. It is a question of the application of the law, but in a way that can be accepted in general. We can also speak of the fitting together of a legalist and an anti-legalist attitude so that the expectations coming from different directions in the legal order can be satisfied as greatly as possible.

2. A SCIENTIFIC APPROACH TO THE CONTENTS OF LEGAL NORMS

2.1. *The Scholar and the Judge*

The authority applying the law has judicial power to give solutions and the obligation to reach a decision in every case that has been delivered up to the law. The official status of the authority obliges it to follow legal norms or run the risk of sanctions. On the other hand, the adjudication always deals with concrete cases. For instance, the judge does not interprete the law for the interpretation's sake only.

The scholar has neither power nor obligation to reach a decision nor does he have the same responsibility of office as does the judge. The scholar may forget the problem for a while, if a satisfactory solution cannot be given with the arguments available. In this very respect, the scholar is in the position of "a bystander". This means, that from the *organizational* point of view the judge works within the official system and the scholar examines legal norms from outside. The judge, but not the scholar, is a part of the power wielding machinery. Hence, only the judge has the internal systemic point of view.

All these differences are, however, only differences of the societal function of, on the one hand, the judge and, on the other hand, of the scholar. As far as the legal *interpretation* is concerned, the similarities are bigger than the differences. Let us begin with an example.

There are always two sides of a legal decision: the establishing of the facts of the case[18] and the clarification of the contents of the legal norm. The decision lies in regarding the facts as belonging to the category of events covered by the norm. The traditional way of legal thinking in statutory law countries emphasizes the difference between the fact-question and the norm-question. Hence, many authors have been tempted to think that the legal decision-making is a *steplike* phenomenon. The decision-maker has at first to establish the facts of the case. In this stage, the central task is the proof of the evidence. After the establishment of the facts the contents of the norm concerning this type of facts will be clarified. The last step is subsumption: facts and the norm will be "combined". The final solution is the conclusion of the subsumptive procedure. The traditional model is misleading at least in two senses.

(1) As a justificatory procedure the decision-making is not a simple steplike phenomenon but a succession of several intertwined thinking operations. The subsumption model can only describe the final stage, the so-called *ex post* rationalization of the decision. Later on, this has been called the internal justification. The most problematic part of the justification, i.e. the external justification cannot be illuminated by this elementary model.

(2) As far as our topic is concerned, the kernel of the judicial decision

is the intertwinement of the fact- and the norm-questions. It is impossible to establish the facts of the case without taking into account the norm information. This information shapes the framework for everything that we regard as a legal fact in the case. The norm information as a "preknowledge" of the judge is like a lens through which the decision-maker, necessarily, has to deliberate the proof of evidence.

The scholar does not deal with the concrete cases. The contents of the scholarly interpretation is the examination of typical cases. Legal dogmatics and the application of the law are, however, in a certain sense on the same side of the fence. Also the judge has to interprete the law. He clarifies the contents of legal norms in order to reach the norm information mentioned above. On the other hand, the special interest of the judge is concentrated on the question what norms bind *him* as an authoritative part of the functioning legal machinery. In this regard, the scholar is "a bystander". He is interested in the content of the valid law *in general*. However, in a certain sense both the judge and the scholar have a similar internal perspective.[19] Let us call it an epistemologically internal point of view. This can be elucidated comparing, on the one hand, the position of a legal scholar to the position of the (other) social scientists and, on the other hand, to that of the judge and other practical lawyers.

2.2. *Legal Dogmatics and Social Sciences*

The perspective of legal dogmatics is essentially different from that which is typical of social science. In the latter field it is normal to put the question "What happens?" or "What regularities can we find here?" The social scientists accept legal norms as given, and then take up for examination for example the problem of how a legal norm is followed. In other words, one of their primary goals is the clarification of regularities (invariances) in behavior. On the basis of these regularities, in turn, something may be deduced regarding the content of some norms: "People generally follow such-and-such a norm."

The social scientist thus normally represents a typically external point of view on the subject on inquiry. The matter has been compared to the study of chess purely by watching others play the game. A bystander may uncover many regularities, such as the fact that the piece called the pawn is generally moved one square at a time, except at the beginning of the game. It remains problematic, however, whether the bystander can learn how to play chess in this way if chess is the *first* game that he has ever observed. In the same way, we can ask whether the bystander, through his interest in regularities alone, can understand the moves of the game, for example why in situation *X* the pawn is moved in manner *Y*.

These questions reveal that a clearly external perspective on society and legal norms is not unproblematic. Peter Winch has analysed the problem in a very illustrative way.[20] His point of departure is that the goal of all science is the clarification of regularities in the subject. What is problematic is how we determine the criteria of similarity. Winch observes that ultimately everything depends on the rules and principles which have been agreed upon in the scientific community. These say what is and what is not required in the investigation of phenomena. According to Winch, the difference between (natural) sciences and social (human and moral) sciences lies in the different origin of the rules. In (natural) sciences, the subject is external to the researcher (in the proper sense of the word), and so the basis for the evaluation of similarity can be found in the scientific community itself. There are no such rules in nature. The rules are rules for approaching the truth, and they have been crystallised on different grounds in the community of researchers.

For the investigation of society, the situation is different. In social sciences, the rules defining similarity are to be found, at least in part, in the subject, in other words in society. If, for example, we must determine whether two forms of activity, praying and greeting, are the same or not, the activity in itself (the movements, the gestures) does not reveal differences or similarities. The basis for the deliberation must be sought in the society where these forms of behaviour take place. They are social usages defined by certain rules, and what is even more important, these rules *constitute* the behavior so that it is, for example, greeting. For this reason, we must know at least some (constitutive) rules before we can classify forms of behavior.

No matter what our opinion is of the details of Winch's thought, he draws our attention to an essential idea from the point of view of our theme.[21] Not even a social scientist can be a *pure* representative of the external point of view. To return to our example of the observer of the game of chess, and to borrow the words of Ludwig Wittgenstein, we can say that in order to learn the game the observer must already be able to play *another game*.[22] If nothing else, the observer must understand what it, in general, means to play a game. The same is true of the understanding of social activities. One must, so to speak, somehow be "inside" of them in order to participate in these activities in general, and it is not possible to even understand the activities unless one has at least at one time participated in them.

The position of the social scientist in regard to legal norms *differs* in a radical way from the position of the judge or of the administrative officials. Even if we were to require understanding of the social scientist in the way Winch does, it remains true that the scientist is studying how *other* subjects are bound by legal norms. The subject group may be lawyers, judges, administrative officials, Finnish citizens or a group of citizens manifesting special characteristics. On the other hand, the social scientists do not have to formulate their questions in the way a judge does: "What legal norms bind *me* as an authoritative decision-maker in this very case?". Approaching the content of the legal order from this point of view is alien to the social scientist.

Here also lies the decisive difference between a typical social science, e.g. sociology and legal dogmatics. The attitude of the last mentioned activity is basically centered to legal *norms* (rules) not to the regularities of behaviour of the citizens, judges etc. The difference in the viewpoint can also be expressed by saying that the research interest of legal dogmatics is normative in quite another sense than the interest of sociology. Ordinarily, legal dogmatics is, at least in the Nordic tradition, defined as the study of the content of legal rules (norms) and of the systemic order of those rules. The common terms referring to these tasks are "interpretation" and "systematization".

Evidently, the typical research interest of the social science does not extend to the understanding of systematic connections. The consideration of these connections belong to the *epistemologically internal point of view*. It is a point of view where knowledge of the internal structure of the system is dominant. It is often this type of knowledge which gives the lawyer the possibility of deciding a problematic legal question. In a sense, it is the core of legal thought, the framework through which the decision can be sought at least on a rough level. Understanding system connections sets those with a legal training apart from those who examine matters from outside of the system. In this sense, the approach of the social scientist is *epistemologically external*. Even in certain quite rare cases where sociology takes an interest in systemic connections, this interest is purely descriptive. For instance, the typical legal sociology does not systematize norms in the sense legal dogmatics does it.

Forgetting this fact has in my view seriously warped the discussion which has taken place on the possibility of "transforming" legal dogmatics into a science which would use the methods of social sciences.

The second main function of legal dogmatics, the clarification of the contents of legal norms, is an expression of the *interpretative interest*. Systematization has its own effect on interpretation, as will be demonstrated later on. At this stage, this connection may be left aside. Interpretation in legal dogmatics always has two facets. Something is said of the *meaning content* of a certain expression (or, correspondingly, a norm) and in addition, it is argued that a norm with that meaning content is *valid* in accordance with (e.g. Finnish) law. In other words, it is precisely the valid meaning content which the researcher is stating. Although the social scientist is, in the Winchian sense, "inside" of the (social) system, he does not have this kind of interest in interpretation. Hence, compared with the social scientist the legal dogmatician sees the problem from a *genuine internal* point of view.

This means that the way a legal dogmatician examines the legal order is similar to that of, for example, a judge. They are both specifically interested in the content of valid law. Even so, they do not deal with this content in exactly the same way. Legal dogmaticians do not answer the question of "What meaning content am I committed to?". They try to clarify what norms the decision-maker applying the law *should* observe or – from the point of view of the citizen's behavior – what norms should bind every (Finnish) citizen. However, epistemologically the legal dogmatician and the judge are in a similar position.

2.3. *Legal Dogmatics and Legal Practice*

This statement raises a number of problems. *Stig Strömholm* observes that a researcher must argue in support of his stand *as if* he were bound ("som om han vore underkastad") to the same sources and the same principles of interpretation as the judge.[23] Otherwise the position of the researcher would have no chance of success. In this way, Strömholm is able to bring up a really important point of view. He, however, leaves his observation partly dangling in the air. What does it actually mean when we say "as if"? My answer is as follows.

It is often said that legal dogmatics is a practical field, or a study that is near praxis. In a sense it also *is* praxis in itself, the societal praxis from which our belief about what is in accordance with the legal order receives its content. If, however, legal dogmatics and legal praxis are equated with each other, and we say that there is no difference between legal dogmatics and other activity which investigates the contents of the legal order, problems arise. These can be expressed briefly as follows: does legal dogmatics have an independent position from legal praxis? Pushed to the extreme, it is a question of whether or not there is any difference between purely practical activity and legal dogmatics.

2.3.1. *Normal legal practice.* I shall begin by examining the relation between legal dogmatics and normal legal practice. In this, I shall regard as normal praxis the activity of lawyers, the legal information given otherwise in society, the activity of legal advisers in industry and commerce, and so on. The administrative acts of nonlawyers also belong to this group; examples could be found in the administration of social welfare.

One way to seek the answer would be to analyze whether or not the *results*, the interpretative standpoints of legal dogmatics could in some relevant sense be "better" than the beliefs and standpoints arising from the normal praxis described above. If there is no such position of "preference", the position of legal dogmatics as a field of academic study becomes suspect. In that case, legal dogmatics truly is *mere* praxis. If the contrary is true, then we must investigate what the "better" nature of the result of legal dogmatics means, and how it can be achieved. It is apparent that such a relation of preference actually exists.

Legal dogmatics as a science differs significantly from practical judicial activity, for example from normal lawyer praxis. On a general level the difference can be characterized by saying that the study of legal dogmatics has been marked by a *scientific attitude*: it is this which *G. H. von Wright* regards as the core of a rational attitude towards all reality.[24] A scientific attitude is something different than the professional ability to carry out some technical tasks in praxis. From the point of view of legal dogmatics, it is a question of two things.

First of all, there is a reason to differentiate between *practical* and *theoretical* legal dogmatics.[25] In another connection I have characterized this difference by emphasizing the systematizing task of theoretical legal dogmatics. This form of legal dogmatics formulates theories which can very much be compared to that of other sciences. The formulation of theory, in turn, is foreign to practical day-to-day judicial activity. Thus, in his opinions, the lawyer does not *create* theory. In the best of cases he *applies* theory to the individual case in question in order to describe exactly the rights (and obligations) of his client.

A scientific attitude is also reflected, however, in the (normal) *practical* legal dogmatics. The content and significance of the attitude can be illustrated by repeating what *Ilkka Patoluoto* has written regarding some studies by *Max Weber* and *Paul Lazarsfeld*.[26] Patoluoto observes,

> The reason why the results may be held to be better or more reliable than the everyday view of the world is based on the fact that the results are not hypotheses, but hypotheses which have been verified through the use of scientific methods . . . The scientific method can be used to 'weed out' bias, and so in principle we can say that the results of the study are better or more certain that our everyday beliefs. The result of the study must be understood here as the result of the correct application of the scientific method . . . Propositions which are supported in a scientific study are more reliable than otherwise, since in scientific method the goal is systematization, consistency, controllability, intersubjectivity, objectivity, and the consideration of factors of uncertainty, exactness and pertinence.

In his observation Patoluoto is able to present much that deserves attention also in connection with interpretation in legal dogmatics. Also for legal dogmatics there are *methodological guarantees* for fulfilling the goals described above. When compared with normal praxis, legal dogmatical interpretation follows at least to some extent every demand in Ilkka Patoluoto's list of criteria. It is here that we find the *scientific attitude* of legal dogmatics. Thus, on the average the interpretations of legal dogmatics are *more controllable* than standpoints in normal praxis regarding the content of the legal order. It is for this reason that legal dogmatics produces "better" results than do practical everyday beliefs on what is right or wrong according to the legal order. The same applies to judicial practice. The judge receives information about the legal order in the same way as the legal dogmatician, and – what is important – the interpretation adopted by the judge is, in principle, reliable to the same degree and in the same sense as that put forward by the scholar.

2.3.2. *Judicial Practice.* In order to summarize our analysis, let us recall the comparison between the positions of the judge and the legal scholar. From a functionally internal point of view, only the judge has a power wielding competence, only he has the obligations to solve every case at issue and the judge, but not the scholar deals with the concrete cases. In the functioning legal machinery all this gives to the judge quite a different position than the scholar has. As was mentioned before, these differences are nothing else but *organizational* ones.

The organizational perspective is insignificant as far as the structure of legal justification is concerned. That is also true, however, that the judge does not intentionally systematize legal norm material. It is not according to his function to obtain a system of concepts which is more useful than what he had before. In this sense he is in the same position as the normal praxis mentioned before. The judge *utilizes* the systematization that legal dogmatics has carried out, but he does this specifically when interpreting legal norms.

On the other hand, the legal dogmatician is necessarily bound to the same epistemological preconditions as the judge. Following Strömholm's terminology, the legal dogmatician has to argue for his standpoints *as if* he were a judge. This means that the content of justification has to be of the same type in both cases. The legal dogmatician has to use the same sources of law as the judge and they should both refer to the same methodological rules. Only on these conditions can legal dogmatics provide relevant information concerning legal order to the legal community. If a researcher would use interpretation rules totally unknown to the community, or if his arguments would be incompatible with those accepted as valid in that community, his results would either be regarded as non-legal or be rejected as legal results.

Summing up, the fact that the legal dogmatician does not decide on concrete issues, the fact that the authority applying the law does not systematize legal norms, or the fact that – contrary to the position of the

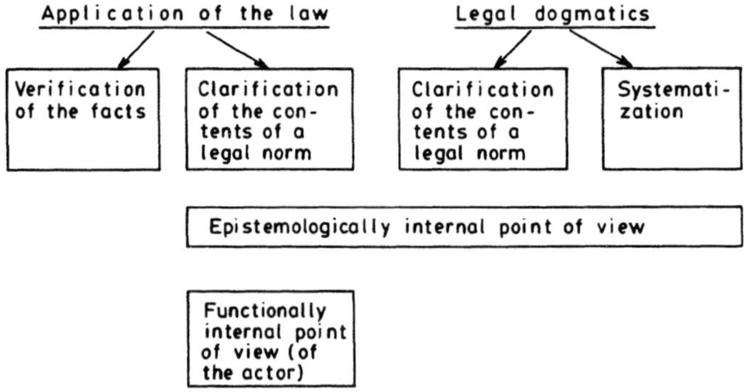

Diagram 3

scholar – only the judge (and administrative officials) use power in the system are irrelevant from the *epistemological* point of view. The structure of the justification (reasoning) is analogous in both cases, i.e. when clarifying the content of the legal order the legal dogmatician and the judge *think* in a similar way.

3. THE CONCEPT OF LEGAL DOGMATICS – A MORE PRECISE FORMULATION

For the concept of legal dogmatics, some of Thomas Kuhn's views on the scientific paradigm are interesting.[27] In its original form, Kuhn's paradigm concept proved to be susceptible to a great number of interpretations. He did not distinguish sufficiently between, for example, the model of a study and the exemplars of a study. Later on, Kuhn gave a more precise formulation of his set of concepts by adopting the concepts of the disciplinary matrix in a field of science. This matrix may be understood as a framework which unites scientists: a framework which explains the fact that the scientific communication between scientists is relatively free of problems, and that there is relatively high unanimity in the scientific community about the "professional opinions" given on studies. In other words, the matrix makes it possible to understand why some level of consensus may be reached on what science is in general, on what science is in the sense of some special field (for example on what legal science is) and even on what good science is.[28] Thus it is the matrix which makes legal dogmatics into legal dogmatics, as opposed to, for example, the social sciences or history. The matrix in legal dogmatics, in other words, helps us to be more exact than before on what the above-mentioned epistemologically internal point of view typical of legal dogmatics means.

Matrixes are composed of, for example, the following elements:

(a) a symbolic generalization,
(b) commitment on certain models that shape the subject,
(c) an agreement on common values and norms, and
(d) a commitment on common scientific models, in other words on paradigmatic problem solutions.

Matrixes, even more than Kuhn's original concept of paradigms, are typified by a conceptual looseness, a certain type of elasticity. There are, however, general forms to be found in every special field of science, and without them that field of science would not be possible. One could also say that the matrix is the basis of the science in question.

It is apparent that the more crystallized the matrix is in a certain field, the more sensitive it is to criticism. It is as if the matrix is used up after all the interesting applications have been presented. Correspondingly, a looser matrix can withstand considerably more criticism, it adapts itself to new circumstances, and with an appropriate reinterpretation of the matrix, it is easy to survive criticism that would otherwise undermine the matrix.

It also appears as if the concept of the matrix illustrates some features of legal dogmatics, even if there is no basis for direct application for Kuhn's terminology in legal dogmatics. One could imagine that the matrix of legal dogmatics is composed of at least four types of factors:[29]

(i) First of all, the matrix includes an assumption about the *subject* of interpretation in legal dogmatics, in other words about what is being interpreted. Furthermore, this means that there is commitment on certain assumptions of the philosophy of law on what a legal norm is, on what one should think about the origin and validity of law, and so on.

In general, at this stage it can be observed that the prevailing conception is colored by a certain type of legal positivism.[30] Legal norms are given by the sovereign in the society who wields power, and the validity of these legal norms has no need of entities outside of positive law. In this sense, the general background assumption of the Nordic legal dogmatics is against natural law.

(ii) Secondly, the matrix contains a number of agreements on the *sources of law*. The practitioner of legal dogmatics have (almost) the same conception of what sources one must refer to, and of what sources one should or may refer to. It is these agreements on the sources of law which most clearly show the type of concept of law and the administration of justice there is in a culture. A restricted list of legal sources is a sign of legalistic tendencies, while a very liberal attitude towards sources of law reveals various shades of anti-legalism.

(iii) The background matrix of legal dogmatics also implicates *certain methodological rules and principles*. They show roughly how legal sources should and can be used in the interpretation. As was noted previously, the methodological rules and principles adopted by the practitioner of legal dogmatics differ from those to be found in, for example, the social sciences. A radical change of the methodological principles signifies thus a considerable reform of the entire concept of legal dogmatics.

(iv) Finally, one can also include in the matrix of legal dogmatics the view that *values and evaluations* can be found in the interpretation in legal dogmatics. Here, the boundary with for example the social sciences is relatively clear. Jaakko Hintikka has observed that the proposition that social sciences are dependent on values can, for example, mean the following:

(1) value judgements and evaluative standpoints can be the subject of social sciences, and
(2) value judgements and evaluative standpoints are a necessary part of the subject of social sciences.[31]

A consequence of the latter view is that value concepts are an essential part of the methodological armament of social sciences, as the subject includes phenomena which cannot be defined, described or explained without recourse to value concepts. But, as Hintikka emphasizes, what was just said does not mean that social scientists would use value concepts in order to present their own evaluations. Presented in this way, social sciences thus investigate values, but it is not a study that presents evaluative standpoints.

The application of law and legal dogmatics (in the sense used here), on the other hand, uses value concepts as the *basis* of interpretation, or it refers in justification indirectly to evaluations. In other words, legal dogmatics is essentially evaluative in a more radical sense than the above.

With the help of these four elements, we can give a more precise formulation of the contents of the epistemologically internal point of view, when compared to the external point of view represented by the social sciences. Legal dogmatics always bind itself to at least some degree of legal positivistic background assumptions, it takes as its point of departure a certain list of sources of law, it depends on certain methodological rules and principles, and in certain situations it makes value-based choices.

The four elements described above at the same time organize the thematics of this study. The goal is the demonstration, on the basis of these fixed points, of the justificatory structure of the interpretative standpoints of legal dogmatics. Seen from another point of view, the question is of an explicit formulation of what is hidden in the concept of the epistemologically internal point of view.

4. THE ANGLE OF APPROACH AND THE BASIC PROBLEMS

As has been noted, legal dogmatics and legal decision-making are *forms of social praxis*. The subject of both is the legal norms that organize social reality. These legal norms can – depending on the classification – be of many types. A third praxis deserving of mention in this connection is legislation, in other words the praxis which creates legal norms (the framework for application). In a broad sense, we can speak of legal policy, i.e. the social planning which deals with legal norms.

Each of these three can be examined on the level of theory. In this way, we can get the theory of research, the theory of the application of law, and the theory of legislation (legal policy). The theory of research can e.g. be either the theory of legal dogmatics, the theory of social sciences (the sociology of law) or the theory of (legal) history or comparative law. The application of law, in turn, can be examined as the theory of the activity of the judge or of the administrative authority. All of these theoretical approaches are ways of engaging in legal theory,[32] which in turn is part of the philosophy of law and, on the highest level, part of general philosophy. Nothing of this type may be said of, for example, the theory of the application of law, as in its general form it does not have any connection with philosophy. There is no separate "philosophy of legal thought". Imagining that there is such a special philosophy is based on a hybrid developed by lawyers themselves.

The focus of this study is on the theory of legal dogmatics as shown in Diagram 4. As was observed above, research in legal dogmatics has some connections with the application of law, especially with the activity of the judge. To this extent, also it falls within the scope of the present study.

In respect of the goal of the theory of legal dogmatics, at least three types can be distinguished. Legal theory can attempt to describe heuristically interpretative activity, it can formulate sets of concepts in order to explain interpretative activity or it can examine the justification of interpretation. In another connection I have dealt with description, explanation and justification in greater detail, and so here it is reasonable to limit the description to brief remarks.[33]

If we attempt to *describe* (heuristically) interpretation in legal dogmatics, the subject often is the reaching of the decision itself. The question is: "How is the result of interpretation found? How does it all take place?" Considered in this way, the difference between the reaching of

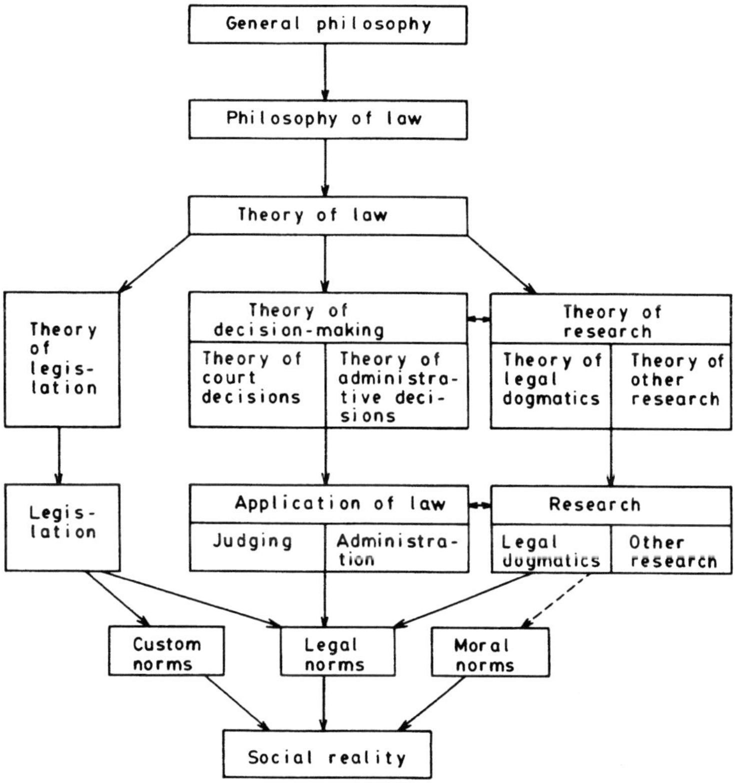

Diagram 4. The hierarchy of the subjects of research.

the decision and its justification is emphasized. From the point of view of the description, the reasoning can either be a true means of interpretation – a means which assists in the reaching of the decision – or a facade of justification which is reconstructed afterwards.[34]

It is difficult to give a heuristic description of interpretation. It is often a question of factors which cannot be observed, factors which belong to the psychological thought processes of the person applying the law. For example the proposition that a decision is (always) based on intuition, and that only afterwards is the decision rationalized with justification, is as a description a proposition concerning the psychology of the individual for which sufficient empirical evidence must be given before it can be accepted.[35] Due to the absence of an empirical foundation, the heuristic picture of legal reasoning, in the sense intended here, is often speculative. It is a theory where the reliability depends – if it depends on anything at all – more on the internal coherence of the theory than on evidence found outside of the theory.

An explanation attempts to render a state of affairs, an event or a process understandable. Explanation may be either causal or intentional. The former is based on the establishment of a relation between cause and effect, while the basis of explanation for the latter is the motives of the actor and the beliefs regarding reality. In both cases, the explanation remains the answer to the question of why something happened or why someone acted as he did. An example would be the explanation of the behavior of a judge.[36] In this, not only is the activity (for example, the muscular movements) described, but a framework for understanding the action is given. In the following, this explanatory aspect shall be left aside.

The theory of *justification* in legal dogmatics can be descriptive, analytic or normative. Descriptive justification theory attempts to describe actual justification activity. It shows what justification or type of justification was used, and describes the rules of inference applied. In this sense descriptive justification theory is always empirical. As the theory is empirical, its validity depends on the empirical data presented in support of the propositions. The data can, for example, be carefully analyzed court decisions. If the examination is not based on this type of data, the entire theory remains speculative.

A description of the justification in fact is valuable, for example in order to gain comparative data on how successfully praxis realizes certain justification ideals. Thus, the examination might be important in the correction of praxis. So far, no proper studies in this direction have been undertaken in Scandinavia.

Analytical justification theory is interested primarily in the concepts used in justification. A typical question would be, "What does analogy mean or what does a precedent mean?"

The examination that follows may be regarded primarily as part of what has been termed normative justification theory.[37] The question is not, however, about normativeness in the strong sense of the word. The intention is not to give norms or recommendations on how justification should or should not be used in interpretation. The study will not, therefore, attempt to define the concept of proper interpretation. It would be better to speak of a *weakly normative* approach. This concept calls for further clarification.

The point of departure in this study is the demand for legal certainty referred to previously. The prevailing Nordic legal ideology is built on the expectation that legal problems are not decided arbitrarily or at random, but through rational consideration ending in an acceptable conclusion. In this way, rationality and acceptability are the cornerstones of the actual ideology of legal certainty. They are, as was noticed before, essential parts of the actual legal culture in societies like e.g. the Nordic ones.

On this basis the functions of a theoretical study include the clarification of *what is required of justification in legal dogmatics for it to fulfill the conditions of rationality and acceptability*. It cannot be only a question of an empirical proposition of how justification takes place in practice. Instead, we should speak of a "technical norm": if you intend to fulfill the expectation of legal certainty, you should act in a certain manner. The most important demand placed on such a technical norm is adequacy.[38] The norm must be relevant from the point of view of praxis in legal dogmatics, because otherwise there will be a gap between theory and praxis. From the point of view of praxis, an inadequate theory is "theory for the sake of theory".

On the other hand, the study in not solely normative even in this weak sense. It is combined with analytical elements, i.e. specifically with questions that were mentioned above as examples. In summary, therefore, one may classify this study as an analytical-normative one, as long as one remembers the relatively weak significance of the concept of normativeness.[39]

Even when limited in this way, the theory of justification includes problematics which are classical in the theory of law. A basic category is formed by ontological problems. We must take a position on what one assumes to be in existence for an interpretation in legal dogmatics to be at all possible. Depending on the ontology adopted, or at least partly in connection with this, we arrive at a position on the question of the nature and possibility of knowledge in legal dogmatics. It is customary to call this the epistemological question. In addition to this, it is also important how one can obtain information in legal dogmatics. The methods of obtaining information "naturally" come to the fore. Hence, the ontological, epistemological and methodological questions have of necessity internal connections with each other. These connections must be taken seriously also as far as legal dogmatics is concerned.[40]

As was observed in the foregoing, the philosophy of law is also concerned with the question of truth. There is nothing surprising about this interest if we remember how important a role the demands for legal certainty play in our society. We demand that our legal conflicts be resolved in a proper manner or, when considered in a slightly different way, that the interpretations are in accordance with the law. But if one considers the matter in this way, it is only natural to pose the question as follows: "Do we demand that the interpretation be true?" If so strong a demand is not placed on interpretation, then we are left with the question of what a "proper" interpretation actually means.

The ontology of law, the nature of knowledge in legal dogmatics, the methodology of legal dogmatics and the concept and criteria of truth thus demonstrate the areas of concern of the theory of justification. At the same time, they show roughly the internal structure of this study. The goal is to find an answer to the following basic questions:

(1) Can the property of *true/false* be attributed to an interpretation in legal dogmatics? If this is possible, what are the criteria of truth/falsehood?	(1′) What *methods* does legal dogmatics have in establishing truth/falsehood?
(2) If it is problematic or (even) impossible to use the concepts of truth/falsehood, is there some *analogous* concept to truth/falsehood in legal dogmatics?	(2′) Through what *methods* is it possible to establish such "truth"?

(3) Is it possible to *know* something about the content of the legal order in cases of discretion?

(3′) What *method* is to be used in obtaining knowledge?

(4) If it is problematic or (even) impossible to speak of knowledge in connection with legal dogmatics, is it possible to use an *analogous* concept?

(4′) Is there some *method* of deduction for formulating such "knowledge"?

(5) Can one argue that the basis for interpretation in legal dogmatics is (internally) proper?

(5′) If it is a proper basis, what are the *criteria* of an internally proper justification?

Later on, we shall observe that in connection with questions (1) and (2) the latter alternative is chosen. Instead of truth, we must speak of the rational acceptability of interpretations. One can also scarcely give an affirmative answer to question (3) if we require that we can speak of knowledge only in connection with a true belief. In other words, we must replace question (3) with question (4). This entails a concession, an admission that in legal dogmatics one can only present more or less justified positions (beliefs) regarding the content of legal norms. Perhaps we can speak of different levels of certainty of a belief. The last question is connected in a way with all of the previous ones. Its significance lies in the fact it gathers together the thematics. Actually, it could be rewritten as follows: "Is a certain decision the (only) correct one from the point of view of its contents?" As is well-known, the doctrine of the one right answer has played a central role in the legal thought of different periods. The present study is, to a large extent a criticism of such doctrines.[41]

CHAPTER II

THE ONTOLOGY OF LAW

1. GENERAL REMARKS

The sector of philosophy termed ontology examines the basic elements and the structure of the world. One basic point of contention in ontology is between nominalism and (conceptual) realism. With reference to Occam's razor (the prohibition against assuming unnecessary entities) the nominalists accept only individual entities in their ontology. D. M. Armstrong describes the nominalist point of view as follows: "The fundamental contention of Nominalism is that all things that exist are only particulars."[1] Only these particulars are really existing. Conceptual realists would grant an independent existence also (yet not necessarily only) to concepts on a higher level, for example to the roundness of a thing. These exist regardless of a conscious subject. Conceptualism has represented a mediating position between these two: general concepts exist in the mind of the conscious subject. The point of departure for the conventionalist is that ontological commitments depend on the language used. This, in turn, is open to agreement, which means that also ontology is a matter of convention.[2]

An interesting touchstone for different positions in ontology is the concept of the *norm*. If we adopt a strictly nominalist position, there is no such thing as a norm as an ideal entity. There are only individuals who behave in a certain way. According to another way of thinking, norms have an ideal existence in the same way that general concepts exist in the ontology of conceptual realists.

To begin with, there is reason to note the following background observations. One of Ludwig Wittgenstein's basic ideas, if I understand him correctly, appears to have been that there is no sense in speaking of existence *in itself*. Such a manner of speaking is not part of any working language game. As Henry Le Roy Finch observes, Wittgenstein did not want to argue that what we cannot say, cannot exist either. He wanted to express something that is even more interesting: "existence cannot be put into words, and, therefore, that 'what merely exists cannot be put into words.' The world that we confront, in so far as it merely exists, is unsayable."[3] Speaking of existence makes sense only within the framework of a language game, and language games, as we shall note later on, are connected with forms of life. In other words, the significance that we attach to an expression is, so to speak, obtained *through* the form of life. For this reason there is no need to bind oneself to something that is mere "pure existence". Such a way of using language simply cannot be found in any practical situation in everyday language.

When we thus attempt to construct an ontology of interpretation in legal dogmatics, we must construct it within the framework of a working legal language. Only within such a framework does it make any sense. "When we speak, we necessarily speak of the common world, in the common language", observes Henry Le Roy Finch.[4] It simply is impossible to construct language which has no foundation in our common world. Thus, to take an example, speaking of the existence of a legal norm receives its meaning content in the language games which we play in legal contexts. Furthermore, if we think in this way, we are easily rid at the same time of the difficulty in understanding the existence of a norm, and we are also rid of unwarranted metaphysics.

Let us bring the matter to a concrete level with an example. A driver, *A*, drives through a red light. We would say that he broke norm *N*. What does this mean? The answer would apparently be that *A* acted contrary to what is decreed in valid law (e.g. in Finland). In other words, norm *N*, which *A* broke, belongs to the legal order of Finland. What does it mean that a norm belongs to a legal order? It means, for example, that the members of Parliament and the President have acted in a certain way, and as a result of this activity a law text expressing norm *N* was passed, or that the legal community has accepted the norm as a guideline for the behavior. We could also go considerably further with our example. This is, however, not essential. At this stage it is important to note only that we understand discussion about the violation of a norm *without* an additional question, "Is the norm *N* existent as a special entity?". This kind of question does not simply fit into that language game. There is no sense for *this* question within *this* game.

Even so, some matters must be scattered as the foundation of our legal language games. What, then, would be the ontological minimum commitments necessarily required by e.g. the interpretation in legal dogmatics?

2. THE ONTOLOGY OF INTERPRETATION IN LEGAL DOGMATICS

The nominalists would appear to be correct in that what amounts to a basic category of existence is composed of individual entities.[5] In this category we can include inanimate natural entities (physical objects) as well as human individuals. In the field of law it is the human individuals who form an important ontological category. They form a category of legal subjects; human individuals create, apply and follow the law.

To such an ontology of entities we could add the properties of entities, for example the property of hardness or the physical properties of human individuals. The structure of our language and the form of life behind it are such that we can freely speak of matters belonging to either category. We can speak in a natural way of, for example, hard objects. Ilkka Niiniluoto terms this types of ontological attitude "moderate realism".[6]

Entities may stand in a certain relation with each other. Thus, individual *A* may have done work for *B* in accordance with *B*'s request; a labor relation is created. *A* has the property of employee and *B* has the property of employer. The relation between them is, at the same time, an example of a social relation. Some social relations are legal relations. In the way, some properties may be legal properties. But what is it that turns a social relation into a legal one? The answer is simple. It is legal norms which imbue a social relation with this quality. This naturally brings up the question of whether or not legal norms should also be accepted as part of the ontology of legal dogmatics. Furthermore, what does the existence of a norm mean in this? The question is important, because norms do not seem to have any existence at all in a nominalist sense of the concept. If, however, a norm is accepted as a category in ontology, then it naturally has "existence" in some relevant sense of this concept. Before I outline my own suggestion for an answer, I shall briefly describe how Hannu Tapani Klami approaches the problem.

According to Klami, a legal norm can only be understood as an ontological connection between a rule and behaviour. "Thus, my view of the essence of law is dualistic. We cannot think of law that would not refer to behaviour; human behaviour must relevantly be examined in the light of legal norms: the behaviour itself is quite apparently something different from legal norms", Klami writes.[7] Thus, norms refer to behaviour, and behaviour receives content from norms. Klami's view is problematic. An adequate interpretation, however, seems to be that there must be a necessary relation between norms and behaviour. The concept of a meaning content acts as a sort of mediating element. The norm as a rule receives expression in a norm sentence (a norm formulation). Vice versa: a norm is the meaning content of a norm formulation. On the other hand, behaviour must always be interpreted. Societal behaviour is not only a "brute" empirical fact, it is also guided by norms and therefore the behaviour gets its sense by means of norms. The meaning attached to behaviour is the same as the norm that "explains" behaviour. In this sense, then, the meaning content connects the norm and the behaviour.

In Klami's ontology, therefore, a legal norm is expressed in two ways, in language and in behaviour. This has meant that Klami has had to expand the collection of ontological entities to also include meanings. On the other hand, he does not expressly state what the concept of behaviour contains, and what the precise ontological status of behaviour is. Does it belong to, for example, the "entity-property category"? This cannot be the case, because behaviour as a physical entity is mere muscular movements. These are, however, not the same as behaviour. From the ontological point of view, behaviour is "more" than a physical entity. It is a conceptual matter that is connected to several kinds of "preknowledge", which is – on the other hand – based e.g. on the rules valid at that area. Behaviour cannot thus have a basic ontological status.

Let us leave these problems aside, even though they should not be overlooked in the ontological point of view. Instead of that, we can limit ourselves to examining the status of meanings as an ontological category. Klami does not deal with this, as I have just observed. My own approach is in general as follows.

Karl Popper has distinguished between three ontological categories, worlds 1–3. The first includes physical objects, the second consciousness and ideas, and the third different products of the human mind. World 3, in other words, consists of, for example, propositions, numbers, theories, institutions etc. According to Popper, World 3 is relatively independent. It cannot exist without the other ontological categories.[8]

Through his own activity, man creates the entities in World 3. They are "products of the human mind". On the other hand, they are independent of individuals as e.g. the language is independent of native speakers. These products have simply been "separated" from their producers. To use Ilkka Niiniluoto's phrase, they have become the common property of humanity. It is also essential that as abstractions they can, at least in principle, be reproduced. In this sense they do not exist merely as mental matters in human minds.[9]

In several respects, Popper's well-known ideas are attractive and they seem to solve many of the burning ontological problems. As regards legal reasoning especially World 3 is of great interest. It involves problems at least in two directions.

First, what does the existence of the entities of World 3 conceptually mean? If we consider, for example real numbers, in Popper's solution they are not the same thing as ideas in the human mind, nor can they be assimilated with mathematical signs. A number is not the same thing as a set of figures on a piece of paper. But if we suggest that ontologically speaking, numbers are human constructs, and that as abstractions they have a relative independence, we have said nothing about what existence means, when compared to the existence of entities contained in Worlds 1 and 2. The semantics of the word "existence" is thus quite different depending on what World is at issue. Naturally, in the philosophical language we can accept a convention according to which the elements of World 3 also "exist". Yet, this is only a convention and thus only a definitional solution to the basic ontological problems. Popper's solution seems therefore to be not only simple but even slightly too simple in order to get a satisfactory answer for legal purposes.

Despite these doubts, Popper's ideas offer an important anchor for further analysis. According to a well-known view point in deontic logic, a norm proposition is true if and only if the corresponding norm exists. This is also definitely the core of Kaarle Makkonen's norm theory.[10] In order to understand this kind of conception and – at the same time – to interprete Popper's ontological point of view let us take World 3 as the starting point.

A norm can be understood, as shall be demonstrated later on, as *a thought (i.e. meaning) content expressed through language*. This thought content is not identical with thoughts in the human mind. We cannot say that a certain mental state *is* a norm. It is another matter that human mental mechanisms, thought contents, which appear as norms, direct human action. In this respect norms have an analogous role to motives or causal beliefs. Also, a norm is not the same thing as the text of an Act, or a precedent, or a decision of a Ministry, and so on. A text is a category on a linguistic level, which has physical existence only in the sense of a row of figures. But this line of figures is not a norm; just as a mathematical line of figures is not a number.

The meaning content of linguistic expressions, referred to above, offers us a foundation for developing the further thematics. If meanings and language in general are entities of World 3 the question is, *in what sense* do meanings exist. Let us try to approach the matter on the basis of Wittgenstein's philosophy of language. Then it is understandable what it does mean to say that "x exists in World 3".

An expression does not have a meaning in itself. If I should suddenly say "cat", my fellow men would at the very least regard me strangely. The situation would be different if, while driving a car, I would observe to my passenger, "cat". In that connection the expression could have the significance of, "I almost drove over an animal." Following Wittgenstein, the matter could be stated as follows: a word receives content only in connection with a language game. A language game, in turn, is a dimension of a so-called form of life. For this reason the language game receives its content from the form of life. Furthermore, the form of life is a sum of acts. Thus we find a construct where language in itself is activity, and this activity receives its content on the basis of activity that is even more primitive. When primitive acts belonging to a form of life have enough in common, a common foundation for understanding is evolved. Those sharing a form of life may communicate with one another.

With reference to these views, we can argue that it is misleading to speak of the independent existence of language and meanings. It easily gives rise to the impression that words have a meaning which, so to speak, "follows" words regardless of how they are actually used. On the contrary, in a Wittgensteinian vein, the meaning is the use of the word in language.

Let us return to the existence of the norm and take a simple example which has been derived from a much more famous example used by Wittgenstein. *A* and *B* are playing some type of construction game. When *A* points to a certain type of component, *B* brings it to him. Here it is a question of a very simple use of language. It is composed of commands and responses to commands. The language does not contain words in the sense that we know words, but even so, we could say that *A* gives commands to *B*. We would scarcely say, however, that *A*'s commands exist in some ideal sense. The command is the fact that there is a certain kind of relation of understanding regarding action between *A* and *B*. These persons know their game of commands when they understand each other. The command "exists" in the actual use of that simple language. It is quite another matter how *A* can have the power position he has in the game. This can also be put in a slightly different way: under what conditions is *B* bound to *A*'s commands? Yet, this question is not a question of existence of norms but a question of validity.

The situation is basically not different if we make the game more complex. Let us assume that *A* tells *B*, "According to Finnish law, a car may not enter an intersection when the red light is on." *B* understands what *A* says and is able to act in accordance with it. *A* expresses an idea, where *A* attempts to get another person (*B*) to orient himself in a certain way. The fact that *B* actually acts as the norm requires him to act is simply part of the nature of this game. In saying this, the purpose is not to give an empirical proposition on the psychological mechanism governing how *B* acts. It is only a question of the description of the structure of the language game. In this game, the existence of a norm *means* the same as the existence of language in general.

It is clear that what has just been said about norms is true also of similar matters, e.g. of general legal concepts involved in the norms or of legal institutions constituted by the legal norms. The existence of them is of the same type as the existence of language. Yet, even if we were to accept Popper's World 3 and even if we interprete the existence of the entities of this World in the above mentioned way, it is not self-evident in what sense a norm exists *legally*. It would seem to be natural to answer that a norm "legally exists" when it belongs to the legal order. But in saying this, nothing new has been brought into the ontology. The proposition that a norm *N* is a part of a legal order *O* can simply be written as follows: "Norm *N* is *valid* in the legal order *O*". Hence, the existence of a norm turns to be a question of validity. This is conducive towards bringing about a problem of how we should react to the problem of validity. What does it mean to say that norm *N* is valid (e.g.) in the Finnish legal order? Which kind of ontological commitments must be accepted as necessary in answering this question?

The same holds true as far as (e.g.) the "existence" of Roman law is concerned. The problem lies in our linguistic usage which comprises such expressions as "Roman law exists as a historical fact." From the point of view of our time Roman law is not valid any more although some norms of Roman origin are included in the modern legal orders, including the Finnish legal order. Roman law was valid only during a certain time period and in a certain geographical territory. Viewing matters from the legal standpoint this validity is a phenomenon that can be controlled in several manners. The problem of the legal existence of Roman norms is thus exactly the same as the above mentioned question concerning the existence of a Finnish legal norm at the present moment. Hence, the concept of validity has a key role in the ontology quite independent of the legal order under consideration.

3. THE VALIDITY OF A LEGAL NORM

In speaking of the law in force (valid law), standard language is tautological in a rather interesting way. Thus, for example, Webster's dictionary defines "valid" as "having (legal) force". "This rule is valid" is the same as "This rule is in force". The definition does not take us very far. When we use language in this way, the problem is the concept of validity in itself. Taking this into consideration, there would seem to be reason to differentiate between three different meanings of the concept of validity. The distinction is important also because it reflects three conceptions in legal theory.

3.1. *Wróblewski's Three Approaches*

Jerzy Wróblewski has denoted these conceptions with the terms *systemic validity*, *factual validity* and *axiological validity*.[11] In the following, this same distinction will be denoted by the terms systemic validity, efficacy and acceptability of legal norms. "Being in force" can thus mean any one of these three. With certain reservations, which will be dealt with later, the different approaches can also be combined.

Presented schematically, the different meanings of the concept can be shown as in Diagram 5.

The law in force (Valid law)		
Systemic validity (Validity)	Factual validity (Efficacy)	Axiological validity (Acceptability)

Diagram 5

3.2. *Systemic Validity*

Systemic validity of a legal norm is often formal. According to Wróblewski, a norm is valid in the systemic sense if it fulfills the following four conditions: (a) it has been accepted and promulgated in due course, (b) the norm has not been repealed, (c) it is not in contradiction with another norm in force in the same system, and (d) if there is a contradiction, there is an accepted rule for resolving the conflict.[12] There are, however, a lot of problems connected with the concept of systemic validity.

First of all, two different meaning contents of the concept "formal validity" must clearly be kept separate from each other. Let us call them *internal* and *external* validity of legal order. The first one of these concepts refers to the validity "inside" the system, whereas the external validity tells something about the validity of the system itself.

In the lawyer's everyday practice only the question of internal validity is normally posed – if the systemic validity in such a context generally is at issue. This question may be written as follows:

'Does the norm N_i belong to the (Finnish) legal order?" In the answer to this question one may refer to a unity of legal norms. N_i belongs to that unity if it has been given in a proper order, i.e. on the basis of a higher norm. The highest of these norms is the Constitution. This is internal validity *sensu stricto*. For instance, for an advocate it is enough to know if the norm is valid in this strict sense of the term.

Hans Kelsen's view of the bindingness of law reflects in an important way the internal validity. According to Kelsen, law is the totality formed by the norms given by legal organs. On the other hand, legal norms are always part of the world of "Ought" ("Sollen"). Nothing that belongs to the world of "Is" ("Sein"), i.e. of the real world can form the basis for the force of a legal norm. A legal norm always receives its validity from another legal norm.[13]

In this sense the legal order always is a delegated unity. A certain norm is (formally) valid if it is given on the basis of the authority created by a superior norm. It is this that is meant when referring to a so-called hierarchy of norms, a hierarchy ending at the Constitution.

However, the problem is left why one has to obey the Constitution. How is it possible to "lock" the delegated unity of legally valid norms? In Kelsen's theory the ultimate basis for internal validity is the fundamental norm (Grundnorm) at the top of the norm pyramid.[14] In its simplest form the fundamental norm can be written as follows: "The Constitution must be followed". Let us denote this type of fundamental norm – according to Aleksander Peczenik – with the sign G_1.[15] This norm gives to the norm hierarchy the internal validity *sensu largo*.

In accordance with Kelsenian tradition, it is emphasized that the fundamental norm does not have content in the sense that the provisions of the Constitution can be substantially based on the fundamental norm. It is not a given norm, either. The fundamental norm has not been selected from several alternative norms by a certain sovereign. However, Kelsen has not given an unambiguous clarification for this very concept. He has called the grundnorm an assumed norm as well as transcendental precondition of the validity of the Constitution. The grundnorm has also been defined (by Kelsen) as a hypothesis or simply as a fiction.[16] In the literature concerning the Kelsenian theory Alchourrón and Bulygin have suggested that the grundnorm can be understood as a conceptual rule which defines the use of the concept of valid law.[17]

All these answers are, in their own way, satisfactory, if we seek an answer to the question: "what does it mean to speak of internal formal validity?" For instance, the notion of conceptual rule as well as the speech about an assumed basic norm is quite understandable if we deal with the validity only from the (internal) systemic point of view. In other words, it is well-founded to "lock" the system of norms by means of an assumed norm.

In certain (empirically rare) situations *external systemic validity* of the norm system can also be questioned. The problem is then of the following form: "Why is the norm system S legally valid?".

Let us take an example. More than one system of norms (S_1 and S_2) can be supported by a proper fundamental norm (S_1/G_1 and S_2/G_2). This is the case e.g. when one has to compare the system of norms established by a Mafia with the legal order of the State. Why is just the last mentioned but not the system of a Mafia legally valid? Here the question is not of the validity of a certain individual norm within the system but the validity of the system as such.

Hans Kelsen has tried to solve this special dilemma by claiming that a fundamental norm gives legal force only to that system of norms which at least by and large ("in Grossen und Ganzen") is *effective*.[18] Of the many possible systems of norms, the fundamental norm gives force only to the most effective one. Thus, a matter belonging to the world of "Sein" – efficacy – becomes a necessary condition of the bindingness of a system of legal norms. From this point of view, systemic validity means that the legal norm is part of an effective hierarchy of legal norms, culminating in a fundamental norm. It is interesting to note that

Kelsen requires efficacy also of each *individual* norm.[19] In this way, cases of desuetude are left outside of his concept of validity. In other words, norm N is valid if it is part of a (by and large) effective system of norms and if it in itself is effective.[20]

The Constitution is the superior given set of norms. Thus the Constitution does not receive its formal validity from any superior norm given by certain authorities, as was the case in the previous examples. Kelsen also emphatically denounces the possibility that the validity of a norm could be determined axiologically. Binding law does not require morality for its validity. For this reason, Natural Law cannot be law in the proper sense of the word. It belongs to the category of morality.

In order to elucidate this, let us accept the following distinction: external systemic validity in the *formal* sense and external systemic validity in the *material* sense. From the purely formal point of view the kernel is how to justify the fundamental norm itself by means of "external" criteria. Dealing with this type of formal validity one comes to the problem of the legitimacy of the norm system as a *legal* order. The interest to justify (legitimate) the fundamental norm is clearly of a social nature. The Constitution and the fundamental norm supporting it (norm system as a norm hierarchy) must also be legitimated from a social point of view and, what is important, legitimated as a legal order. For instance, a merely assumed fundamental norm is not enough for that purpose. We are in a circle: the Constitution must be obeyed because it is assumed that the Constitution must be obeyed.

Let us begin, following Aleksander Peczenik[21] – with two special norms:

G_1 The Constitution must be (legally) obeyed.

G_1^j If certain underpinning reasons (U), certain social facts (F) and certain minimum moral criteria (M) prevail, then the norm G_1 must be obeyed.

The norm G_1 is, as was noticed before, the most elementary formulation of the Kelsenian fundamental norm. On the other hand, the norm G_1^j is an example of a general justifying (legitimating) norm. It is a conditional norm which makes possible a transformation from (social) "Is" to (legal) "Ought". When interpreted in this way, the justifying norm G_1^j is an expression of the external validity in the formal sense. As a justifying norm it "locks" the chain of norms and gives the legitimacy to the Constitution.

Written in this general form, the justifying norm G_1^j does not say anything about the material criteria by means of which a certain individual norm system, e.g., the Finnish legal order can be legitimated as a legal order. Only in the case where the variables *U*, *F* and *M* are replaced with certain material criteria can the legitimacy of a certain norm system be evaluated. On the basis of this kind of substitution we can formulate the external validity of the norm system in a material sense.

The underpinning reasons refer to matters such as the acknowledgement of the necessary conditions of social order. For instance, if in general we wish to avoid chaos in our societal relations, we must accept some system of norms as generally valid.[22] This very general reason makes it possible to speak of social (and legal) order.

The social facts, on the other hand, assumed by the justifying norm G_1^j can be of several types, for example:

(a) the Constitution has been given by a *sovereign*, i.e. by an organ wielding political power in society.

(b) It is in principle possible that there are two or more such centers of power existing at the same time. Condition (a), therefore, is not enough. What is important is that the Constitution has *territorial* validity.

(c) Furthermore, the set of norms in the Constitution must be *general* in the sense that it affects all citizens in the territory referred to in (b).

(d) A further necessary condition of law is that the norms have *temporal durability*, in other words the content of the legal norms does not change continuously and at random.

(e) Pure formal validity of the Constitution, for example as an internal relation of delegation in the system of norms, does not guarantee legal validity. As was observed in connection with Kelsen's ideas, there is a demand for *efficacy* of the totality of norms. In general, the norms of the Constitution must be followed.

(f) In addition, a requirement of a *preciseness* must, to some degree, be placed on the Constitution. A completely open set of norms does not create the conditions for a sensible use of social and legal power.

The list is not exhaustive. It provides guidelines for understanding which *types* of social facts (F) are preconditions for accepting G_1.

According to Peczenik, the justifying basic norm (G_1^j) contains also at least some moral (minimum) demands. The legal order is legal order only if these moral criteria are fulfilled. Let us recall, e.g., the legal orders during Hitler's or Pol Pot's regimes. In these situations one necessarily is faced with serious questions of the acceptability of the legal order. In the extreme case, the whole system of norms must be renounced as a legal order.[23] The external validity in material sense belongs, however, to the problematics of the acceptability. Therefore it will be dealt with later on.

To sum up, the concept of formal validity used in this contribution can be defined as follows:

(1) Norm N_i is legally valid in the *internal systemic sense*
  (*a*) *sensu stricto*: if the norm N_i can be derived through an (internal) transformation from a formally valid norm, in other words from a norm given in accordance with the Constitution and
  (*b*) *sensu largo*: if the legal validity for the Constitution can be justified with a fundamental norm G_1.

(2) The norm system based on the fundamental norm G_1 is legally valid in the *external systemic sense*.
  (*a*) formally: if the legitimacy of the fundamental norm G_1 can be justified by the norm G_1^j ("if the underpinning reasons, U, the social facts (F) and moral criteria (M) prevail, then the fundamental norm G_1 can be accepted as the basis of a legal order).
  (*b*) materially: if a special norm system (e.g., Finnish legal order) can be legitimated by means of certain identified underpinning reasons, social facts and moral criteria.

According to these specifications, the legal order established by Hitler's regime was valid in the internal systemic sense as well as from the formal external point of view. On the other hand, it cannot be called materially (legally) valid in the external systemic sense of the concept.

3.3. *The Efficacy of Legal Norms*

A distinction must be made between the factual validity and the systemic validity of the norm. In legal philosophy, the term "validity" is often used in such a way that it refers to *both* of these phenomena. The validity of a norm in factual sense means its actual *efficacy* contrary to a (formally) given norm. In spite of this somewhat confusing way of using language, this use of the term "factual validity" has been accepted. This is also quite normal usage, for instance, in Finnish legal language.[24] The concept of factual validity in itself, however, can be understood in many ways. One could think that norm *N* is factually valid in a society if and only if the *citizens* regularly follow it in their behaviour, i.e., if the norm is in this sense effective in society. In more precise terms, regularity means that if anyone has to make a choice in how to behave, it is probable that he will choose the behaviour which is in accordance with norm *N*. The term "anyone", in this, refers to the category of individuals affected by the legal norm.

Efficacy is not always defined in this way. The point of departure has often been the application of legal norms by *authorities*. The law is realized in society when it is applied by the appropriate organization wielding power. This idea is connected with the view that the possibility of a reaction by a social organ is usually considered essential, and it is here that the position of the legal order as a coercive order finds expression. Such a reaction is closely connected just with the concept of coercion.[25]

A typical view of efficacy is represented by legal realism, which has also been called pragmatic instrumentalism. The basic view here is well described by Oliver Wendell Holmes' famous words, "The prophesies of what the courts will do in fact, and nothing more pretentious, are what I mean by the law".[26] According to this, it is the intention of legal science to investigate the practice of authorities, and especially, to predict what the authorities who apply the law will do in the future. This point of view has at times been depicted by speaking of the so-called problem of the "Bad Man".[27] It is always possible to uncover the content of the law by placing oneself in the position of a law-breaker (the "Bad Man") and asking not the content of abstract rules, but what sanctions the authorities will set in the case of the law-breaker.

G. H. von Wright has added precision although not an authentic interpretation to legal realism.[28] He notes that it is *not* always natural to say that a norm "exists". Instead, one could speak of, for example, the existence of obligations. What, then, does it mean that individual *i* has the obligation to do, shall we say, *O*? According to von Wright, this means that *i* belongs to a category of actors, *C*, where it is (very) probable that if some *C* does not carry out *O*, then some *A* will consequently do *R*.

In this, it is assumed that *A* is an authority and that *R* is something unpleasant for *C*, something "bad". According to von Wright, this means that for most *C*'s, the unpleasantness resulting from the performance of *R* is greater than the benefit to be derived from not doing *O*.

If *i* then has the obligation to do *O*, we can see according to von Wright, that such a norm is valid according to which every *C* should do *O*. This norm is usually called a primary norm. The legal order may also include a norm that obliges the authority (*A*) to perform, *R*, if some *C* does not perform *O*. In norm theory, the term secondary norm has been reserved for this type of norm. It would appear that it is not a necessary consequence of the validity of a primary norm that there is a valid secondary norm. On the other hand, the validity of a secondary norm (logically) implies the validity of a corresponding primary norm.[29]

The legal realists have not presented their view in so precise a manner. Even so, the core of the prediction theory is well presented in von Wright's analysis. On the other hand, we must remember that legal realism contains a number of different shades. Some of its extreme American forms denied in general the "existence" of legal norms. There exist only regularities of the behaviour. This approach was taken by, for example, Jerome Frank, who emphasised that written statutes were primarily tools, instruments from which the judge could get hints at the solution – good or bad – if he thought he needed such hints.[30] What is essential is that the judge, when faced with a difficult case of discretion, makes his decision on the basis of intuition, and only then justifies his decision, for example by reference to statutes. In such a conceptual world we cannot speak of either the existence or the validity of a norm.

Alf Ross, a representative of the so-called Scandinavian realism, analyses the concept of validity from the point of view of legal science. His point of departure is that if the knowledge regarding law is to attempt to be scientific, it must be based on experience. Legal norm statements say something about reality.

Ross himself has written:

> the real content of the assertion "*P* (the Bill of Exchanges Act, Section 28) is valid law of Denmark at the present time" is a prediction to the effect that if a case in which the conditions given in the section are considered to exist is brought before the courts, and if in the meantime there have been no alterations in the circumstances which justify *P*, the directive to the judge contained in the section will form an *integral part of justification* of the judgment.[31]

This sentence must be read together with the other part of Ross's theory, especially together with the following formulation:

The working hypothesis implies that the *law*, like the rules of chess, is a *supraindividual*, social phenomenon in the following sense: Legal patterns of action constitute a common ideology, operative in many persons. Consequently, an interpersonal complex of meaning and motivation is created. *The law is legal norm and legal phenomenon (law in action) simultaneously*. Legal norms constitute the abstract, normative content that, used as a scheme of interpretation, makes it possible for one to understand legal phenomena (law in action) as a meaningful complex of legal acts and to predict law in action within certain limits.[32]

Thus, the line of reasoning is as follows. When Parliament gives a norm, it does not provide information on any special state of affairs, it only directs social behaviour. A norm is always a *directive* not a proposition. Through the norm, people acquire certain images ("handleforestillinger") defining the activity. As social activity, they are above the level of the individual, and through them, a significance and motivation-connection which links people is created. Normative ideology is born, and this ideology is experienced as being binding. Decisions are made in accordance with this ideology. As was noted above, authorities are in a decisive position from the point of view of the validity of law. For this reason, the *normative ideology* that the authorities adopt determines what is valid law in society.[33]

The validity of a legal norm (in a certain legal order), means that this norm is to be found in the normative ideology that is experienced as binding.[34] In Ross's own set of concepts the matter should apparently be presented as follows. A norm is an abstract, normative idea content that expresses action images experienced as binding. In legal science, a norm functions as an *interpretation model* ("tolkningsschema"), through which it is possible to understand the significance and motivation-connection that prevails in society. By saying that a norm is effective we can adequately present the ideology that the decision-maker experiences as binding. Thus, only law which actually guides the activity of the authorities is effective.

The theory of validity as efficacy thus contains both an ideological and a behavioural element. The validity of a legal norm depends on the authorities' behaviour (according to Ross especially on the behaviour of the courts). A norm is valid if the authority behaves itself in the way the norm demands and the authority will do this if it regards the norm as binding; the norm motivates the action of the authority in a certain manner. This is the ideological side of the theory. On the other hand, we can acquire information about the validity of a norm e.g. by examining the authorities' actual behaviour. Consequently, a statement "Legal norm *N* is valid in legal order *O*" is correct or not depending on whether the authorities act in the way the norm prescribes or not.

The idea of efficacy as a criterion of validity is a very natural one. It can also be theoretically justified. The linking of validity of efficacy is thus, no doubt, *one* possible way of speaking of validity. There are, however, certain difficulties hidden in this way of thinking. They clearly arise also in Alf Ross's ideas of validity. In this context the only attention is paid to the very concept of validity and to its significance for the present study. The problem of predictions will be dealt with later on.

As was noted above, Ross examines the matter from the point of view of *legal science*. His basic question is: "How is it scientifically possible to understand valid law?" The same approach is also connected with other predictive theories. This means that on the basis of these theories it is not possible to give the *judge* an answer to the question of whether or not a certain norm binds him.[35] Even so, our expectation of legal certainty starts from the assumption that the judge in some way clarifies for himself the proper content of the legal order. From the point of view of the judge, it is not important – as Stig Jørgensen observes – to receive information on how a judge (in other words, also he himself) will act.[36] The decision-maker must know already before the decision what binds him and what does not. Theodore M. Benditt writes pertinently, "An observer may predict what a judge is going to do, but a judge cannot, in deciding a case, merely be predicting what he is going to do; he is doing it."[37] Kaarle Makkonen views the matter in the same way.[38]

The point of view of the judge would thus appear to strongly defend the view that the validity of law cannot be defined as efficacy. In doing so, the definition loses its internal logic, and covers only certain situations. According to such a definition, the judge becomes the measure of what he himself must regard as binding.

It may be that a legal realist would interrupt me and say that in any case, it is always the Supreme Court that decides what is "right" and what is not in society. In this point of view the Supreme Court cannot err. Thus, all law must ultimately be realized law. There is no organ other than the Supreme Court which can dictate what the "given" norms are in society. H. L. A. Hart has answered this line of argument by saying that also the Supreme Court can criticize its own previous decisions in connection with an analogous case.[39] In fact, this may indeed be what it does when it later gives a precedent with a different content even though the case itself remains basically the same. As the judge can thus "learn from his mistakes", there must be some reason which demonstrates *that* a mistake has been made and which also shows *why* the decision is to be considered erroneous.

One could add to this that, as a matter of fact, one of the traditional tasks of legal science has been to follow and criticize legal praxis. The research praxis of legal dogmatics is not the description (and acceptance) of already given decisions, just as it is not – at least to any greater extent – merely prediction. It would be impossible to think that such criticism could be correct, at least sometimes, if at the same time we did not acknowledge that the criticism has justification which is *independent of* the court decisions themselves, "outside" of legal praxis. We thus come to the concept of axiological validity.

3.4. *The Acceptability of a Legal Norm*

Axiological validity is often connected with the so-called Natural Law. In doing so, values such as justice are not merely the yardstick of a given (positive) legal order, they form a basis that gives the system of norms its ultimate legal validity. In a way, natural law lies above the positive law and forms the basis of its force.

The theories of Natural Law do not form the basis for this work. In spite of the external material criterion of validity, there are no legally relevant criteria outside of the positive law giving legitimacy to the legal order as such or to the individual norms belonging to this very order. However, different kinds of axiological criteria play an important, sometimes even decisive role in legal dogmatics and in jurisdiction. This can be clearly understood if we rephrase the question as follows: "Why does legal norm *N*, which was formally valid in society *X*, remain systematically unapplied?" One explanation may be found in the idea that this norm, even though it has never been formally repealed, no longer corresponds to the generally accepted system of values.[40] All legal norms which are formally valid, therefore, do not have a guarantee of axiological acceptability. Here can we find the core of axiological validity.

One could also think that a norm which is regularly applied by an authority stands in conflict with a system of values which is regarded as relevant. In other words, the norm is both formally valid and effective without its being acceptable from the point of view of a certain value system.

This result is deeply connected to the very concept of legal certainty that consists of two different elements. The demands (or expectations) of legal certainty are fulfilled if: (a) an artbitrariness can be avoided and (b) the result is in accordance with the value code, i.e., "right" in the substantial sense of the word. Avoiding arbitrariness means roughly the same as predictability. Furthermore, predictability can be defined by means of rationality. Every procedure that fulfills the criteria of rational discourse results in predictable decisions (see pp. 185)

It is another matter that reality does not always or even usually correspond to our ideal. Social life is full of illogical elements, very indefinite persuasion, secrecy and attempts to influence others. All this is part of the nature of life. Legal ideology (of the law in our utopia), however, cannot be built on such elements, no matter how real they are. We are seeking something better, something more. For this reason we are justified in considering specifically rational acceptability as one relevant way of speaking of the validity of law.

In any case the scholars, for instance, lean on such points of view when they criticize an interpretation the validity of which is based either on purely formal grounds – rules as such – and/or norms which have proved to be or which are argued to be effective in society.[41]

To follow the model outlined by Ilkka Niiniluoto[42] but rewriting it, we get the following formulation for axiological validity. Norm N_i is valid in community C if

(1) N_i belongs to the norm system given by the authorization of the Constitution of C;
(2) The Constitution has to be followed because of the basic norm G_1;
(3) The norm G_1 must be followed on the basis of a justifying (conditional) norm G_1^1 and
(4) N_i is acceptable in C in the sense that the majority of the members, after having rationally considered the matter, would bind themselves to accepting N_i as a legal norm to be followed.

The elements (1) and (2) in the formulation refer to the internal formal validity of the legal order. The precondition (3), on the other hand, deals with the criteria of the external validity, both in the formal and material sense. The axiological element – acceptability – concerns specifically the last element (4) of the formulation. Hence, it can easily be seen that Peczenik's definition of external validity is – in the end – nearly the same as the formulation presented above. It contains also, as point (4), certain moral (evaluative) criteria characterizing the valid legal order.

The difference lies, as far as I can see, in the fact that for Peczenik the external moral justification is a justification of the legal order as such. Here, on the contrary, the whole problem is connected with individual norms. The question is as follows: is *norm* N_i acceptable (valid in this sense) in the community *C*?

Validity as acceptability is a type of counter factual state of affairs. Norm N_i of the content I_i *would be* valid in society *X* if people would be rational in their argumentation and if a certain value-basis would be prevalent. This is not always the case and therefore the acceptability is only an ideal. The acceptability is our interpretation of what law is in a "good" (Western) society. The contents of acceptability will be dealt with later on in Section *IV*.

What is essential is the insight that we can speak of validity in *all* three senses: as formal validity, efficacy and acceptability. Theoretical problems arise when we try to use one of the alternative sides of this concept as the *genuine* type of validity. The same difficulty arises when the definition is constructed on a combination of the above three senses. "Reine Rechtslehre" is a good example of an attempt to define the bindingness of a legal norm through the use of one or some meanings of validity. Kelsen's definition covers formal validity and, to some extent, efficacy. Someone else might define validity solely on the basis of formal validity. It is equally possible to regard a norm as legally binding if, asides from formal criteria, it fulfills certain value-based requirements.[43]

Apparently a weakness in every definition of this type is that they confuse *the logic of the ordinary language that we use*. In practice, we do not speak in the cut-and-dried manner that legal philosophers would have us use. Differences of opinion arise from our deeply-rooted tendency to search for clear definitions of words i.e. when we begin to philosophize. In the ordinary legal language there are several interlocked language games dealing with validity. It depends on the context which one is the most adequate way to present the validity problematics. Let us take an example.

When the point of departure is efficacy, formal validity must normally be included. In spite of the customary law only norms that have been given in the proper order can be effective. The authorities have the obligation to follow the systemic valid law. In this very language game there is no place for axiological validity. The same holds true if the attention is focused solely upon the systemic validity, either in the internal or external sense. The game has been changed. The concepts of efficacy and acceptability do not play any role in this use of language. For these reasons, no attempt has been made in the following to define the very notion of validity.

However, axiological validity proves to be the most significant as far as the *justification* is concerned. The justificatory basis of an interpretation is often consisted of "extra-legal" arguments, among them references to a certain value code. Only in the light of axiological validity it is therefore possible to comprehend, for instance, the relativity of interpretations. Systemic validity, both in the internal and external sense, is only one of the preconditions of acceptability. Efficacy, in turn, is one, but not the sole criterion of acceptability. But even so, argumentation theory attempts to show, all things considered, what norms should be accepted in a legal community if the matters are considered rationally. In this, it always is a critical theory of law.

Regardless of how the language of validity is used, there is no reason to supplement the *ontology* of legal dogmatics in respect of what has already been done. The language games dealing with validity function without the necessity of adopting new entities. And *vice versa*: when all the validity games have been explicated an exhaustive description of the notion validity is at hand. We do not need any assumption of the ideal existence of legal norms in order to understand our language games. In this sense, the ontological problem of independent existence of legal norms disappears, when it is turned around to the problem of validity, i.e. to all the different validity games that can in practice be played by this very notion.

CHAPTER III

THE METHODOLOGY OF INTERPRETATION IN LEGAL DOGMATICS

1. BASIC CONCEPTS

1.1. *Two Research Strategies*

The problematics of interpretation may enter the question in two types of situations in legal research praxis. I shall call these *a law text centered research strategy* and *a problem centered research strategy*.[1]

The point of departure of text-centered research is a certain expression; in a system of written law, this is usually a law text. The task is to justify an alternative interpretation of this text. The subject of interpretation may be the ambiguity of the text or the fact that it can be interpreted in different ways. The question may appear in the following form: "What does the expression 'in writing' mean in the context of Chapter 17, Section 3 of the Finnish Decedent's Estate Act?". If we denote the law text with the letter *L* and the alternative interpretations with the letter *I*, the result can be shown as in Diagram 6.

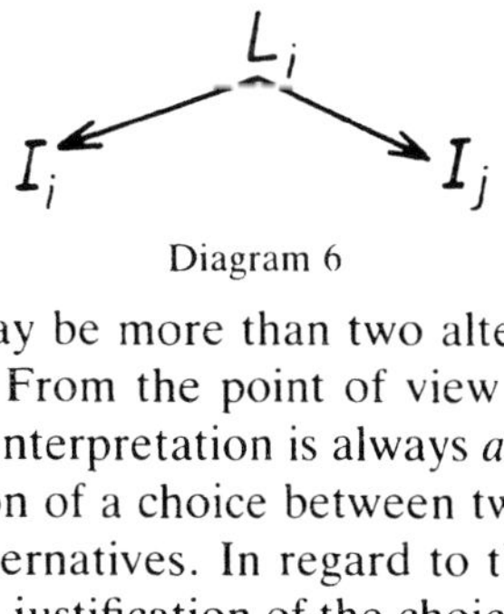

Diagram 6

In practice, there may be more than two alternative interpretations. This is not important. From the point of view of our subject, what is significant is that here interpretation is always *a decision which involves a choice*. It is a question of a choice between two or more semantically and legally possible alternatives. In regard to the accepted legal ideology, the problem is the justification of the choice which has been made. Only an interpretation which has been justified in the appropriate manner has relevance from the point of view of legal certainty. Thus, the theory of interpretation in legal dogmatics is partially the justification theory concerning the choice of an alternative interpretation.

In problem-centered research the point of departure is a concrete or, as is more common in scholarly interpretation, an imagined but in

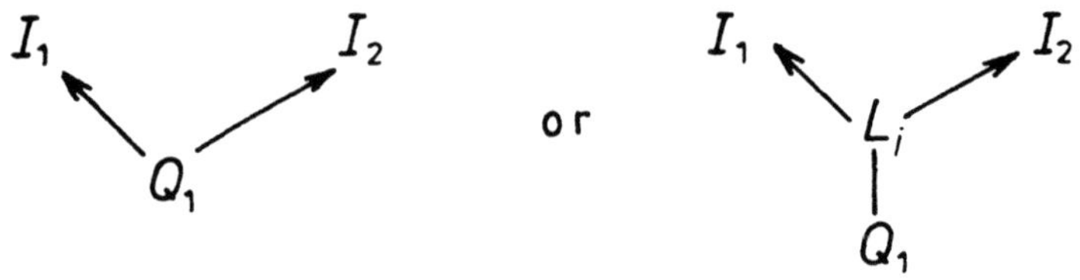

Diagram 7

reality possible legal problem. Let us denote it with the letter Q. The researcher may try to clarify which interpretation (I_1, I_2) of a known law text (L_i) deals with the problem in question (Q_i). The situation can be presented as in Diagram 7.

The problem may just as well be that, initially, the same problem is regulated by two or more law texts. It may be a question of a conflict between the contents of the law texts. The situation is the same also when there is uncertainty as to what law text is to be applied (Diagram 8).

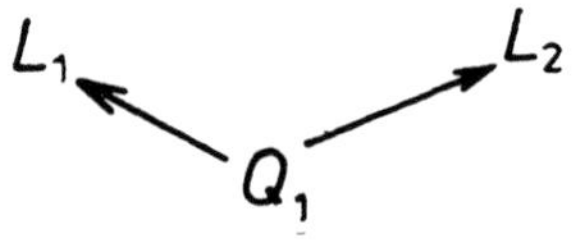

Diagram 8

Even though the points of departure of the two research strategies are different – in one, it is a text, in the other, a legal problem – in regard to the *structure* of the interpretation there is no essential difference between the two. Ultimately, problem centered research leads to the same or to the same type of basic question as does text centered research. In both, the scholar deals with the clarification of the unclear meaning content of law, or to be more precise, with the clarification of the formally valid law texts. The similarity can be graphically depicted as in Diagram 9.

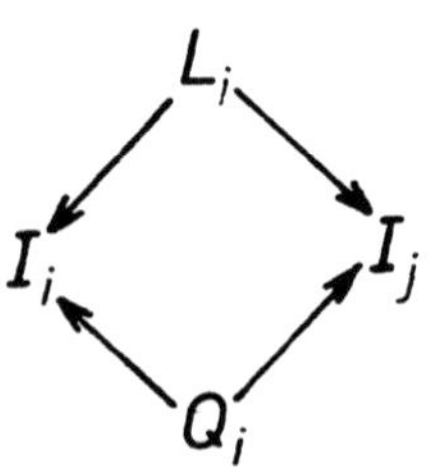

Diagram 9

In this line of thought, the difference between the research strategies lies in the fact that they, so to speak, start out from different ends of the same problem, one from a law text with an ambiguous content and the other from a category of problems which has proven to be difficult. With this taken into consideration, in the following, law text centered and problem centered research have not been subjected to a separate analysis. Unless otherwise noted, attention will be directed solely at a situation where two alternative interpretations, I_1 and I_2, can be given to one and the same law text. Everything which can be said of this research strategy can also be said *mutatis mutandis* of more complicated situations and of problem centered research in general.

1.2. *A Norm Statement and an Interpretative Statement*

1.2.1. *The concept of the norm statement.* The legal order can be defined as an entity which has been formed in a certain way out of legal norms. If the legal order is denoted with the letters *LO* and legal norms with the letter *N*, then, following Ilkka Niiniluoto, we can draw Diagram 10.

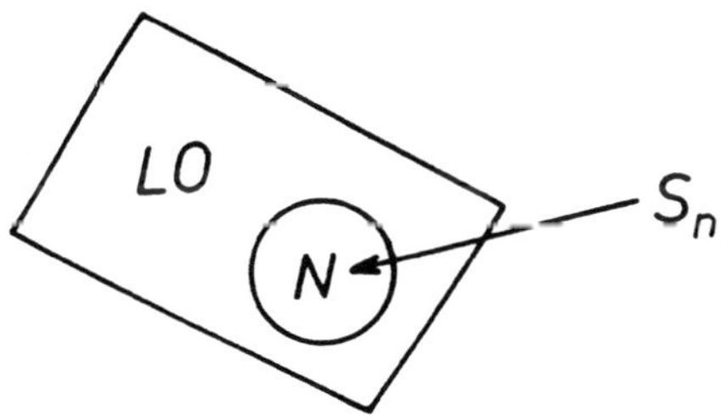

Diagram 10

In the diagram, S_n is a statement which says something about the content of the legal norm *N* which is part of the (valid) legal order. I shall call such a statement a norm statement. In order to clarify the meaning of this concept ('norm statement') the following general analysis concerning the semantics of different types of statements may be useful.

The common way to classify statements is to divide them in two groups: *theoretical* and *practical* statements. Theoretical statements may be either empirical or logical ones. Normally, these statements have been called propositions. Semantically, a proposition is usually defined as the intension of the sentence. In this connection, another feature of the concept 'proposition' is important. It can and must be possible to assign the property *true/false* to the proposition. This property may, on the other hand, be an empirical or logical one. Empirical propositions refer, in this sense, to reality. Either the proposition is or it is not in correspondence to reality. Hence, the very concept of truth has often defined just on the basis of the correspondence theory (the so-called Tarskian truth). It is simply a question of the correspondence between the proposition and the world outside of the proposition. Logical propositions, on the other hand, do not refer to reality at all. They are valid in all possible worlds.

Practical statements are of different type. The concept of correspondence cannot be applied in connection with practical statements. In this very context it is enough to divide practical statements (sentences) into two groups: (a) sentences intended to produce an *effect* ("effect sentences"), and (b) *expressive sentences*. In the first group can be counted both prescriptive sentences (norms and commands) and persuasive sentences (e.g. recommendations, manipulative expressions etc.). The other main class consists of either "pure" expressive sentences (e.g. expressions of attitudes, dispositions etc.) or standpoints (contentions). As far as the content is concerned, standpoints may be, for instance value standpoints or norm standpoints.

The division between "pure" expressions and standpoints is based on a criterion quite independent of the classification criteria used above. For instance, the difference between effect sentences and expressive sentences refers to the different *function* that these sentences have in language and in human communication in general. By means of prescriptive and persuasive sentences one tries to influence the other party. Expressive sentences, on the other hand, mediate information from the sender of the message to the addressee. The difference between pure expressions and standpoints (in the above mentioned sense) lies in the fact that the last one is supported by reasons, i.e. only the standpoints are justified. As we will see later on, there can also be certain "mixtures" between different types of sentences. However, this is not important as far as the concept of norm statement is concerned. Before we deal with norm statements in a more detailed way, the above mentioned classification form is presented schematically in Diagram 11.

Let us recall now the norm statements. They can be of (at least) the following kind:

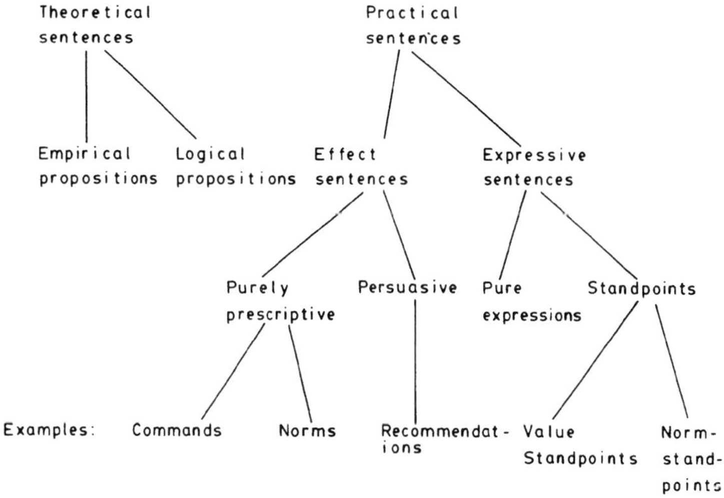

Diagram 11

(i) First of all, the interpreter can present a norm proposition.[2] The proposition would then be as follows:

P_n "Norm *N* with content *I* is part of the (valid) law of Finland".

In this case the proposition is compared – in accordance with the definition – to a certain social state of affairs. This means that the validity of the norm must be defined in an empirically verifiable way. The proposition states something about the real world. With reference to the above discussion of the concept of validity, we can note that realist theories, which define validity on the basis of efficacy, satisfy the conditions set in the definition of the proposition. Realist norm statements are propositions. This is true not only of the approach of American realists, but also of the predictive theory supported by Alf Ross. Ilkka Niiniluoto's realistic approach, that will be dealt with later on, can also be counted in this group.

The systemic validity (in an internal sense) may also satisfy the truth conditions of the norm propositions (type P_n). This is the case regardless of whether we adopt Hans Kelsen's view of the hierarchy of norms or whether we come to the conclusion formulated in the foregoing on the basis of Aleksander Peczenik's ideas (as long as one stays within the limits of the transformation into the law and indentification of legal sources).

The concept of acceptability as the criterion of validity is considerably more problematic. Acceptability comprises not only the legal but also extra-legal aspects. In this point of view, (rational) acceptability is not an empirical state of affairs in the same sense as, for example, the acceptance of a legal norm or the efficacy in general. Thus, the statement expressing something about rational acceptability cannot be a (norm) proposition. As a matter of fact it is here that the entire core of the interpretation problematics is to be found.

(ii) A norm statement regarding rational acceptability has in this work been termed a *norm standpoint* (norm contention). The statement says something about a valid norm (valid law), but it is a standpoint, since it contains not only propositions regarding reality but also value judgements. The interpreter not only presents a statement regarding an empirical state of affairs, he *presents* an evaluative standpoint. For this reason, a norm standpoint can (for example) be written in the following form:

(1) P_s: "It is rational and right to accept norm N with the content I as part of valid law."

In this form a norm standpoint can be called an axiological statement. Since the value judgements which intertwine with norm standpoints are not objectively right or wrong in the same way as beliefs about states of affairs relating to experiential reality, a norm standpoint cannot be true or false as can a proposition. The "rightness" of a norm standpoint – if there is any justification for the standpoint – is relative, as shall be described below. It is thus possible to present two or more well justified norm standpoints for the same problem of interpretation.

Let us now assume two such standpoints, P_{s1} and P_{s2}. The former states that it is rational and reasonable to accept the content I_1 to norm N_1. The latter says the same about the content I_2 to norm N_2. The difference between these two standpoints lies in the fact that even if we bind ourselves to exactly the same principles (and rules) of rationality, it still can be quite justified to disagree about what is right in this very case. Thus, there is no universal basis for stating in regard to either P_{s1} or P_{s2} that they are true when compared to the "legal reality".

In certain cases it may be strange to say that a norm statement (P_s) provides us with information of the valid legal order. As Ilkka Niiniluoto points out, there may be "underdeveloped areas" of legislation (e.g. environmental laws) such that most rational persons *would* accept new statutes or interpretations (e.g. protecting the nature) *if* someone first invented and formulated those statutes or interpretations. "There may be norms which are rationally acceptable but no one has ever even thought about them", writes Niiniluoto. This is right. Therefore, a norm standpoint can also be formulated in gap situations where the standpoint produces really "new information" of the proposed content of the law.

In regard with definition (1) of a norm standpoint Niiniluoto also states that this standpoint is nothing else but a consequent of certain *technical norms*.[3] As is well known, a technical norm (N_t) is of the following form:

(2) N_t: "If you want A, you ought to do B".

According to Niiniluoto, a norm standpoint is just a conclusion of a deductive inference:

(a) If sources G and values V are accepted, norm N should be accepted as valid in this legal order
(b) G and V

Hence: It is rational to accept norm N.

Norm standpoints are, as the first premise points out, justified only in relation to a certain group of persons (to an audience). The conclusion "It is rational to accept norm N" is thus a technical obligation for those persons who share the common values V. It would be possible to say also that the norm standpoint as a technical ought is *true* for this group of persons. This truth is, however, not the truth in the correspondence-theoretical sense. Instead of that a descriptive statement "It is rational for person A to accept the norm N as valid" is true also according to the theory of correspondence.

In his remarks, Niiniluoto has presented a lot of remarkable ideas. It is true that a legal scholar can formulate technical norms as well as norm standpoints. Yet, norm standpoints cannot be reduced to such sentences as technical oughts. A norm standpoint not only states that *if* you reason rationally and if you have bound yourself to certain values, then you ought to accept a certain norm or certain interpretations of a norm. A genuine standpoint does not consist only of theoretical elements. There are also value commitments included in them. Norm standpoints are simply contentions: it *is* rational and reasonable to accept norm N as valid. Therefore the norm standpoints are not conclusions of the syllogism referred to above; the standpoints express contentions about the valid legal order.

In this respect, legal dogmatical interpretations as norm standpoints say something of the *ideal* world regulated by the law. It is the world that is rationally acceptable for those persons who commit themselves to the rules of rational discourse. This is the reason why the world can be called ideal. G. H. von Wright points out that the task of legal dogmatics is just "to expound and make clear the exact nature of the ideal state of affairs which the envisages. It clarifies the content of the law". The proposed content is stated, von Wright says, in true or false propositions – but the proposal itself cannot be assessed as true or false. "It can, however, be justified by various means of legal argumentation, and it may be assessed as reasonable or not according to a variety of standards which need not, incidentally, mutually agree".[4] Hence, even if the goal of a norm standpoint is to give information about the ideal world, it is only a proposal. The wider acceptability the standpoint has, the greater societal value it has as an interpretation of the valid law. Rational acceptability is thus a "measure" by means of which it is possible to deliberate the "success' of the standpoint.

(iii) Norm *recommendations* can be either strong or weak as to their nature dependent on whether the recommendation is justified or not.

If in addition to a norm standpoint, a person recommends that other people also accept this standpoint, he has presented a norm recommendation in the weak sense of the term. The fact that a certain expression is a recommendation in nature does not remove the possibility of justifying the standpoint. Regardless of the recommendation aspect, the conception either is or is not acceptable on the basis of the justifying arguments. The element of having been recommended does not increase or decrease the acceptability of the conception.

Thus, a norm recommendation in a weak sense has two sides: a justified conception of the content (and validity) of the norm *and* an element of recommending acceptance (persuasion). One can also say that there is a recommending operator in the expression.[5]

If, on the other hand, the person in question presents his opinion of the content of the norm without having a justification for it, he recommends – for example on the basis of his formal position – that this standpoint be accepted. The standpoint is norm recommendation in the strong sense of the term. It can also be called a *genuine* recommendation. The author tries to persuade other people but the relevance of the standpoint lies solely in the authority of the person making the statement. With an eye on legal certainty, its value is of the same level as any "taste-based judgement". A genuine recommendation may not be questioned rationally, as in the absence of justification there can be no rational discussion of its content and scope.

1.2.2. *Conclusion.* Norm standpoints do not have a privileged status among the statements of legal dogmatics. As the research praxis easily reveals, legal dogmatics is composed of a numerous cluster of norm statements, for instance:

(a) Empirical statements ("Norm *N* is accepted by the legal community");
(b) Technical norms ("If you want *V*, you ought to accept norm *N*");
(c) Norm standpoints ("It is rational to accept norm *N* as valid");
(d) Norm recommendations ("Norm *N* should be accepted as valid").

For the further analysis of legal interpretation it is not relevant which one (ones) if none, of the sentences is (are) the most *common* in scholarly practice. More important is to remind that all of these language-games can be adequately played in legal dogmatics. However, special attention will here be paid to norm standpoints (group (c)). There are two reasons for this. First, as regards the application of the law it is not natural to say that the judge presents norm statements of the type (a), (b) or (d). In order to apply the law to the facts of the case the judge has to interprete legal norms at issue. The interpretation is a necessary precondition for the subsumption. Yet, for this purpose the judge is not interested in e.g. technical oughts or in mere recommendations. He simply has to make a *choice* between the interpretation alternatives and this choice expresses his opinion of the "right" answer.

As we have seen, the scholar is, from the epistemological point of view, in a similar situation. There are a lot of cases where the scholar must take stand. The proper function of society presupposes that scholars "guide", for instance, the judges in giving information of the rationally acceptable states of affairs. On the other hand, norm standpoints will be used in this work only as examples by means of which we can clarify the content and the role of rational acceptability in legal justification. The same problematics could be elucidated also using technical norms or recommendations. For instance, rational acceptability has a key role in the technical norm "If you want *V*, you ought to accept norm *N*", as well as in the recommendation "It should be rational to accept norm *N* as valid".

1.2.3. *A meaning statement and an interpretation statement.* Every statement regarding the meaning contents of a linguistic expression can be defined as a *meaning statement*. In this, a meaning statement is an expression which says something about another expression. In other words, its focus in language in itself. A meaning statement may be one of (at least) three types:

(i) It may refer to the *unambiguous* content of another expression, term or sentence. For example in the law of inheritance, "widow" = "surviving female spouse". The concept of spouse, in turn, is made more precise in the appropriate sections of the Marriage Act.

(ii) A semantical proposition may also content itself with presenting an expression's *alternative contents* which can be considered or which in the interpretation situation in question enter the question. For example, the often mentioned expression "in writing" in Chapter 17, Section 3 of the Decedent's Estate Act can refer to an unsigned document, a signed document, a signed and witnessed document, and so on. By listing the logically possible alternatives of the concept of "document", we can analyse the alternative contents of the law in question. In a statement that analyses contents in this manner, no special position on what contents are "right", "legal" or "most justified" is taken.

(iii) It may be considered that a meaning statement is used to make the range of meaning *more exact* by cutting out possible alternatives or alternatives which enter the question. After the range has been made more exact, the expression in question will have one or more possible contents.

In the following, the meaning statement referred to in part (iii) will be called an *interpretation statement*. According to our definition, an interpretation statement is therefore a meaning statement which clarifies the meaning of the focus expression. The interpretation statements, in turn, may be of a variety of types.

(a) In some cases an interpretation statement may express a *stipulative definition*.[6] In this it is a question of a "convention" of the meaning of a linguistic expression. A stipulative definition may be likened to the baptism of a child: something is given a new name.

A stipulative definition can never be true or false: Its task is to add to, simplify or clarify the "agreed-upon" use of language. In this view a stipulative definition corresponds to a norm recommendation. To be more exact, it is a question of defining stipulatively a term in a law text so that a norm recommendation with a corresponding content can be given. Thus, if "surviving spouse" is defined as being similar to the term "widower", we can arrive at norm recommendations where all legal instructions pertaining to surviving spouses express norms that deal with widowers.

The weakness of a stipulative definition, in regard to interpretation in legal dogmatics, lies specifically in the fact that it is "open to agreement". An interpretation statement constructed on such a basis leaves open the question of whether or not the statement is in accordance with the legal order. In order for the interpretation statement to serve the ideology of legal certainty referred to previously, it must therefore in some sense be "more" than just a stipulative recommendation or a proposal for a convention. Otherwise, even a completely arbitrary stipulation will fulfill the appropriate conditions of an interpretation statement.

(b) An interpretation statement may also express an *analytical definition* in a special sense. Such a definition is based on the conceptual system in legal context. The meaning of a certain legal expression is analysed through the use of other legal expressions so that the intensions of the expressions are equal. For example, in the Decedent's Estate Act "the contesting of a will" means the same as "a suit based on Chapter 13, Section 1 of the Decedent's Estate Act". The term "contesting" thus receives a definition which is essentially more limited than what is usually referred to in ordinary language.

An analytical legal definition, when understood in this way, in principle is always true or false. It is true if and only if the expression is used in the language in question (in the conceptual system in question) in the way referred to in the definition. The truth of an analytical definition can therefore be called "empirical".

Doubtless in legal dogmatics many situations may be recognized where the way in which language is used can be defined analytically and so that the definition is, in the sense referred to above, true. Despite its possible widespread nature, interpretation statements which express an analytical definition are not very central from the point of view of the subject of this study. As was noted in the beginning, decisions involving discretion pose a greater challenge to the theory of interpretation in legal dogmatics. In these decisions, in turn, it is a question of the interpreter having to take a standpoint on the meaning content of the expression. He does not simply describe the prevailing ways in which language is used.

(c) In a way more interesting than in the case of "pure" analytical definitions, the interpretation problematics is brought out by *non-analytical* and, at the same time, *nonstipulative* definitions. Such a definition is descriptive. It states that the *extension* of a certain expression is the same as the extension of another expression. The definition thus states in the true sense of the word something about reality. Hence, such a descriptive definition says something essential about what is meant by so-called *real definitions*. Its truth is synthetic.

An example of a descriptive nonanalytical definition in law is the following.

(1) "The transfer of an inheritance share is a legal act through which an heir transfers to another heir, a member of the decedent's estate or a third party his share in the estate."

The definition may also be written in another form which more clearly than the first definition reveals the "real definition" nature of the definition:

(2) "The term 'transfer of an inheritance share' refers to the same phenomenon in the system of the Decedent's Estate Act as the term, 'a legal act through which an heir transfers . . . his share in the estate'."

In definition (2), it is stated that the sphere of legal acts covered by the first term is the same as the sphere covered by the second. A *legal* real definition, however, is problematic in two different ways.

First, the line between it and analytical definitions is not clear. The difficulties in drawing this line come up very well if we were to rewrite definition (2) as follows:

(3) "In the terminology of the Decedent's Estate Act the term 'transfer of an inheritance share' *means* the same as the term 'a legal act through which an heir transfers . . . his share in the estate'."

This last definition does not say anything directly about the extension, i.e. about the states of affairs belonging in "legal reality." It is a statement about the terminology of the Decedent's Estate Act, in other words about legal language. As was just observed, such a statement as a description is not very interesting from the point of view of decisions of discretion. We will come to see that the terminology of the Decedent's Estate Act as well as legal terminology in general can be so semantically open that nothing can be asserted, even in principle, regarding its truth or nontruth. It is a question of interpretation *standpoints*, not interpretation propositions.

A significant difficulty is to be found also in definition (2), regardless of the fact that it seems to have the form of a *real* definition. Transfer of an inheritance share as a legal act is not a phenomenon of reality which would fall in the category of "pure" observation. It is an institution that is heavily marked by legal concepts. For us to know what institution is in question, we must already know the system of the Decedent's Estate Act. The contents of this system, in turn, depends on interpretation. Thus, the concept of "transfer of an inheritance share" is an *interpreted* matter. The same is true of the right-hand side of the definition. In the definition, it is thus a question of legal interpretation. In the case of discretion, the interpretation assumes a choice between possible meaning alternatives. For this reason, a "real" definition of type (2) does not give a theoretically sound foundation for further analysis in this study.

(d) There remains a fourth interpretation statement, which is the most important one from the point of view of our subject. This category is connected most closely with interpretation standpoints. In the following, I shall refer to this category when I speak of *nondescriptive analytical definitions*. As this term may lead to misunderstandings, there is reason to deal more closely with it in at least two respects.

First of all, the term "nondescriptive" does not mean the same as "normative". It is not a question of the setting of a norm, at least in the strong sense of the term. We can not speak of a stipulative definition either in the sense referred to above. A point of comparison is offered by the norm standpoint discussed above. *Justifiability* is typical of norm standpoints. It is not merely a recommendation or a convention proposal but a justified or a least a justifiable standpoint on the contents of a system. On the other hand, it does not solely describe the system. It is a question of a standpoint which falls outside of the category of true/false.

1.2.4. *A norm standpoint and an interpretation standpoint.* In order to clarify the relation between a norm standpoint and an interpretation standpoint, there is reason to remember what was said about text centered research strategies. According to the statutory law system, interpretation in legal dogmatics, as a rule, is the interpretation of legal texts. The intention of the scholar is to give an exact meaning content to a law text.

In this view, the law text is thus the focus of interpretation. When in a situation of uncertainty one alternative meaning of a law text is chosen as the "right" one, an interpretation statement is made. If value judgements are added to this, it is a question of an interpretation standpoint. It is presented in the following form:

(1) Expression "E_1" in law text L_i means the same as expression "E_2".

On the basis of such a standpoint we can formulate *a norm standpoint with a corresponding content*, in other words a standpoint on what content of a norm is part of the legal system. A norm standpoint is thus of the following type:

(2) According to valid (Finnish) law, norm N, which is expressed in text L, has content E_2.

If it is rational and right to interpret a law text in the way presented, it is rational and right in this sytem of language and in this legal system to accept a norm with the corresponding content as part of the (Finnish) legal order. In this sense, interpretative standpoint and norm standpoint are two different ways to speak of the content of legal order.

1.2.5. *Summary.* In the sense noted above, the interpretative definition is always nondescriptive. It does not merely describe the prevailing way in which language is used, its current use. A second specification has to do with the analytic element. Interpretation is always a linguistic matter. It is a question of clarifying a meaning. This, in turn, takes place through other expressions. Since an interpretation standpoint always deals with the relation between (legal) expressions, it may be called analytical. The intension of the law text term is the same as the intension of the alternative expression presented by the standpoint. In other words, the law text *has* the content that is presented. Since the relation between the intensions is as has just been described, we can also speak of a definition, the justification of which consists of both factual propositions and evaluations. The definition is analytical, but not descriptive.

In summary, the types of interpretation statements may be gathered together as in Diagram 12.

Interpretation statement	
Analytical and descriptive definition	Stipulative definition
Nonanalytical and descriptive definition	Analytical and nondescriptive definition

↑ Interpretation standpoint (below "Analytical and nondescriptive definition")

Diagram 12

1.3. *The Concept of the Norm*

In accordance with the terminology adopted above, the focus of an interpretation posititon is a law text and the focus of a norm standpoint is a (valid) norm. Law texts are an important part of the information on the basis of which we come to a conclusion regarding the valid legal order, in other words about the content of legal norms. In this point of view, law texts are also important official material. In accordance with Chapter 1, Section 11 of the Finnish Code of Judicial Procedure, every decision regarding the valid legal order must (ultimately) be based on a law text. In other words, law texts and comparable linguistic data are the material which aid us in *coming to grips* with legal norms. It has been noted in the foregoing that discussion of the existence of a norm turns into discussion on the validity of a norm. In the same way, the *methodological* problem of validity appears as a question of the interpretation of linguistic expressions. Even though the methodology of legal dogmatics, in this point of view, is the methodology of interpretation and it lies in connection with the problematics of language, it is still natural to regard norms as the main focus of legal dogmatics. After all, the legal order is usually defined specifically as the entirety formed by legal norms. In accordance with this, the task of legal dogmatics is the clarification of the contents of norms and the systematization of norms.

The norm in turn, is formed of certain linguistic expressions (norm formulations) and, in addition, of thought contents.[7] For example, when we write out the norm "Thou shalt not steal", it has two sides:

(1) The expression "Thou shalt not steal" and
(2) the thought content which says *that* one is not to steal.

Together, these two sides form a matter which in the following shall be briefly termed "a norm".[8]

A norm in the form "Thou shalt not steal" can easily be understood as a prohibition directed at an individual citizen. This type of norm has at times been referred to as a *primary norm*.[9] The same is true of other types of norms with which we shall soon be dealing. We can regard also their addressees as individual citizens.

If, on the other hand, we wish to precisely clarify the structure of this very regulation mechanism of society, the legal norm must be given another form; i.e. as a *secondary norm* which corresponds to the primary norm.[10] It is directed at the authorities. This type of norm always has two elements:

(a) The description of the behaviour demanded, and
(b) the description of the consequences facing a person who behaves in a different manner.

In the terminology of legal theory, the former has been called the description of legal facts and the latter the description of the legal consequences. In a simplified form, our example may be written as follows: "Whosoever steals shall be sentenced."

The *relation* between the legal facts and the legal consequences is not the same as the (causal) relation in nature between facts and consequences. The connecting factor "ought" separates this legal relation from that of cause and effect. In this sense there is a clear demarcation line between "Is" and "Ought".[11]

By applying the scheme to the previous example of stealing, we can write the secondary norm as follows: "If someone takes the property of another without permission, he shall be sentenced to *X* time units of imprisonment". When presented in this form, the following relations of correspondence prevail:

(1)	"If someone takes the property of another without permission"	=	description of facts (legal facts)
(2)	"he shall be sentenced"	=	element of "ought" (deontic operator)
(3)	"to *X* time units of imprisonment"	=	description of consequence (legal consequence)

Schematically presented, then, the structure of a legal norm is as follows:

legal fact (F) element of ought (O) Legal consequence (G)

The same matter may be presented even more concisely with symbols:

$$N_i\ (x)\ (Fx \rightarrow OGx)$$

This formula may be read as "it is true of all (x) that if someone (x) acts in manner (F), he shall be sentenced to legal consequence G". The symbol "————→" expresses the relation of ought ("Sollen") in "if . . . then . . .". According to Alchourrón and Bulygin we could also say that a norm "consists" of two elements:

(a) the propositional element (propositions describing the facts and consequences) and
(b) the deontic operator (element of ought to e.g. do something).[12]

On the other hand, the *meaning* content of the propositional element is connected to the deontic part of the norm. A proposition P (e.g., description of facts) does not have the same meaning when it merely describes a part of reality or forms an element in such a description as when used for prescriptive purposes. The deontic operator *qualifies* the reality.

In its simplest form a law text expresses norm in an unambiguous manner. This is the case when the text of the law contains an explicit definition of a term. Normally the law is not written in this way. It expresses two or more norms each of which *can* be part of the legal order. The task of the interpreter is to select from these norm alternatives the one which is "in accordance with the legal order." The scope for interpretation can be connected either with the description of the legal facts or with the description of the legal consequences or with both.

(i) The scope for interpretation affects the legal facts. In this, the norm receives the following form:

$$N_i\ (x)\ (F_1xV\ .\ .\ .\ F_{n'}x \rightarrow OGx)$$

where the symbol "V" can be read either as "and" or as "or". The individual characteristic elements can thus either be alternatives (and which thus rule each other out) or it can be possible to combine them.

Such a scope for interpretation prevails in, for example, many cases in civil law. There is a clear description of the legal consequence – the legal consequence is G – but there is no certainty as to what state of affairs or what configuration of states of affairs the consequence is connected to.

For example, Chapter 21, Section 11 of the Decedent's Estate Act regulates the liability for the debts of the deceased. The provision states, "if the parties of the estate have . . . sold, pawned *or otherwise* used or destroyed property of the estate . . . they shall be held liable . . . for the debts of the deceased." In the system of the Decedent's Estate Act, there is no uncertainty as to the content of the consequence of liability. On the other hand, the set of legal facts has been expressed in part with open elements: ". . . or otherwise . . .".

(ii) Often, however, the situation is different. The scope for interpretation is connected with the way in which the legal consequences are defined. Presented schematically, the situation is thus as follows:

$$N_i\,(x)\,(Fx \rightarrow OG_1x\ V\ .\ .\ .\ \ G_{nr}x)$$

One example which is often used in discussions of legal theory, that of the punishment latitude in criminal law, suits rather well for illustrating this type of scope for interpretation. The punishment scale is expressed only as a maximum and a minimum, and so every decision which fits within these limits is legal. Even so, one cannot say that the legal consequence has been described in a precise manner.

An even better example is the case where more than one type of consequence, for example nullity and a liability for restitution, follow on the same facts. Yet another example: the norm states that, for example, either a fine or imprisonment follows the set of facts in question.

(iii) The most problematic case arises when both the description of the legal facts and the legal consequences give scope for interpretation. We may write this as follows:

$$N_i\,(x)\,(F_1\mathrm{x}V\ .\ .\ .\ \ F_{mr}x \rightarrow OG_1xV\ .\ .\ .\ \ G_{nr}x)$$

Many cases of interpretation at the heart of civil law are of this type. For example, according to Chapter 7, Section 8 of the Decedent's Estate Act, a person who has received property from the deceased in certain ways is obligated to return to a heir the amount that the heir is missing from his "compulsory legal portion." In this situation, the problem of interpretation is aggravated by the fact that not only must we determine what the phrase "receiving of property obligating the person in question to return the property" refers to, but we must also determine what the "return of property" is. Is it a returning of the property "as such", or can the person for example give a sum of money corresponding to the property in question?

When we attribute content on this basis to the choice of the interpretation alternative – the choice between contents I_1 and I_2 – we could imagine for example the following situations:

$$\text{(i)}\ N_i\text{: } (x)\ (F_1x \rightarrow OG_ix)$$
$$N_i\text{: } (x)\ (F_2x \rightarrow OG_ix)$$

$$\text{(ii)}\ N_i\text{: } (x)\ (F_ix \rightarrow OG_1x)$$
$$N_i\text{: } (x)\ (F_ix \rightarrow OG_2x)$$

$$\text{(iii)}\ N_i\text{: } (x)\ (F_1x \rightarrow OG_1x)$$
$$N_i\text{: } (x)\ (F_2x \rightarrow OG_2x)$$

The basic problematics of the interpretation is the same in all of the cases in the examples above. It is a question of a choice between two alternatives. The cases (i) and (ii) differ from each other as far as the focus of the interpretation is concerned. In the former case, the problem lies in the type of the consequences and, in the latter one, in the description of the facts. On the other hand, case (iii) represents (even though in a rather schematic form) a very complicated situation. In order to simplify the presentation we shall only deal with the methodology of interpretation in case (i). Here, the description of the set of legal facts permits two different content alternatives, interpretations I_1 and I_2.

In accordance with their contents and functions, legal norms can be categorized in a number of ways. In the foregoing, we have already discussed primary and secondary norms. A classification which in broader than this divides norms into *rules* and *principles*.[13] In this study, legal norms will be examined specifically as rules. Rules, in turn, may be either *constitutive* or *regulative*.[14] The difference may be illustrated by taking an example from the rules of a game. Constitutive rules define, for example, which piece (in chess) is the king. The regulative rules define how the player ought to behave. In the field of law, constitutive rules are used to define for example legal institutions. Thus the institution of a (valid) marriage is constituted as marriage specifically through certain rules.

One type of constitutive rules is *competence norms*. They define, for example, who has the (legal) power to make a valid transaction. In the administrative law the competence norms have also been called organizational norms: they lock the system of competent organs, for instance, of the organs of the State.

Regulative norms may be called *norms of conduct*.[15] They define how one ought, ought not or may behave. In other words, they are commands, prohibitions or permissions. A well known problem is formed by the question of the relations among commands, prohibitions and permission. Is one of these categories primary in the sense that the other categories can be reduced to it? I shall not deal with this problem here. Also the problem of the "imperative status" of behavioural norms will be bypassed, for example, the question of whether or not behavioural norms are the expression of the will of some authority and, if they are, in what sense they are of this type.

Much attention has been given in legal theory to the relation between norms of conduct and competence norms. At times, the independent position of competence norms has been questioned, and it has been observed that they only define the conditions in which norms of conduct can be applied.[16] Thus a norm which entitles *A* to transfer his real estate to *B* only gives a condition of the application of those norms of conduct which define the position of the purchaser, *B*, in relation to third parties. I shall bypass a closer examination of even this question in norm theory.

The same is true of the classification of norms into norms of conduct, reaction norms and reaction manner norms (procedural norms). This classification has been developed by Kaarle Makkonen in a very important manner.[17] The distinction between these different categories is significant for the analysis of the structure of a legal decision-making situation, but from the point of view of the interpretation the classification is irrelevant. It makes no difference whether or not the scope of interpretation pertains to norms of conduct, reaction norms or reaction manner norms. In any case, the method of justification is similar for all three types of norms.

In all modern Western societies one can identify a development according to which different kinds of *discretion norms* are becoming more and more important. Discretion norms cannot be classified either constitutive or regulative because they simply define a decisional framework for an administrative organ. For instance, the law may only provide a certain authority with certain financial resources but the same law leaves open the criteria of allocation of these resources. The legislator has delegated the final decision to a lower authority. A great number of problems is involved in this type of legislation. From the point of view of Constitution the "open" delegation of the legislative power is not unproblematic at all. On the other hand, the whole structure of the justification is in this discretion of quite another type than in the traditional interpretation cases. First, the justification is not born out the sources of law and, second, there are no standards of the proper legal interpretation that give the guidelines for the application of the law. The decision is merely based on the discretion of expediency.

Irrespective of the increasing general importance of the discretion norms, the entire analysis of legal justification is in this study focused only upon the constitutive and regulative norms. This is partially due to the fact that the very concept of jurisdiction does not cover the mere discretion of expediency. According to its function the court has to apply the law and the discretion of expediency belongs to the administrative organs. Furthermore, in order to elucidate the core of *legal* justification, constitutive and regulative norms are of special importance, because only here we meet the problem of alternative interpretations and of the choice between them. Hence, the ambit of the study will not suffer from the restriction of the scope although, for the sake of clarity, only constitutive and regulative norms have been chosen as examples of the justification cases.

2. A GENERAL CHARACTERIZATION OF INTERPRETATION AND INTERPRETATION THEORY

2.1 *Interpretation as a Hermeneutic Process*

In the foregoing, it has been seen that a central task of legal dogmatics is the justification of norm standpoints, in other words the justification of why it is rational and reasonable to accept norm N as part of the valid law (in Finland). Interpretation, in turn, has been understood as a linguistic matter. It is primarily the clarification of law texts through the presentation of interpretative statements. Of interpretation statements, interpretation *standpoints* state what meaning content of the law text it would be rational and right to choose. The interpretative standpoints that are thus produced can always be turned into norm standpoints. But as interpretation is a linguistic matter, it is more natural to speak of the interpretation of law (texts) than the interpretation of legal norms.

From a *procedural* point of view, however, the nature of the interpretative process is not unproblematic. It is a question of how a justified interpretation of a rationally acceptable meaning content is produced. How can we render believable that a certain meaning content is rationally justified and right? One anchor is offered by the so-called *hermeneutic approach*.[18]

The interpretation of a linguistic expression is typically hermeneutic, or to be more specific, a phenomenon which belongs to the sphere of text hermeneutics. This means the general theory assigning meaning to language, and to the theory of the philosophical conditions of the assignment of meaning. Without entering into the development of hermeneutic philosophy or into its different tendencies, I shall give some general remarks on hermeneutics as the theory of text interpretation in order to guide the reader to the thematics of this study.

The representatives of hermeneutics regard all understanding as being based on *pre-understanding* ("Vorwissen"). From the point of view of general hermeneutics, pre-understanding can apparently be characterized as a meaning entity or a meaning unity understood in advance. In order to illustrate this, reference has been made to, for example, the understanding of a work of art. In order to identify a work of art we must already be in possession of the concept of art, some impression of what art is. This impression may be rough, simplistic and unclearly delineated. It may contain much bias and unjustified assumptions. But even so, we *need* some kind of impression of art and works of art so that in general we could be able to discuss these matters.

The same applies to the understanding of different texts. Even they must be approached from "somewhere". The understanding of texts cannot be free of presuppositions, it cannot, so to speak, take place in a vacuum. The act of understanding, in turn, can be described in many ways. One way is the following. A certain text (for example the unclear/ambiguous expression L_i in a law text) is rendered understandable by connecting it with other expressions. These other expressions are used as the basis of the interpretation; they are, for example, expressions in the legislative history of the law, the texts of precedents, written standpoints taken in the legal literature, and so on. When brought into connection with the sentences referred to, L_i becomes sensible for us. We *understand* the meaning of L_i.

In this case, understanding is based on two factors: the relation between the part and the whole, and the insight into new meaning connections. It is often emphasized in hermeneutics that an individual expression receives meaning only *as a part of a whole* and that, correspondingly, the whole is rendered understandable when the part falls into place. The latter position, which seems somewhat enigmatic, is understandable when we consider that the connecting of different expressions with each other opens up new meaning connections. Both the expression which we must interpret and the expressions which form the foundation of the interpretation "fall into place" in a new way. This is what is added by the interpretation. When the expression we are interpreting falls into place in the whole, we believe that we understand the meaning of that expression, at least in *that* connection. Later on, in connection with some other expressions and through the realization of a new meaning entity we are prepared to reevaluate our position. The expressions has received a new shading, without any subtraction from the content of the previous case of interpretation. Thus, interpretation, depending on the meaning connections (the whole), receives what amounts to layers of meaning. Each layer is connected with the whole just referred to.

It is essential to note that the finding of the relation between the part and the whole, and the insight into new meaning connections is not based on the application of a closed set of rules of procedure. The meaning of the expression we must interpret does not result from the application of unambiguous rules to a set of propositions used as the basis of the interpretation. The sentences used as the basis and the result (the interpretation) are connected with each other in a nondeductive and yet plausible manner. Hermeneutics is thus not deduction in the precise logical sense of the word. It is here that hermeneutic philosophy offers its most interesting anchor to interpretation in legal dogmatics. As we shall see later on, this view needs a more precise element in order for it to be suitable for the theory of interpretation in legal dogmatics.

The nondeductive and yet believable connection of expressions has often been presented as follows. Expressions *make sense* only when they stand in relation to other expressions: the way partial expressions are read depends on how other expresssions are read and ultimately on how the whole is read. A *hermeneutical circle* is formed, a phenomenon which has been compared to the reading of poetry. When we have come to the end of a poem and are able to form an impression of the whole, it may be that a detail opens up better than at first reading; this detail affects the way in which we understand the whole, and so on. We continue in this way until we are tired of reading the poem. But all in all, after we have done all of this we can say that we understand the poem or that we at least understand it better than before.

It has been said that a typical feature of a hermeneutical circle is that the interpreter cannot break out of it. He, so to speak, is enchained by language. When we wish to present justification for an interpretation or the interpretation of an interpretation, we must resort to language, to an expression or to the interpretation of an expression. We simply cannot get rid of words and sentences: words are interpreted *through other words*. No empirical observation or anything similar (for example a "real" legal argument which has been shown to be valid) can simply solve our problem; our only refuge is language.

We can say that expression L_i has been interpreted successfully only when the person with whom we are speaking understands the interpretation *in the same way* as we understand it. In other words: a proper interpretation is an interpretation which makes the interpretation understandable to the recipient, to the person at whom the interpretation is directed.

The hermeneutic circle can be described also in accordance with system theory. Interpretation is a feed-back phenomenon. At a certain stage in interpretation, feed-back occurs, and the result is "tested" in the light of the previous information. When the feed-back no longer brings anything new to the available information, we have reached the point in the hermeneutical circle that we can reach in those circumstances.

Some authors have, at times, wanted to make a sharp distinction between the hypothetical-deductive model used in the (natural) sciences and hermeneutic interpretations (and the interpretation circle).[19] In so doing, they have generally tried to illustrate the hypothetical deductive model with a spiral. On the basis of a certain preliminary insight and on the conditions set by certain theoretical concepts, a hypothesis is formed which one attempts to support or reject on an empirical basis. A supported hypothesis creates on its part the basis for new hypotheses and new testing, in other words for the formation of empirically controllable theory. With the use of a diagram, the situation can be shown as in Diagram 13.

One can scarcely consider it an essential feature of the "hypothetical deductive spiral" that the supporting/rejecting of hypotheses takes place with the help of certain proof or empirical facts given from *outside*. Taking into consideration the theoretical content of empirical observations, they cannot be regarded as a basis for testing given once and for all, in the same way that, for example, logical empiricists imagine of observational data. One should instead say that one breaks out of the

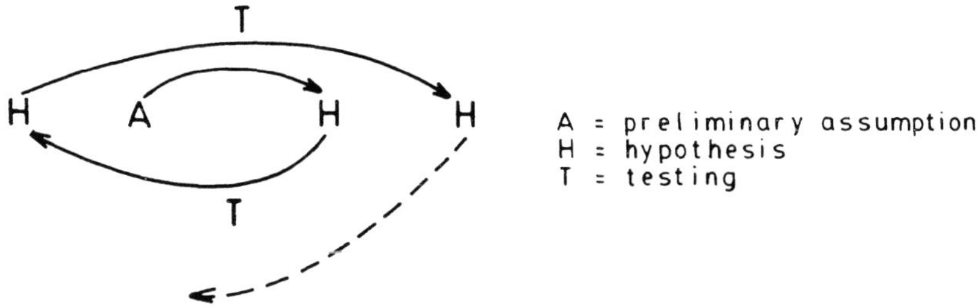

Diagram 13

spiral in the hypothetical deductive method by referring to the *theoretical* conceptions. These conceptions, rather broadly accepted in the scientific community, state with what type of data we can regard the hypothesis as having been confirmed, i.e., which one of the tested hypotheses is a scientific result.

In the hermeneutic circle the property of "theoretical conception" is in a somewhat different position. In interpretative sciences we do not have the same very *uniform* "theories" as to the basis for testing as in the natural sciences. It does not follow from this, however, that the interpreter would have to wander without end around the interpretative circle. At the stage when the interpretation becomes acceptable in the interpretative community, we have come to much the same position as when a hypothesis has become supported in the natural sciences. Here, acceptability is based on (often rather ambiguous) conceptions on how expressions are to be understood in the connection in question.

When these points of view are considered, it would seem to be justified to draw parallels between the structure of the hypothetical deductive spiral and the hermeneutic circle. In the former, there is a dialectic interchange between hypothesis and testing, while in the latter the interpreter constructs the situation on the basis of the interpretative connection between the part and the whole. The interpretative standpoint which is the point of departure is the hypothesis which, during the interpretation process, in part changes and in part is either confirmed or rejected.

With reference to the views of Peter Winch, we can state that the two methods are joined by a common "basis of testing". This is ultimately tied to certain conventions adopted in a human community (in a scientific community or another social community). From this point of view the most significant difference between research in the sciences and the doctrine of interpretation would seem to lie in the fact that in the former the "conventions" behind the testing (1) have been agreed upon in the scientific community and (2) are relatively stable, while the "conventions" in the doctrine of interpretation are (1) based on the positions of the entire social community and, in addition, (2) their content is often considerably ambiguous.[20] In the doctrine of interpretation there can exist at the same time many "conventions" which shut each other out without any of them lacking justification.

If, however, it is possible to produce conventions also in the doctrine of interpretation on some criteria of interpretation, some natural explanation must be given for this fact. It must be possible to justify philosophically the possibility of conventions itself. And in connection with this, if it is possible in the doctrine of interpretation to have several valid conventions in existence at the same time, the question of whether or not it is possible to cross the boundaries of conventions and find greater unanimity becomes important. My view is that this is one of the most decisive philosophical problems in hermeneutic interpretation theory in legal dogmatics.

2.2 *The Special Nature of Interpretation in Legal Dogmatics*

Two matters may doubtless be credited to hermeneutic theory. The theory justifies the connection between interpretation and language in a way that is deserving of attention, and at the same time is it shown that interpretation is nondeductive and at least partially nonempirical. With an eye on legal dogmatics, these observations have the important significance that it is possible to locate interpretation in legal dogmatics in the basic classification of the various sciences. Generally speaking, we can say that legal dogmatics belongs to the so-called interpretative sciences and, in this view, to the tradition of the humanities, rather than as a neighbour of the empirical social sciences.

Such general characterizations may easily lead to misunderstanding. One of the most fateful misunderstandings is the impression that interpretation in legal dogmatics is something that can clearly be classified, i.e. that there exists a core which is typical of proper interpretation. According to this view, legal interpretation is not, for instance, the same as presenting empirical statements (predictions, technical norms etc.). As we already have noticed, legal dogmatics is composed of a cluster of language games. These language games have family resemblance: games *A* and *B* may strongly resemble each other, as may *B* and *C*, and *C* and *D*. This need not mean that *A* and *D* would have significant common features other than the fact that they are interpretation games. The descriptive statements, technical norms, recommendations and norm standpoints belong all to these variegated games. Yet, the interpretation game that is constituted of norm (interpretation) *standpoints* is not an internally homogeneous one, either. In actual research practice, there can be a variety of ways to reach the solution. Sometimes the reference to the text of law is enough. In other cases, the result of the interpretation can be deduced from the concepts mentioned in the law. However, normally, different kinds of the sources of law and evaluations are needed for getting an answer. In this regard, interpretation can be illustrated as in Diagram 14.

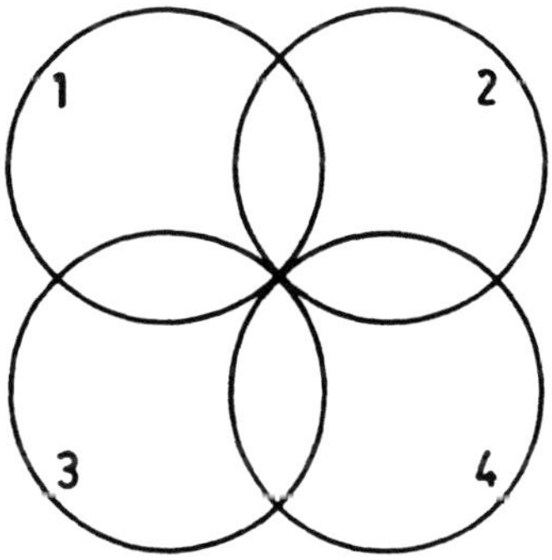

Diagram 14

The numbers in the diagram have the following meanings.

1 = the reference to the text of law (literal interpretation)
2 = conceptual analysis
3 = the presentation of empirical data or the sources of law
4 = the presentation of evaluations [21]

The diagram attempts to illustrate two matters. On one hand, interpretation in legal dogmatics can be connected with parts of each numbered sector. In a way, it is a combination of any of the four language games illustrated. The weight of a certain language game, shall we say of conceptual analysis, can vary with the situation. In one case the analysis of concepts may be totally unnecessary. Even so, conceptual analysis can have a part in some other case of interpretation. On the other hand, the diagram shows that in complicated situations the language games involved have a common area where each partial factor has an influence in accordance with its relative weight. One cannot say, however, that this is the true content of interpretation in legal dogmatics. To an equal degree, interpretation is something that is only affected by sectors 1 and 2, 2 and/or 3 and/or 4 just to take some examples. Thus, an interpretation consisting of the interpretation standpoints cannot be defined on the basis of any individual part or any special combination of these parts. Interpretation is simply the *family resemblance entity* formed by various language games.[22]

Even so, there must be some way of analyzing interpretation. One possibility offered by the application of Wittgensteinian linguistic philosophy is gaining insight into the construction of language games. Let us again begin from the idea of legal certainty. Each of us expects decisions to be rational, and the results to be acceptable. In this, a natural point of view in legal thought is offered by the attempt to construct an interpretation game where, in as problematic a situation as possible, one attempts to maximize the expectation of rationality and produce an interpretation result which has as broad an acceptance as possible. This sets certain preliminary demands on the game we are to construct.

First, we must assume that random factors are eliminated from the justification situation. We must construct a language game where

(i) all the feasible and relevant justification is *available*, and
(ii) the participants are able, *despite random factors*, to evaluate the justification which they are using and bring it to a conclusion.

An interpretation game constructed in this way is, as we have noticed, ideal. But why construct such an ideal game? Would it not be more natural to examine interpretation in legal dogmatics as it is in practice? In principle, we really should proceed in such a fashion. This, however, is prevented by many factors. First of all, research is often unprecise. Different interpreters disagree or agree on a problem simply because the concepts that they use are not sufficiently precise to distinguish between the actual subject of the disagreement or agreement. It is also not unusual that interpretation is not justified, or is justified only very briefly. In some cases, the interpretation is actually used to reach a certain goal, or it reveals the pre-set attitudes of the interpreter towards the matter being interpreted. The most important difficulty, however, is presented by the language being interpreted itself. If we try to form a total picture of interpretation games we should try to describe the entire group of games. This, however would be impossible. First of all, justification games as a totality, form a changing, dynamic whole. Individual language games are discarded, others take their place, and yet the over-all change is so gradual that in day-to-day life it is impossible to notice any clear limits. There is also another reason. The group of language games is so complicated that a description so to speak falls apart on its own accord if no attempt is made to concentrate and simplify it artificially. The interpretation language in legal dogmatics is hidden in all of its many shades with a fog that prevents understanding of the nature of interpretation.[23] In order to disperse the fog we can consciously *construct* either a game that is more primitive than ordinary language, or games that shed light on some features of this ordinary language; games which, in the light of what we have learned, appear to be possible and at the same time adequate justification games.

In saying this, it is not being argued that a constructed language game would represent such-and-such an actual justification situation. No attempt is being made to give an empirical example; it only describes a possible method of analysis. On the other hand, the purpose is not to produce a "deepstructure" of interpretation in law which would amount to a "Natur der Sache" of interpretation, a core which is latent in all justification of interpretation statements.[24] This would mean much the same as the view that, after all, every justification game must have something in common with every other game. In this sense, the construction of a language game is not the systematization of the background which unites the different methods of interpretation.

On the other hand, the goal is not, as already observed, the setting of a recommendation (*sensu stricto*): this is what interpretation in law should become. It is not a question of a methodological technical ought, either: this is how you must reason if you wish to reason correctly. An idealized example does not at the same time try for a definition of what proper argumentation is. The concept of the ideal argumentation game expresses a "weaker" technical norm: *if* you want to fulfill to expectation of maximal legal certainty in society, you ought to follow the pattern of rational justification. On the other hand, one can reasonably defend the position that rationality is the core of legal certainty.[25] The games played in reality have a more or less family resemblance with the ideal game. The significance of this pattern (ideal game) lies in its property to offer one single thread of interpretation which makes it possible to enter into the fabric of the games formed by the research language in everyday praxis. The purpose of an idealized interpretation game is to give us a *hold* on the language that we use, so that we can understand – and also criticize – in a better way than before our own language and through this our activity in the legal community; ultimately, so that we can understand ourselves better as members of society. Wittgenstein's famous sentence, "Denk nicht, sondern schau", in this point of view, comes close to the old exhortation from classical times, "Know thyself."[26]

The comparison with games has much to say also in another sense. The minimum equipment of every game includes both the pieces, tokens or whatever, and the rules of the game. As has already been observed, the rules of the game are either constitutive or regulative. The "pieces" in interpretation games are the basis on which the interpreter gives the result of the interpretation, his conclusion. They are the parts of the whole with which the expression being interpreted is brought into contact, as the matter can be expressed in hermeneutic language. The rules of the game, in turn, are formed by the rules of legal interpretation.

In the theory of law, it is usual to call the interpretation basis the sources of law. The rules (directives) of legal interpretation are the rules that define how to use the sources of law in connection with the interpretation. The result of the interpretation "follows" from the sources of law when they are used in the way required by the rules of interpretation. Thus, the point of departure in the interpretation game is as follows:

$$S \xrightarrow{TR} I_i$$

In the formula, the letter S refers to the sources of law, I_i to the interpretation alternative chosen and TR to transformation in the sense used by Aleksander Peczenik. According to Peczenik, it is a question of transformation from p to q if and only if the following conditions are fulfilled:

(1) p is the justification of q
(2) q does not deductively follow from p and
(3) the transformation from p to q cannot become deductive through the addition of an analytic proposition.

Peczenik distinguishes between many types of transformations. The most important is the distinction between "transformation *into* law" and "transformation *in* law". The former type has already been dealt with in the discussion about the systemic validity. Norm *N* is valid in systemic sense if and only if it belongs to a norm hierarchy and this hierarchy is legally valid if and only if it is based on a fundamental norm and, furthermore, on a justifying fundamental norm.

A basic example of the latter type of transformations is a "jump" from legal sources to legal interpretation (justification), in other words, the formula referred to above. The result is not entirely a deductive consequence of the justification material but the interpreter "moves" from the basic material to the conclusion so that the conclusion is

1. rationally considered and, at the same time,
2. generally acceptable (reasonable).

Hence, legal justification is the same as transformation from the sources of law (and evaluations) to the final interpretation alternative. Problems in the theory of justification can be found in two areas: (1) what is the structure of justification and (2) what guarantees can be given of the rationality of the justification and the acceptability of the result? Before I deal with these matters I shall present briefly the basis of interpretation, i.e., the sources of law and the interpretation rules, and the ways in which the sources of law are used.

3. THE SOURCES OF LAW AND THE DIRECTIVES OF LEGAL INTERPRETATION

3.1. *On the Concept of the Sources of Law*

3.1.1. *The source of information.* From a practical point of view the interpreter needs different kinds of information media. For instance, a collection of the statutes (Law book), text books, collections of the precedents etc. On the basis of this material the interpreter tries to identify the relevant *texts* for finding out the solution or for justifying it. In this regard, the source of information may also be called the source of law. However, this terminology does not fit if one attempts to analyse the structure of legal reasoning. The source of information is only a technical tool, not a material source, for the interpreter.[27]

3.1.2. *The source of reasoning.* In the context of discovery the focus lies on the criteria by means of which one finds out the answer to a legal problem. This means that there is a causal relation between the criteria and the final choice of the interpretative alternative. In other words, the source of law is a cause that results in the solution. As was noticed before, the context of discovery has been left outside of the scope of this contribution. Hence, in the following the concept "source of law" does not refer to the causes of the interpretative activity but the reasons that are used to justify a legal interpretation (context of justification).

The reasons for the legal justification may, on the other hand, be understood either in the strict or in the broad sense of the concept (*sensu stricto* versus *sensu largo*). Traditionally in the statutory legal systems the former category covered only such authoritative reasons as the law texts (statutes) and as is the case, for example, in Finland, the customs of the land. These are, as will be pointed out later on, the obligatory basis for the justification of the court decisions. It is, so to speak, the minimum justification. An authoritative source of a corresponding type in the common law system is a precedent. As far as the Finnish court traditions are concerned, the statutes and, in some quite rare cases the customs of the land, have normally been also the only manifest justification of the court decisions.

However, the actual legal justification, in the courts as well as in the scholarly work, uses sources other than merely the statutes and the customs of the land. In legal practice, the functioning concept "source of law" is generally used in the broad sense (*sensu largo*). The notions "reason for the legal interpretation" and "source of law" are equivalent. Referring to this practice, the notion of the source of law is in this contribution defined as follows: *every reason that can – according to the generally accepted rules of the legal community – be used as the justificatory basis of the interpretation is a source of law*. Preliminarily, the following catalogue of the Finnish sources of law can be listed.

3.2. *The List of the Sources of Law*

3.2.1. *The Finnish catalogue of the sources.* (a) *Law texts.* In this connection "law text" refers to every statute or provision that has been given on the basis of the authority of the Constitution. The category of law texts in the Finnish legal order includes not only Acts of Parliament, but also decrees given by the Council of State, Ministry decisions, and so on.

Often the use of a law text as a source of law means a reference to the *systematic relationship* between two or more texts. The law texts and the norms that they express are seen to form a system. Every provision has its place in connection with this system. For this reason, not only individual law texts but also systematic points of view can be presented as justification for interpretation.

(b) *Travaux préparatoires*, i.e. the legislative history of law text (statutes). The idea that the goal of the legal interpretation is to reach the will of the legislator more generally: *ratio legis* – is already expressed by C. H. Eckhardus in 1750. He writes e.g. that the legal interpretation is nothing else than to clarify the will of the legislator on the basis of his words and ideas. During the 19th Century Thibaut and von Savigny as well as Windscheid and Bierling (in the beginning of the 20th Century) emphasized the same idea as one of the basic strategies of the legal interpretation.[28]

According to the traditional English doctrine, the will of the legislator has no place among the sources of law. However, in all common law countries the significance of the *travaux préparatoires* is gradually increasing. The reason for this recent phenomenon is quite natural: the amount of written law is increasing, it covers still more sectors in society and thus the significance of the written law as a steering mechanism in society is increasing more and more. On the other hand, the dynamics of society is such that it simply is impossible to write the texts of law so that they directly express the area of the application. The legislative procedure is often the only source from which the interpreter can get additional information.

The concept of *travaux préparatoires* covers, e.g. the following documents as the source of information:

- various basic studies published as Committee reports, reports of the legislative Council, reports of different ministerial working groups, the memorials of the officials etc.
- Government Bills to Parliament,
- the minutes of the Committees of Parliament and, in some cases, the reports of these Committees, and
- the records of the discussions in plenary sessions of Parliament and the results of votes in Parliament on various questions, as published in the Diet Documents.

In addition, one could mention unpublished notes, the minutes of (non-Parliamentary) committee meetings, the statements of individuals participating in the drafting of legislation, and so on. Much of the material mentioned here also has subsidiary material, such as statistical reports, on the basis of which some of the tendencies in the proposals may have been formulated.

(c) Customary law is often mentioned as a source of law. One subcategory of customary law is commercial praxis. As Aatos Alanen observed, the acceptance of customary law as a source of law is based on "that which is continuously repeated becomes in the general view a binding rule of behaviour, especially when it is found to be appropriate and reasonable."[29]

In Chapter 1, Section 11 of the Finnish Code of Judicial Procedure, "the custom of the land" is accepted as a source of law, but it is subject to written law: "The custom of the land, if it is not unreasonable, shall also serve as a guide to him (i.e., the judge), if there is no written law."

There has been continuous debate in the philosophy of law on the birth and binding basis of customary law in the statutory system. Much support has been given to the view that the binding nature of customary law is based on the tacit acceptance of the legislator. In the historical school doctrine, this is not accepted as such; the binding nature of customary law is seen to lie in the legal conviction of citizens.[30] In later thought it has often been observed that the binding nature is simply based on the fact that a certain custom has been applied in praxis for an extended period. In so doing, the interest of legal certainty demands that the custom be "legalized", or at least that the custom be accepted as a binding rule of law.[31] The extent to which a custom must continue before it becomes a binding source of law has been left to discretion in the individual case.

At times the custom of the land may set aside written law. This is the case when circumstances change and the law text is left without any scope for application. This is one, although not the only, example of the so-called *desuetude*. The norm expressed in the law text and the norm produced through customary law are in conflict, and the former steps aside. This kind of desuetude has a somewhat different meaning in legal dogmatics and from the point of view of the courts. As Makkonen points out, every formally valid norm in fact gives the judge the possibility of applying it.[32] The possibility of acting on the force of a "desuetude rule" has not been eliminated. On the other hand, in research, desuetude in fact forms a justification which must be taken into consideration in arguing either for or against an interpretation. This is especially evident when the researcher attempts to predict in advance the behavior of the court. Desuetude speaks strongly in favor of the view that the norm will not be applied. And yet: the judge can – even though it would be extremely rare – follow that norm.

Finally there is reason to recall the reservation in Chapter 1, Section 11 of the Finnish Code of Judicial Procedure: the custom of the land must be reasonable. Alanen notes that this is a well-founded reservation, as the norms of unwritten law are not based on planned decision-making in the same way as the norms of written law are. The principle of reasonableness, as it were, controls the custom of the land.[33]

(d) *Court Decisions*. In this connection much has been mentioned concerning the precedents.[34]

When a legal decision is considered to be a precedent, it is always judged so from the point of view of some later judicial decision. The former decision always precedes the latter one. I take an example from the Common Law system. Within the Common Law system, it is not conceived possible that a judicial body has the authority to decide whether its own decision will have the status of a precedent. That will remain for the later jurisdiction to decide.

In the widest use of the term, a precedent may refer to any judicial decision which has some kind of *significance* for later jurisdiction. It may, for instance, serve as one argument among several reasons for reaching a certain kind of outcome in the case. Widely speaking, any legal decision may have such significance for later jurisdiction. In the strict (and proper) sense of the word, however, only the decisions given by the *highest* national courts of justice – in Finland, the Supreme Court and the Supreme Administrative Court – may be truly called precedents. See however p. 85.

The binding strength of a precedent may be of two kinds: either *legal* (*de jure*) or *factual* (*de facto*).[35] The former one means that a judge may be charged with misconduct in office, if he neglects a precedent when making a decision in a later case of the similar kind. The observance of the precedent, in other words, is legally sanctioned. On the other hand, the factual binding strength of a precedent is only directive. A strong binding weight of a precedent may thus signify that if a precedent is not followed at a lower court of justice, it is highly probable that the case will be decided differently – and in accordance with the precedent – at a higher court, i.e. the Court of Appeal or the Supreme Court.

A precedent may be said to be *horizontally* binding, if it binds (*de jure* or *de facto*) the later jurisdiction of the very same jurisdictional body, say that of the Supreme Court. For instance, according to the Internal Working Order Act for the Supreme Court of Justice (§ 22), a deviation from an earlier Supreme Court precedent requires that the case has to be decided either by the plenum composition of the Court or by a so-called strengthened composition of a Court Section. The *vertical* binding strength of a precedent refers to the effect which the decisions given by a higher court have on the jurisdiction of the lower courts. For instance: a precedent issued by the Supreme Court binds (*de jure* or *de facto*) the judicial praxis of the Courts of Appeal and the Courts of First Instance.[36]

In the Finnish (and Swedish) legal culture there is an old principle that not even the decisions given by the highest national court of justice have any *legal* binding effect – either horizontally or vertically – on the judicial praxis of the lower courts. Deviation from a precedent has not been considered punishable as misconduct in office. And that old legal principle is still valid law today. Therefore, deviation from a precedent is allowed always when there are material grounds for doing so, and the judicial praxis is kept alive and flexible consequently. That important legal principle can in fact be traced back to the 17th century, stating that a judge cannot decide a case on the sole ground of an earlier precedent. Each legal dispute is considered bearing such individual characteristics that all the relevant legal source material has to be taken into account in the legal discretion.[37]

On the other hand, the factual binding effect of the precedents has generally been acknowledged, with the strength of the binding effect differing from case to case. The binding strength of a precedent depends on the *weight of the arguments* presented for the decision. The matter has been stated very clearly in Sweden so that only the weight of the arguments of a precedent shall have decisive influence on the judicial praxis of the lower courts. The factual binding effect of the precedents has been thought to strengthen the unity of national jurisdiction, and thereby also to increase the legal security enjoyed by the citizens. The Code of Judicial Procedure refers to the issue, too. A party in a dispute has for long had the right to ask for permission to appeal to the Supreme Court in his case, if the case may have significance for other legal disputes of similar character. The precedential nature of the case, in other words, has been the cause for appealing to the Supreme Court. At present, however, the system is slightly different. The law reform which entered into force in 1980 (see Code of Judicial Procedure 30:3) has significantly restricted the right of a litigant to have his case decided by the Supreme Court. A permission to appeal to the Supreme Court may be allowed either because of the precedential character of the case or (e.g.) because the unity of national judicial praxis justifies it. Since only a very limited amount of cases now enter the Supreme Court, the precedential weight of the decisions given in those cases has increased accordingly.

The matter has some highly significant consequences as far as the legal certainty of the citizens as well as the very concept of a precedent are concerned. It has been stated in legal dogmatics that the more *interesting* the problem of legal interpretation that the petitioner can present in his case, the better are his chances to obtain the permission to appeal to the Supreme Court on the ground of the precedential nature of his case. The interests of the petitioner are not the key issue – the "interesting" character of the norm interpretation problem is. Thus the protection of the rights of an individual citizen may be ignored so that a legal interpretation issue of a more general nature may be solved. The Supreme Court of Justice therefore receives more and more the status of a general norm interpretation and norm giving body.

It has also been mentioned in this connection that the Supreme Court often seems to grant the permission of appeal in such cases when the unity of jurisdiction is thought to require it. An inherent danger, however, is concealed therein. The unity of national legal praxis is thought to be in danger always when a lower court has deviated from a precedent issued by the Supreme Court. The Supreme Court controls especially closely the observance of its *own* judicial praxis. That may have a "closing" side effect on the whole legal order: the Supreme Court quite autonomically dictates what is to be considered *right* in society. Let us yet return to the concept of a precedent.

In the discussion of the binding effect of a decision, the rubrication of the case has received the central status. Representatives of the Supreme Court have in several contexts emphasized that it is just in the rubrication that the precedential norm is given. It is a "nutshell" description of what is considered *legally relevant* in the case. The rubrication of the case, however, can be interpreted in (at least) two different ways.

Firstly, it is very well conceivable that the rubrication of the case no more than states the solution given to an individual legal problem: as the existence of the facts T_i has been made evident, the legal dispute between persons *A* and *B* has been decided in the way R_i. What is concerned is the description of an individual legal case and the decision attached to it – not a norm having a general character. The rubrication of the case, in other words, gives information of the decision reached. The true meaning of the short rubrication of the case is revealed only after having taken acquaintance with all of the documentary material of the case – beginning from the writ and ending to the letters of appeal and their enclosures. Such an interpretation would seem to match well with the ideas that underline the unique character of each legal case. The case under consideration has been solved in the way R_i *just because* the case description of the case is T_i.

If the rubrication of a case is understood in this way, i.e. as a description of a singular case, one can hardly speak of a precedent at all in this connection. The description bears rather closer similarity to such an "explanation" of a historic event with the help of a singular "law" that is commonly known as Dray's paradox. As an example, the outburst of the First World War has been mentioned. A historic "law" on the matter might sound as follows: a war is always the outcome of such a chain of events that an archduke gets shot in his automobile in such-and-such circumstances. The description and the historic "law" are bound to that particular case. Thus, there is consequently no rule that could be followed in the explanation of any other event.

The very concept of a precedent in fact does require another kind of interpretation of the rubrication of the case – one that the Finnish Supreme Court itself seems to have defended. According to this alternative, the rubrication of the case indicates the *norm* (legal rule) that has been followed in the case. In other words, the rubrication counts up to a norm formulation the contents of which is the legal norm that has just been duely enforced. As a norm formulation, the rubrication represents a higher degree of generality than the description of the facts or the arguments put forth for the case. The rubrication defines a certain *class* of cases to which a certain type of legal consequences is to be attached. The rubrication gets "detached" from the original decision, and – so to say – begins to lead its own life.

In legal language, the term precedent often gets the meaning of a precedential *case* instead of a precedential legal decision. The choice of the term, however, does not blur the matter to a significant degree. Properly speaking, though, the notion of a precedential case does not fit very well with the idea of the rubrication of the case as a norm formulation. The case itself, i.e. the fact description of the case, does not have any precedential weight – only the legal rule attached to the case has. Moreover, the rubrication of the case does not reveal anything of the facts of the individual case, *if* it is thought to have become detached from the original case and to have received the status of an independent norm formulation. In order to grasp the problematics related to the rubrication of a case as a norm formulation, I will explicitly refer to the legal *decision* in question when using the concept of a precedent.

In accordance with this way of thinking, the precedential character of a legal decision lies therein that the jurisdictional bodies are bound to the norm issued in the rubrication of that case when making a decision in a later *similar* case. The strength of such factual binding effect then depends on the probability that the courts in fact will adhere to the decision in their own judicial discretion. In some fields of law, e.g. tax law, the repetitive character of the cases to be solved may emphasize the binding weight of the precedents. In some other fields of law, e.g. civil law, the fact descriptions are usually highly unique, and so the binding effect of the precedents becomes more problematic.

The norm issued in the rubrication of a case may be of two kinds. The rubrication may define an explicit rule to be applied to a certain *type* of legal cases. However, that the rubrication fails to offer such explicitly is quite a common-place. More often it is open to several alternative interpretations. For instance: the Finnish courts have the authority to enforce a deviation from a valid civil law contract, if the stipulation in case is considered to violate the principle of equity. What is then the meaning of the expression "against the principle of equity"? The width of the expression becomes the key issue.

Summing up, one can regard the following types of decisions as sources of law:

– *the decisions of the highest courts* (the Supreme Court, the Supreme Administrative Court). In connection with the Supreme Court, it should be noted that there is legislation which limits the possibility of appealing to the Supreme Court. For this reason mainly such cases which have general significance for the application of law are channeled to this court level. Thus, this legislation disposes with a large number of decisions where the decision of the lower court becomes final. This means that, especially in the long run, the actual precedental value of the decisions of the Supreme Court will increase.

– *Intermediate court level decisions*, for example decisions of the

Courts of Appeal, especially if no appeal can be made from these courts to the supreme level. This would be the case either due to the legislated limits on appeals referred to above, or because the law expressly prohibits appeals in certain matters. Recently, the actual precedental value, especially of the decisions of the courts of appeal, has been increasing.

– In some cases also *lower court praxis* may have precedental significance or at least significance as justification for a decision. This is the case whenever the matter is dealt with solely on the lower court level. A typical example in the Decedent's Estate Act would be court decisions on the appointment of the administrator or the executor of estates.[37] These decisions have in fact solely created the praxis which now constitutes the entire institution.

(e) *General principles of law* and *moral principles* (values). In the philosophy of law, the nature, content and position of general legal principles have often been questioned. In this connection I will only refer to the views expressed on the matter by Otto Brusiin and Kaarle Makkonen.[38] On the other hand, it is undeniable that in legal reasoning one refers to such principles as *pacta sunt servanda*, *Treu und Glaube* and *nulla poena sine lege*. These and similar principles are considered to be "derived" from existing legislation. They express unwritten and yet valid legal rules. Chaim Perelman writes, "Mann kann demnach sagen, dass dieses allgeimeine Prinzip in Gesetz begründet ist."[39] General legal principles are part of the legal tradition which, through decisions and their justification, are transferred from one generation to the next even though they are not written down in law.

General moral principles are partly in a different position. In some cases, however, they have value as a basis for justification, and they might also be mentioned. As an example we might point to the discussion on abortion, where the principle of the respect of life has an important role. To an equal extent one can imagine that in certain connections reference to justice would be an argument in a decision of discretion.

In a moral context the principles mentioned have only moral value. When the same principle is used as justification for a legal decision, it receives legal relevance. This shows that nothing is connected with these principles as such which would justify us in categorizing them as either legal or moral.[40] Their status as sources of law depends solely on the context in which they are used. The matter has significance even beyond the scholarly interpretation. Our example of the extent to which moral principles are tied to the context shows how ambiguous the line is between law and morals, when that line is examined from the point of view of a legal decision. Already the fact that moral principles can be a source of law – in some relevant sense of the concept – shows that it is impossible categorically to draw a line. I shall return to this matter in connection with the analysis of value theory.

(f) *Doctrinal opinions*. In Finnish interpretation of law, one normally sees references to legal dogmatics only in scholarly works. It is not part of the court tradition to refer to individual legal scholars or even to so-called prevailing opinions. This does not mean that in the deliberation that takes place within the court, behind closed doors so to speak, the views expressed in legal dogmatics may not have an important role.

To this category belong not only the opinions of valid law but also references to the comparative law, to the history of law (e.g. the information concerning the development of the law text at issue) and other material that is a subject matter of doctrinal study (e.g. Agreements of the International Organizations, as EEC).

(g) Practical reasons or so-called *real arguments*. Especially since the 1950's it has been usual in Finnish legal thought to take several kinds of practical reasons into consideration. From the Finnish point of view, the presence of this type of justification is tied to the break-down of the so-called constructivist way of thinking (conceptual legal dogmatics; *Begriffsjurisprudenz*) since World War II. This approach was strongly disputed by the so-called analytical jurisprudence.[41] As the ties between the constructivist tendency and German legal science at the end of the 19th Century were close, analytical jurisprudence and legal dogmatics based on this way of thinking found, in turn, support from Anglo-Saxon analytical philosophy and from the Scandinavian legal tradition.[42] One, although indirect, consequence of this was that justification in legal dogmatics and in law in general was opened up to practical reasons.

To this group of reasons belong e.g. several kinds of comparison between different interests: the interest of vendor/purchaser, of employer/employee etc. In certain cases the comparison is concentrated upon the interests of the state (or society) versus the individual member of the community.

The use of this kind of argument normally follows the form of so-called consequental reasoning.[43] The interpreter refers to a consequence (e.g. the interest of the vendor), evaluates this consequence in a positive way and argues on this basis for a certain solution. For instance: if solution I_1 would be accepted, the consequence will be C_1, if I_2 then C_2. The final choice is based upon the priority order of C_1 and C_2. This type of reasoning will be clarified later in paragraph 4.6.5.

3.2.2. *General remarks*. The history of legal thought teaches us that the doctrine of the sources of law has an important position both in decision-making activity in the courts and in the understanding of research in legal dogmatics. The view of what decision-making activity – and, correspondingly, of what legal dogmatics – is in each period depends decisively on the content of the doctrine of the sources of law which is adopted. A few examples will illustrate this point.

The exegetic school, which flowered for example during the period following the Napoleonic Codes (at the beginning of the 1800's), tied itself to a very limited doctrine of the sources of law. In its most radical form this doctrine only accepted law texts as sources of law. A natural consequence of this was that the interpretation of law was unknown to the pure form of exegetic school. The purpose of decisions is to note the contents of law and apply the provision to the facts which have been demonstrated to be true. Perelman writes about the theoreticians of the exegetic school that they tried to concentrate themselves on the establishment of the facts of the case and to a simple subsumption.[44]

A slightly more liberal doctrine of the sources of law accepts the possibility that when the text of the law is unclear the decision-maker can turn to the purposes of the legislator. Such a mitigation of the doctrine already existed in embryo in the views of the exegetic school, and it is clearly expressed for example in Section 6 of the Austrian civil law, the ABGB. The doctrine of the hypothetical will of the legislator was later developed as a supplement to this historical interpretation: the goal of the interpretation is to clarify what *would have been* the will of the legislator *if* this type of a problem would have been under the discourse in the legislative procedure. In the very sense of the term the hypothetical will does not deal with the legislative history (the genuine will of the legislator). However, it is a manifestation of a doctrine that explains the legal norms as the results of a will (act of will, *Willensakten*).[45]

All of these doctrines of the sources of law tended largely, in the methodological respect, towards syllogistic thought. A legal decision is understood as the connecting of clear superior norms to statements which describe the facts. The conclusion is thus the result of a logical operation. It is not necessary to enter into criticism of this syllogistic thought. The discussion that has taken place on this subject has clearly shown the limits of the doctrine.[46] It is enough when it is emphasized that the extent of the doctrine of the sources of law is connected to the way in which legal reasoning is understood and through this with the way in which for example it is determined what legal dogmatics is and what it is not.[47]

As can easily be seen from the above list of the sources of law, the functioning Finnish (and Scandinavian) doctrine of the sources of law is very liberal.[48] This has decisive significance from the point of view of our subject. A liberal doctrine of the sources of law is a necessary condition of the type of justificatory theory which is presented in this study. For example the idea of the audience and the criticism against the doctrines of one right interpretation are not possible within the realm of the type of limited doctrine of the sources of law which is represented by the exegetic and similar schools.

3.3. *The Categorization of the Sources of Law*

Aleksander Peczenik has grouped the sources of law into three categories with reference to the strictness of the rules to which these sources are tied.[49] In other words, the basis of the categorization is the extent to which the sources of law are binding. Without taking a prejudicial position on the general significance of such rules in the justification, the classification suggested by Peczenik can be used as a basic categorization of the sources of law.

3.3.1. *The bindingness of the sources of law.* (*a*) There exists a principle in the different legal communities, either written or unwritten, according to which in a certain situation one must refer to a certain source of law. This source of law is binding in the strong sense that disregarding this source will lead to official liability being incurred by the decision-maker, for example by the judge. On the other hand, in regard to researchers, and against this background, there is an *epistemic* obligation to follow a binding source of law. As has already been mentioned, such a source of law on the basis of Chapter 1, Section 11 of the Finnish Code of Judicial Procedure is law (statutes) or, from the linguistic point of view, a law text. In connection with this rule, in Finland one greatly feels one's self tied to, for example, the principle of "*nullum crimen sine lege*". This background principle in criminal law is apparent in Finnish praxis in that certain authorities (the prosecutors of the courts of appeal) closely supervise the use of punishment latitudes.

In civil law, a similar principle has not been acknowledged in a strict a form. If, however, an unambiguous law text exists, and there is no uncertainty about its applicability to the case, the judge who neglects to apply this provision is guilty of a breach of office.[50] On the other hand, the reference to a wrong provision is not a failure to perform the judge's duty, if the behaviour is not voluntary. Thus, in practice the decision-maker is very seldom open to charges of a breach of duty.

If there is no law, the decision must be made with reference to the customs of the land, in accordance with Chapter 1, Section 11 of the Code of Judicial Procedure. The court must always take judicial notice not only of the custom of the land which has become fixed through legal praxis, but also of such custom as has in general become binding in social praxis. An example of the latter would be, as was noted, various forms of commercial praxis.

The bindingness of the custom of the land as a source of law is not of the same degree as that of law texts. First of all, it is more problematic to ascertain that a custom is valid than it is to ascertain that a law text is valid. The custom of the land has simply not been written down anywhere – with the exception, perhaps, of some principles which have been formulated in some fields of business. Secondly, the extent to which the custom is followed, its nature as the custom of the land is difficult to study. A third problem is related to the requirement of "reasonableness" set in Chapter 1, Section 11 of the Code. Even though we can observe that there is a general custom valid in regard to a certain matter, it may still be that, with due consideration to all the circumstances, this custom is unreasonable in that particular situation. If so, the custom cannot be used as a binding source of law. Our principle of the bindingness of customary law must therefore be formulated in the following careful manner: *if* there is valid a general custom concerning that area and *if* this custom is not unreasonable and *if* there is no law text dealing with the matter the judge *must* take judicial notice of that custom and apply it to the problem at issue.

(b) A second group of sources of law consists of those which should be followed in the interpretation, i.e. to which the interpreter has only a "weak duty" to refer to. Disregarding the source of law in the justification of the decision can never lead to liability for a breach of office. The term "weak duty", however, must be made more specific.

It is a question of the obligation for *giving proof* regarding the justification. If a reason that belongs to this second group is not referred to, then the rationality of discretion requires that the interpreter gives reasons why this source of law was disregarded. Through this, the "weak duty" is connected with the concept of rational discretion. In order to be rational in his discretion the interpreter must follow rules regarding this kind of the burden of proof. Formulated in that way, a weak duty to refer to this category of reasons has its roots in the legal ideology accepted by the (e.g. Finnish) legal community. It is expected that the interpretation will be justified, and it is justified only when the available sources of law have been utilized in the appropriate manner.

Material arising in the legislative history of law texts and court decisions belong to this second category (b). In regard to court decisions, it has already been noted that in Finland court decisions do not have the character of precedents. On the other hand, Chapter 1, Section 11 of the Code of Judicial Procedure does not mention material prepared in the legislative history of law texts as binding. Thus, when the law text does not provide the final decision on the matter, the interpreter must refer to the *travaux préparatoires* if the question has been dealt with there. Disregarding the *travaux préparatoires* does not amount to a breach of office, for which reason, by the way, *travaux préparatoires* are used quite seldom in Finnish court praxis. A person who neglects them, however, is acting contrary to the burden of proof rule laid down by rational discretion.

In this regard, the Finnish system differs quite clearly from the Austrian one. In ABGB § 6 there has been written a norm: "Einem Gesetze darf in der Anwendung kein anderer Verstand beigelegt werden, als welcher . . . aus der klaren Absicht das Gesetzgebers hervorleuchtet". The goal is thus the clarification of the historical will of the legislator. The wording of ABGB § 6 is strictly normative: " . . . darf . . . kein anderer . . .". It is a binding norm.

As far as the appeal is concerned, the breach of the weak duty means that the decision will probably be changed in the higher court. For instance, if there is a recent decision of the Supreme Court and the decision-maker does not solve the problem according to it, although there is a clear analogy between the case at issue and the case solved by the decision, the probability that the decision will be changed on appeal is quite high. The same holds true concerning the other sources mentioned in the second category. However, the probability of the decisions being changed differs depending on the case. If the source, for instance, is ambiguous and/or the applicability of the source is problematic, the degree of the probability cannot be very high.

The reason for the probable change on appeal lies in the nature of the weak duty as a manifestation of the burden of proof. In order to argue in a rational way, i.e. in order to fulfill the expectations of legal certainty, one has to refer to this type of source. The Court of Appeal and the Supreme Court are, on the other hand, social institutions that are especially established to maximize the expectations of rationality in the decision-making procedure. Hence, the probability of the weak duty being fulfilled is quite high on appeal. The degree of the probability naturally depends, as always in human behaviour, on whether those institutions really act in a rational way or not.

(c) A third group of sources of law is formed by those to which one may refer according to the established practice. It is a question of permissable sources of law. The interpreter does not have either a strong or a weak duty to refer to them. Permissable sources of law, however, have factual weight in legal reasoning, hence especially in the scholarly interpretation they often have an important role.

All the sources of law except those specifically mentioned above belong to this category. In other words: general principles of law, moral principles, opinions of law professors and practical arguments. Mention may also be made of such justification as reference to points of view in the history of law, comparative law aspects and justification in the sociology of law as well as "the nature of the matter" (*Natur der Sache*) — no matter what is meant by this.

3.3.2. *Authoritative reasons and substantial reasons.* Some sources of law have an authoritative position.[51] By this, the strong or weak bindingness of the source is not referred to. The idea is that some sources of law have what amounts to an institutional position in society. Such a reason receives the function of a source of law on the basis of its authority. A typical example is a law text. It has been "made official", as it is a source of law which is specifically mentioned in Chapter 1, Section 11 of the Finnish Code of Judicial Procedure. This means that the law text has the greatest authority as justification. Sources of law with an authoritative position may be divided into categories according to their bindingness, as noted above. Law is the most authoritative (strongly binding), *travaux préparatoires* and court decisions are weakly binding, and (for example) legal dogmatics is only a permitted source of law.

There is no doubt that legal dogmatics is also specifically an authoritative source of law. This is easy to observe when we try to imagine whether or not another opinion expressed in society could receive the same significance in the interpretation of the legal order. Certainly not. In this respect, legal dogmatics, when compared with the other sources of information in society, undeniably has the status of an authority even though its status relative to law, travaux préparatoires and court decisions, is less authoritative because doctrinal opinions are not official in the same sense as e.g. *travaux préparatoires*.

Certain sources of law enter the justification background on the basis of their material (substantial) significance. For this reason, they can be called substantial reasons or, to use the terminology of sources of law, substantial sources of law.[52] If a law text is ambiguous, it still has a basic binding force regardless of whether or not its content is felt to be satisfactory in some respect. In this sense, the authority of law texts is not dependent on its content. On the other hand, a substantial reason can never have justificatory power other than on the basis of its content. It is also important to note that a law text as an authoritative source of law is enough as justification to the extent that the minimum demands of Chapter 1, Section 11 of the Code of Judicial Procedure are fulfilled. A substantial source of law alone is never enough to fulfill the minimum demands of legal justification. A substantial reason must at least be connected with a law text, it must support the choice of the meaning content given to this law text, or a choice where one law text is preferred over another.

We can see the nature of the sources of law in Diagram 15 where the degree of bindingness is shown on the vertical dimension and the

	strongly binding	weakly binding	permitted sources of law
authoritative justification (authoritative sources of law)	LAW TEXTS CUSTOM	TRAVAUX PRÉPARATOIRES COURT DECISIONS (PRECEDENTS)	LEGAL DOGMATICS FOREIGN LAW etc.
Substantial justification (substantial sources of law)	CUSTOM		GENERAL LEGAL PRINCIPLES MORAL PRINCIPLES, PRACTICAL ARGUMENTS

Diagram 15

distinction between authoritative reasons and substantial reasons is given on the horizontal dimension.

Robert S. Summers has distinguished not only between authoritative and substantial sources of law (reasons) but also between factual reasons, interpretative reasons and critical reasons.[53] Such supplementary justification categories, however, do not appear to be necessary from the point of view of the structure of legal interpretation.

First of all, the category of factual reasons used by Summers is connected with the application of the law in individual cases. It is a question of reasons which are used to substantiate statements concerning facts which have occurred. Scientific interpretation does not deal with the factual side of matters, and so the factual reasons have no bearing on the matter from the point of view of legal dogmatics. They may thus be left aside in this study.

As for the interpretative reasons mentioned by Summers, they can be reduced to either authoritative or substantive reasons. Critical reasons, in turn, enter the question when we are evaluating valid legislation, a certain court decision or the scholarly interpretation of the law in force. Thus, in the clarification of the structure of interpretation in legal dogmatics, critical reasons are also lacking in significance. We are therefore left with two of the five categories suggested by Summers: authoritative and substantial sources of law.

One point, also suggested by Summers, should be made more specific. Substantial reasons can be either *rightness reasons* or *goal reasons*. Rightness reasons include (a) general principles of law, (b) moral principles when they appear in a legal context, and (c) the custom of the land. It is thus a question of a content and normative reasons. An example would be reference to justice. This category also includes value judgments on the basis of which one matter, for example a source of law, is preferred over others. In the category of goal reasons we are left with only one source of law, real arguments. They are part of this category, as real argumentation ultimately turns into consideration of consequences, where certain consequences are preferred over others. They are the consequences that are sought. It should be observed, however, that they become goals because they are preferred: they are not only valuable, they are to be preferred more than other consequences which enter the question. Thus, there is an internal link between goal reasons and rightness reasons. It is the same type of link as that between values and goals in general. All in all, we can give the set of categories originally suggested by Summers the following illustrative interpretation:

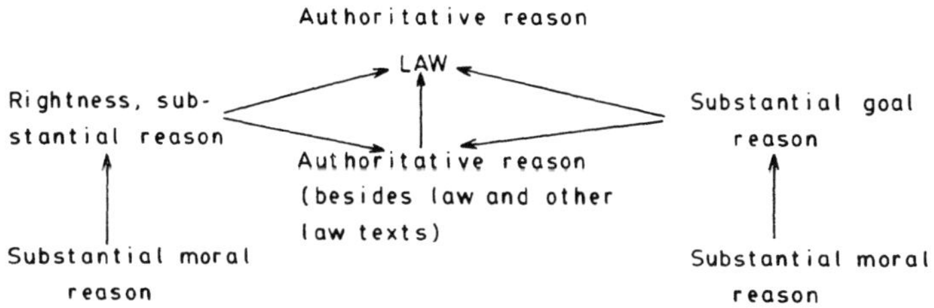

Diagram 16

Diagram 16 is an attempt to summarize and systematize the "strategy" of interpretation. The task *is* interpretation. The reasons can be either authoritative reasons or substantial reasons. Depending on the situation, the latter can be included among either rightness or goal reasons. Substantial moral reasons "become legitimate" when they enter into a legal context, in other words when they are either used as rightness reasons or they define the sought-after consequences. When separated from a legal context, moral principles are only moral principles.

3.4. *Directives of Legal Interpretation*

The directives of legal interpretation consist in two categories of rules: the rules *constituting the sources of law* and the rules defining the *procedure of discourse*. The first category can be called constitutive and the second one regulative rules of legal interpretation.

All those rules have family resemblant connections with each other. Typical for that resemblance is that no single one of the rules *as such* is a necessary condition for an interpretation to be just a *legal* interpretation. In this respect, it is impossible to give a general definition for a proper interpretation using a rule of interpretation as a criterion. However, depending on the legal culture, a certain cluster of those rules is always a minimum basis for legal interpretation. This cluster belongs to the paradigmatic character of legal reasoning as was pointed out when the paradigm of legal dogmatics was dealt with. Legal reasoning as legal reasoning can be identified by means of this cluster of the rules. From this point of view, it seems adequate to say that the constitutive rules of the sources of law are always a necessary element of the cluster mentioned above. If all constitutive rules are lacking, the interpretation is not a legal one fundamentally. Which kinds of procedural rules belong to the cluster depends on the paradigm of the time. However, if all procedural rules (rules of inference) are replaced by e.g. the methodological rules of empirical sociology, the research activity is not legal interpretation any more. In this sense, at least some procedural rules of interpretation are necessary for genuine legal reasoning.

The directives concerning the use of the sources of law are often called the principles of interpretation. This expression brings up the question of their normative status. Are these directives, in the end, rules or principles? As is well known, this distinction, which has received much attention in philosophy of law, has once again become a current subject for debate thanks to Ronald Dworkin. He has defined the concept of rule on the basis of an either/or-situation: either a rule is followed or it is not followed. A principle, in turn, logically belongs to a different category. A certain principle may be followed or not followed without either procedure being considered a violation of the principle. Torstein Eckhoff and Nils Kristian Sundby have approached the problem, in part, in the same way. Their terminological proposal covers "rules" ("regler") and "guiding standards" ("riktlinjer").

Both distinctions have been criticized. A major argument has been that the assumed difference in category between rules and principles is illusory. A more moderate form of criticism has started from the view that it is a difference of degree, while the more uncompromising critics have said that the nature of rules and principles is exactly the same.[54]

It is true that rules are of either/or-character. In the Wittgensteinian sense they are like railroad tracks.[55] Let us take the rule "If *F*, then ought to be *G*" as an example. If the state of affairs *F* prevails, then *G* "follows" from the rule, except when the rule is violated. Furthermore, the rule is the reason, for instance, for a judge to sentence *G*. The judge behaves in this way because the rule has such a content.

Principles are different as to their nature. Following Robert Alexy's terminology one can characterize the principles as maxims: try to reach an optimal application of the principle. For instance, the principle of the freedom of speech can be understood as a maxim according to which this freedom ought to be protected *as effective as possible*. If this principle is in conflict with another principle, e.g. with the principle of protecting the privacy a compromise between them is a necessity. Both principles cannot be followed at the same time in an optimal way. Hence, even if a certain principle, say the principle of freedom of speech, is accepted as valid, it is permitted to deviate from the principle without any threat of a sanction. This is not the case when a rule is followed. If the rule "If *F*, then ought to be *G*" is a valid legal rule, the judge is obligated to follow it. In the opposite case he is guilty of a breach of his duties. According to Alexy, a rule either belongs to the legal order or is outside of it (inside-outside-problem). The same does not apply to principles. Also a principle which cannot be followed to its full extent is inside of the system. As Dworkin says, principles have only "a dimension of weight", and dimension of weight differs from case to case.

The so-called rules of legal interpretation – as they are called in the philosophy of law – are clearly principles as to their status. They only point out the factors that should be taken into account in legal interpretation. There is no legal obligation to follow them. However, they are *necessary* in the sense that they ought to be followed in an optimal legal justification. In other words, if one wants to be rational in one's legal discourse, one ought to follow the principles of legal interpretation as long as possible. In this respect, these principles are typically maxims in the above mentioned sense. What is also important, the legal decision or the scholarly interpretation is not justified with reference to the principles of interpretation. In the justification only the reference to the sources of law is necessary (and normal).

From the linguistic point of view, there is no difference between the rules and principles. The rules as well as the principles may be *formulated* in an ambiguous or unambiguous way. Very often the formulation of principles is more general than that of the rules. However, also the rules are sometimes vague or otherwise difficult to clarify. Let us only recall the flexible norms or the so-called open texture problematics. In this very respect, the rules may be as difficult to interprete as the principles. At the most there can be difference of degree between these two categories.

In the following, the term "*interpretation standard*" will be used as a characterization of the principles of legal interpretation. It resembles the expression "guiding standard" proposed by Torstein Eckhoff and presents, to my mind, in an adequate way the very nature of these principles.

3.4.1 *The Order of Preference of the Sources of Law*

The Finnish interpretative community has accepted certain *standards of preference* regarding sources of law. Two of them, (*i*) and (*ii*) below, are given in Chapter 1, Section 11 of the Code of Judicial Procedure, a provision which has been cited above in many connections. The rest, (*iii*) and (*iv*), have become formulated through praxis.

(*i*). A *law text* (statute) has priority over other sources of law, no matter whether these are authoritative or substantial.

As to the *internal* order of preference, for example the following standards have become accepted in praxis:

- *Lex superior derogat legi inferiori*: a hierarchically superior provision sets aside an inferior one. For example, an Act of Parliament supersedes a decree.
- *Lex posterior derogat legi priori*: a later provision over-rules a previous one, unless the provisions given in the enforcement of the later provision decrees otherwise.
- *Lex specialis derogat legi generali*: a less general provision is regarded as an exception to a more general one, or in other words a special provision supersedes a general one.
- *Lex posterior generalis non derogat legi priori speciali*: unless otherwise decreed, a later general provision does not supersede an earlier special provision.

(ii). If there is no statute on the matter, the custom of the land takes precedence over the other sources of law. It is thus preferred over *travaux préparatoires* and court decisions. The custom of the land, however, has this privileged position only in cases of gaps in law. If, on the other hand, a formally valid statute is applicable to the case but there is uncertainty as to its content, the customary law does not have a privileged position as a basis for interpretation. On the contrary, the custom of the land is in the same position as so-called unprivileged sources of law. Its weight as justification in interpretation is noted in connection with each individual combination of reasons.

(iii). *Travaux préparatoires* go before other sources of law other than statutes and the customary law.

The priority, however, is not of the same degree as that of a statute and custom as expressed in Chapter 1, Section 11 of the Code of Judicial

Procedure. Peczenik has observed that the Swedish doctrine of the sources of law does not contain an established standard according to which an interpreter, for example a judge, would unconditionally be bound to *travaux préparatoires*.[56] However, in the Nordic countries *travaux préparatoires* seem to have a more important role than in many other legal cultures. This is especially the case in Sweden where *travaux préparatoires* have received a special place in legal reasoning in the 1970's. In the discussion concerning this type of reasoning the following arguments have been presented for the use of *travaux préparatoires*:

(1) It is democratic to take into account the ideas that the persons participating in the legislative procedure have presented. In the statutory law system the role of the sovereign is decisive from the democratic point of view.

(2) The expertise of the legislative staff is of a high level. Therefore, the standpoints about the meaning contents of the statutes expressed by these expertise are of a special importance.

(3) There are no reasons to claim that *travaux préparatoires* cannot elucidate the meaning contents of the statutes. All material that is useful for this purpose must be exploited. This is especially important because the text of the statutes is normally formulated very briefly. It is natural to think that the authors of the text are the genuine source of information as far as the meaning content is concerned. The situation is the same as in all literal interpretation.

The Swedish tradition is thus based on the principles of loyalty and democracy. In Finland the role of preparatory materials is clearly weaker. In the Code of Judicial Procedure Sec. 1 Art. 11 it is said: the judge has the obligation to examine the right purpose of the law and give the decision by this purpose. This does not refer to the preparatory materials (historical purpose). According to the prevailing opinion the purpose of law mentioned in Sec. 1 Art. 11 means the objective purpose of law (*ratio*). Therefore e.g. the courts do not explicitly or even implicitly refer to the documents produced by legislative committees etc. In the Supreme Court, however, the draft or the final decision may include also references to the legislative history but this argument is only one single reason among others. It has no primacy compared to e.g. the precedents or the doctrinal opinion. The emphasis on the independence of the courts is to be seen on the background of this reservedness. They are independent of the other state powers. Therefore they do not easily accept a situation where a written report of a certain official (public functionary, a secretary of a legislative committee or other single person) reaches the status of an authoritative reason. The power balance between the governmental employees and judges would be disturbed because the real legal power would be in the hands of a small group of officials.

As we remember, *travaux préparatoires* belong to the so-called weakly binding sources of law. This means that *if* the interpreter does not refer to *travaux préparatoires*, he has the burden of proof to justify why he proceeded in this fashion. This burden of proof formulates a number of non-established interpretative standards, for example the following:

(a) Travaux préparatoires which are internally inconsistent or ambiguous may not be used as arguments.
(b) Of several interpretations of a statute which all accord with the everyday language, the one that clear *travaux préparatoires* point to must be preferred. There must be special grounds to depart from this preference.
(c) If *travaux préparatoires* which are clear as far as the interpretation of a certain statute is concerned are in conflict with a prior court decision the decision cannot be used as an argument.
(d) If *travaux préparatoires* which are clear concerning the content of a statute or of an interpretation, are in conflict with a later court decision, the interpreter must justify the departure from the *travaux préparatoires*.
(e) If *travaux préparatoires* which are clear concerning the content of a statute or of an interpretation are in conflict with a substantial reason, a departure from the *travaux préparatoires* must be justified.
(f) If the position of the *travaux préparatoires* on the matter is clear, it can be used as a basis for departing from the meaning content of a statute in accordance with everyday language, if there are no special reasons to remain with the everyday meaning of the text.

It is possible to present a number of other standards, too. The above list of examples, however, already demonstrates two matters. The priority of *travaux préparatoires* is decided on the basis of an essentially more complicated collection of standards than is the case with the priority of law texts and customary law. On the other hand, the priority standards of *travaux préparatoires* are typically burden of proof rules.

(iv) As for the preference of court decisions, we can refer to the standards pertaining to *travaux préparatoires*. It is possible to formulate corresponding burden of proof guidelines for court decisions to the extent that it is a question of the relation between court decisions and other sources of law. The principal idea in standards is to assign the burden of proof to any divergence from the interpretation given by courts on the basis of sources of law other than *travaux préparatoires*.

(v) The other sources of law have an equal order of preference. What is decisive is the reasoning power of the source either on its own or used together with the other sources in this group.

3.4.2. *The Standards of the Reasoning Procedure*

A. The standards of grammatical interpretation. At times in this connection, one also speaks of literal interpretation. No matter which term is used, it is a question specifically of the principles of interpretation.

Examples of the standards of grammatical interpretation are the following:

(i) A law text should not be interpreted so that part of it is left without use or meaning. Thus, grammatical interpretation starts out from what amounts to a principle of the economy of regulation: no element in a law text is lacking in significance.

(ii) An expression in a certain text should not be given a different meaning in different connections unless there is sufficient justification for proceeding in this manner. Behind this principle one can imagine that there is the idea of the consistency of regulation: if possible, the same expression is used in different connections in the same way.

(iii) The expression to be interpreted should not be assigned a meaning that departs from the general usage in language, unless there is sufficient justification for proceeding in this manner. Legal language is itself ordinary language, and for this reason, in a way, there is a "burden of proof" that any deviation from ordinary language usage – something that actually happens quite often – must be justified. Let us call this the privilege of ordinary language.

(iv) If the terminology of a statute deviates from the ordinary usage in language, special terminology takes precedence over ordinary language. This principle, the privilege of the technical terminology, is derived from the principle (iii) that is more general as to its nature.

B. Extending interpretation refers to the application of a statute beyond the core of its wording. The situation is thus similar to the analogy that will be dealt with later on. The difference between extending interpretation and analogy has thus often been questioned in recent legal theory.[57] In principle, one can, however, draw a line between those two forms of reasoning. In analogy there is either a gap in the law or a genuine uncertainty if the case at issue is covered by the text of law. According to Peczenik, the extending interpretation does not cross the limits of "true judicial meaning" and thus it only applies to those situations which are not shut out on a grammatical basis.[58] In practice, however, the limit is not so simply drawn. The difficulty in differentiation is due to the fact that with many expressions, for example the semantical uncertainty is so large that it is not possible grammatically to draw a line between interpretation of the text and the use of analogy. In any case, with an eye on argumentation, there is every reason to emphasize the very close relationship between extending interpretation and analogy.

C. Restrictive interpretation is involved when the law text is given a more limited meaning than what could be assumed on the basis of the "normally interpreted" wording. An example would be "high quality wool goods" as a definition of quality. If we assume that according to ordinary language (in the field in question), a product that is 80–90 % wool is considered to be "high quality wool", then a restrictive interpretation would be that only 100 % wool goods would be covered by the term.

The extreme form of restrictive interpretation is to be found when certain additional qualities are used to reduce the meaning beyond what would be demanded by normal restrictive interpretation. Peczenik calls this type of interpretation reducing interpretation.[59] In our example, these additional qualities would be (in addition to the purity of the wool) the length of the fibers, the evenness of the quality, and so on.

If extending interpretation and analogy are characterized as an "extension" of the field of application of a law text, it would be proper to speak of a cutting down of the field of application in connection with restricting and reducing interpretation. Actually these latter two forms are modes of reasoning which complement the so-called reasoning *e contrario*: the field of meaning contents is made narrower and at the same time the cases that remain outside of the field of interpretation are left out.

D. There are also e.g. two forms of *argumentum a fortiori*.[60] One is argumentum *a maiore ad minus*, of reasoning from the large to the small: if law text L_i applies to case A, then with all the more reason L_i applies to case B, as B is a "smaller evil" than A. The other form is argumentum *a minore ad maius*, or reasoning from the small to the large: if act A is prohibited, then also act B is prohibited, as A is a "smaller evil" than B.

Structurally, these forms of reasoning are decisively similar to analogous reasoning. For this reason there is no need to consider here their details to any greater extent.

E. The principle of analogy. In analogy, the focus lies on the comparison of similarities. This can enter the question in two situations. I shall call these case analogy and norm analogy. The former one deals with the similarities between different cases, i.e. between two or more court decisions, and with the drawing of conclusions on the basis of these similarities. The purpose of the latter, norm analogy, is to demonstrate that the categories of cases covered by two or more legal norms are analogous. In this, the statutes (or provisions) provide interpretative support in relation to each other.

In both situations, referring to analogy requires the use of two different principles. First of all, the interpreter must know the principle of analogous reasoning itself, in other words he must know what analogy is. On the other hand, an understanding is needed of how analogy can be utilized. In the following, the principle of analogy itself will be dealt with more closely whereas the use of analogy will be analysed only in passing.

(i) As has been said, case analogy is the comparison of the similarities of two or more court decisions.[61] It is not essential which cases are taken as the focus of the comparison. For comparison to be possible, each case must be analysed into its basic elements. In other words, one must look for the elements of the fact descriptions in each case, on the basis of which the case can be reconstructed. This means the dissection of the basic elements of the fact description into significant and insignificant elements. One must be able to pick out the essential elements. In comparing decisions regarding last wills and testaments with each other, the sex of the testamentor or the locality are not essential, but the type of the testament might be.[62]

If the elements of two cases which are logically of the same type correspond to each other, then the cases can be called analogous on the condition that the similarity is significant with an eye on the totality of the basic elements of the cases.[63] Such a comparability, however, demands a basis on which the comparison can take place. Expressed somewhat differently, there can only be comparability in relation to an analogy key.[64] This key tells us which elements in case A correspond to a significant degree to elements in case B, and which comparability between these elements is significant from the point of view of the analogous relationship.

The matter can be illustrated with an example. Court X has given three decisions, decisions A, B and C. Of these, A and C represent interpretation I_1 of law text L_i, while in decision B, the interpretation of the same law text is I_2. The elements of the cases are as follows:[65]

$$A: K_1, K_2, K_3 \qquad = I_i$$

$$B: K_1, K_2, \qquad K_4 = I_2$$

$$C: K_1, \qquad K_3, K_4 = I_1$$

It can be seen from the systematization that the decision are not contradictory if we choose K_1 and K_3 as the analogy keys. Cases A and B have a similar set of facts only through keys K_1 and K_2. Correspondingly, cases B and C can be compared with each other in relation to keys K_1 and K_4. In both of the latter cases, however, one would either have to say that the court had been inconsistent or that it had changed the tendency of its decisions. On the other hand, keys K_1 and K_3 render decisions A and C analogous: they manifest the same view of the content of the legal order. Lacking of K_3 in case B explains the solution I_2.

Even so, it is not an isomorphic relation.[66] First of all, the elements of cases A and C are not identical, no matter that they are assumed to be of the same logical type. In case C, we can also identify element K_4 which does not appear in the set of facts in the first decision. On the other hand, the elements taken from the fact description do not completely represent these cases. As has already been noted, they are just the essential elements of the cases.

We have said that two cases can be analogous only through a certain key. The key, in turn, is not objective, for example something that can be verified through observation. For this reason it is not possible to verify statements concerning the existence of a relationship of analogy merely through factual propositions. An analogous relationship is (in part) a matter of values.[67] The terms "significance" and "essential", just referred to above, demonstrate in a graphic way this degree of values. One person may regard key X as the proper one, while another may prefer key Y. Neither has an objective testable measure of the order of preference of the keys. For this reason, analogy always remains "dependent on the subject", at least to some degree.

The normal chain of reasoning in case analogy is somewhat different from what has been presented above. The point of departure is a decision where we know the set of facts and the legal interpretation. Let us refer to a case as A. Interpretation I_1 has been connected to the set of facts formed by K_1 & K_2 & K_3. We must now interpret case B – in legal dogmatics, this case is often imagined or reconstructed on the basis of an actual case. The interpretative problem receives the following form: are the legal consequences in case B also I_1 or not? The decision to this depends on the analogy key. If there is, on the basis of the key, sufficient similarity between the essential elements, interpretation I_1 can also be given to case B, even though the set of facts in case B is not identical to that of case A.

(ii) In norm analogy the question is the uncertainty of the content of a given statute, L_i. The application area of L_i, however, is analogous to the application area of another statute which we will denote L_j. We know the detailed contents of this latter statute. Thus the interpretative support offered by L_j can be used in ascertaining the contents of L_i.

An example will again be taken from the law of succession. The concept of "in writing" in Chapter 17, Section 3 of the Finnish Decedent's Estate Act, referred to above, is unclear. The juridical act referred to in the provision, the transfer of a share in an inheritance, resembles in important respects a partial distribution of an inheritance. In any case there is a considerable resemblance between the transfer of a share in an inheritance and renunciation of one's share in the distribution of an inheritance. We know that the document used in the apportionment of an inheritance, referred to in Chapter 23, Section 9 of the Decedent's Estate Act, must be signed and witnessed, and so we are justified in thinking that the same form is to be used in the transfer of a share in an inheritance. Thus, Chapter 17, Section 3 of the Act is interpreted through analogy with Chapter 23, Section 9 of the same Act.

F. Conclusions e contrario. In this the interpreter shuts out from the range of application of the law text all cases that the text does not specifically deal with. This means, in effect, that conclusions *e contrario* are a form of grammatical interpretation.[68]

No clear rules on *when* one should use analogy and when arguments *e contrario* have developed in the legal community. Alanen observes that material justice (for him: the principle of equitable treatment) supports the use of analogy, while predictability in turn speaks for argument *e contrario*.[68] On the other hand, e.g. in Finnish criminal law the use of analogy is in general prohibited, and so the problem of the relation between analogy and *e contrario* conclusion can especially pertain to situations in civil law, administrative law and other comparable situations.[69] The following, relatively rough basic principles have been defined in order to simplify the drawing of a line:

- In connection with relatively old legislation the use of analogy is more justified than with laws which have just been passed. This is due already to the simple fact that the development of society constantly creates new situations which could not have been considered when formulating the older legislation.[70]
- In the interpretation of procedural provisions, the ensurance of legal certainty is foremost. This is the case with procedural provisions proper as well as with all rules that concern legal forms. In their connection, analogy must be used with greater care.[71]
- In interpreting exceptional provisions, one must be very careful in using analogy.[72]

In those cases where one does not turn to analogy, an opposite conclusion readily enters the question: if the case does not belong within the range of application specifically noted in the law text, the text cannot be extended to cover this case.

Peczenik has described the (rough) relationship between the different principles of interpretation with circles.[73] This description bears repeating here as a summary. The illustration does not reveal the conditions of the use of the principles, nor does it show the difficulties of distinguishing between the principles.

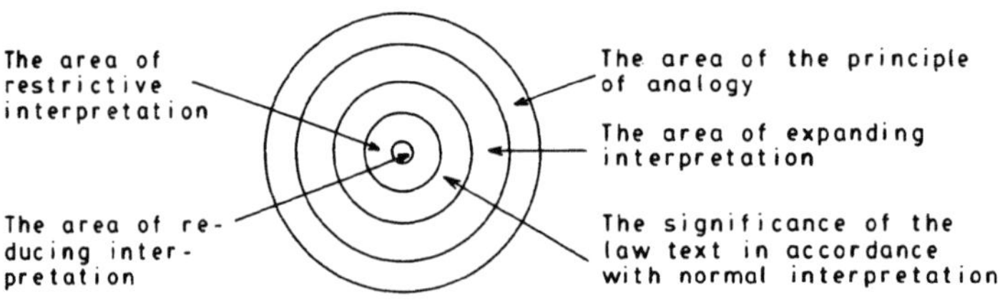

Diagram 17

The methodological principles briefly characterized here do not, any better than other similar guides for reasoning, form a closed system which would always guarantee the acceptability of the interpretative standpoint. There simply are no more exact standards of reasoning which would have received a precise formulation in legal dogmatics. On the part of each one of them, it is easy to agree with what Alanen has said of analogy and reasoning *e contrario*: they are more like roads for legal thought than arguments for decisions which, through their logical imperative, would unconditionally define the interpretation.[74] The same matter is referred to by Alexy when he emphasizes that these standards do not guarantee the sureness of a conclusion, but they provide a number of conditions, criteria and principles which can be used as a guide. Even so, Alexy continues, they can provide a framework for what can be regarded in the legal community as proper interpretation.[75]

For example, legal dogmatics does not recognize any principles that would unambiguously state how a semantically ambiguous text should be interpreted, what specific reasoning should be used, how one *should proceed* if there are reasons that point in different directions, and how different justification elements should be combined when formulating an interpretative proposition. From this point of view, the structure of interpretation in legal dogmatics is open.

4 JUSTIFICATION OF THE INTERPRETATIVE STANDPOINT: STRUCTURAL ANALYSIS

4.1. *The Point of Departure: Disagreement on the Result of the Interpretation*

Let us return to the point of departure of this study. Legal norms can be formally valid and effective, in other words valid in these senses of the word, and yet some ultimate expectations connected with legal certainty are not fulfilled. A formally valid and effective set of norms is not always legitimate from this point of view. It is not fully acceptable in society. Furthermore, in order to evaluate the legal acceptability on a justified basis, the discretion must be rational, and there must be a material basis for the discretion. Only a legal order which, rationally considered, can be accepted as reasonable is legitimate.

A second point of departure of this study is connected with the interest in legal knowledge. This is a societal matter, the contents of which is the acquiring of information on the legal order. To an important extent, legal dogmatics satisfies this interest in knowledge by presenting standpoints on the contents of valid law. It is a consequence of this that such a standpoint is directed (also) at legitimacy. One natural task of legal dogmatics is to answer the question of what rules in society are rational and reasonable when accepted as valid legal norms.

A central problem from the point of view of the methodology of legal dogmatics is thus the problem of how to justify (legally) the result of the interpretation. "The essential notion is that of giving (what are understood and presented as) good justifying reasons for claims, defences or decisions", writes Neil MacCormick.[76] In the following, this problem has been dealt with starting from the idea that legal justification is a discursive procedure that follows the principles of rational discourse. In this, it would appear to be simplest to understand the discursive process as a *dialogue* between the person presenting the justification (*A*) and the person who judges the validity of the justification (*B*). *B* can be an individual, as we shall assume in our simplified example. In practice, however, the justification is directed at all times to a group. In the following, this group will be called the audience.

As a result of the dialogue, *A*'s interpretative standpoint acquires a combination of justifications. *A* attempts to use this combination to convince the recipient, *B*, on a rational basis of the justification of the interpretative standpoint. If *A* succeeds in this, in other words *A* and *B* agree on a rational basis after the presentation, the justification has succeeded.

When presented in this way, the matter may appear to be clear. However, there is a number of problems connected with the theory of justification which is difficult to solve. In the following, an attempt will be made to systematize these problems by beginning with the procedure of justification itself. For this reason, we shall first outline the point of departure, in other words, the situation in which *A* and *B* are initially. After consideration of the structure of justification, an attempt will be made to deal with the question of what the success of justification means. In this direction, a preliminary question is that of the preconditions of the success of justification, and also the question of how the justification can succeed at all, even though it is a question of the justification of an interpretative standpoint which in part is based on values.

In its most simple terms, the point of departure of the dialogue is a *disagreement* between *A* and *B* on the subject of the interpretation. The disagreement can be linguistic or factual (or both).[77] It is a question of a linguistic disagreement when the persons use the same linguistic expression to refer to different matters or when they use different expressions to refer to the same matter. There is material disagreement when the persons, regardless of the terms used, have adopted different views of the object (matter) denoted by the language. Schematically presented, the situation can be as shown in Diagram 18.

	Material agreement	Material disagreement
Linguistic agreement	True agreement	Apparent agreement
Linguistic disagreement	Apparent disagreement	True disagreement

Diagram 18

Who observes the agreement or disagreement is irrelevant as far as our point of departure is concerned. The problem of disagreement may be brought to the attention of the parties by a third party, or they may themselves become aware of the matter. What is important is that somehow, the apparent agreement or disagreement is observed. If true agreement is found behind apparent disagreement, no justification is necessary any longer, as we noticed. It is enough to point out the "technical" agreement, i.e. the mere disagreement regarding language. In the latter case, the parties may retain their different ways of using language, but this is not essential from the point of view of our subject as long as another agreement is apparent. When there is true disagreement or true disagreement is found behind an apparent agreement, further justification becomes necessary. Thus, one can note that the column at the far right ("material disagreement") gives us a preliminary outline of the area which we will be discussing in the following.

There are many types of material disagreement. First of all, it can be theoretical or nontheoretical. Broadly speaking, it is a question of theoretical disagreement when there are differences between the cognitive systems adopted by *A* and *B*. Nontheoretical disagreement, in turn, is based on the fact that the persons have different values or goals.

There are, in turn, two types of theoretical disagreement. *A* and *B* may have a different view of what the state of affairs is in reality, or in other words what reality is. This can be called a difference regarding facts. Such a difference exists, for example, when *A* and *B* have a different view of the empirical prevalence of a phenomenon in society.

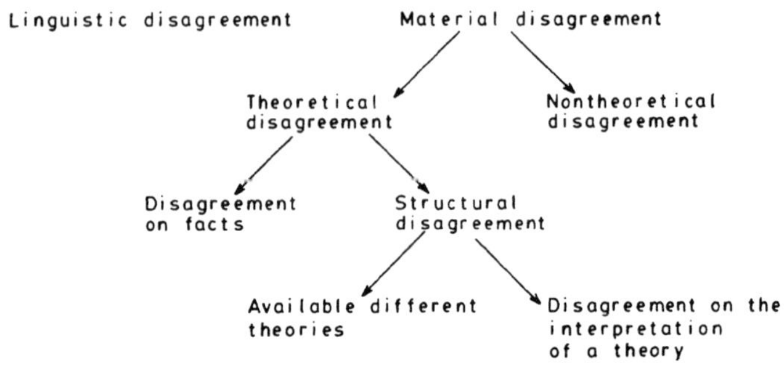

Diagram 19

Another type of theoretical disagreement can be called, to use the terminology of Dag Victor structural disagreement.[78] This exists when *A* and *B* have adopted a different theoretical view on the world. They have different theories of the structure of nature and/or of society or they give different interpretations to the same theory. Furthermore, following Victor's ideas, we can give as an example a material disagreement on whether or not there is democracy in a certain society. If *A* and *B* have the same facts about the society in question, any differences in views between them can be reduced to different theories about what constitutes democracy.

As is well known, the relationship between factual and structural theoretical disagreement is very problematic. It ultimately turns into a question of the position and nature of so-called theoretical terms[79] in human knowledge, i.e. into a question of in what conditions we can say that a matter is a fact. In social sciences the problem is actually much greater than in the natural sciences. We must ask whether or not our theoretical views on society are purely theoretical or whether or not our theories are intertwined with evaluations and, on a broader level, with ideological elements.[80] In this connection we must bypass these problems and satisfy ourselves with listing the different disagreement situations in the form of the following tree of terms.

4.2. *The Scope for Interpretation: Gaps and Conflicts in the Legal Order*

A true material disagreement between the interpreter and the addressee may deal with a situation where *A* interprets the expression L_i in a way I_1 and – correspondingly – *B* gives an interpretation I_2 to the same expression L_i. They do not make any mistake concerning the linguistic usage. Therefore the disagreement is not apparent but substantial as to its nature. This material disagreement – material as far as the content of the legal order is concerned – may be caused by several factors, all connected to the deep nature of our language.

4.2.1. If the statute is linguistically exact and unambiguous, there is no need for justification in regard to the content of the text itself. It is not a case of discretion. A legal decision made e.g. by the judge may, however, prove to be problematic also in such a situation. The decision-maker must always decide whether or not the unambiguous law text in question *applies* to the concrete case. There is no interpretational issue at hand but the problem of the applicability of the text.[81] In the following, this question will not be dealt with.

4.2.2. Normally natural languages and the legal language as a part of them have some degree of *overgenerality*, i.e. of vagueness and inexactness. The terms do not have such genuine meanings that make it possible to decide in each case to which object the term refers. The expressions of natural language are *contextually bound*. They get the meaning in the use of the language. In this sense the semantic character of linguistic terms is not the proper or even the deepest origin of the interpretational issues. In some cases extremely general expressions may have an unambiguous meaning content because of the contextual circumstances. On the other hand, a very technical term can cause intepretational doubts in the penumbra area.

The context of legal statutes is always *systemic* as well as *political*, i.e. extra-legal. Every statute emerges from political activity and it functions in society. Through the application procedure the "output" of the statute is necessarily of social, cultural or political nature. Therefore the interpretation is connected, on one hand, to the normative context (to the legal system as a system of norms) and, on the other hand, to the social and cultural values.

However, the linguistic terms can be classified at least in the following subgroups depending on which type of doubt they produce for the interpreter:

(a) A term can be and often is *vague*; it has an imprecise meaning. Linguistic expressions have often a special penumbra area, i.e. there is a doubt if the term covers a certain case or not. In penumbral situations one can speak about vagueness.

A typical vagueness situation is that when an expression is *unclear*. This is the case, first of all, when the meaning content of the term is inacurrately specified.[82] It is inexact. The interpreter cannot identify the possible meaning alternatives and therefore it is impossible to know to which cases the expression refers. Another subgroup of vagueness is *openness*: there simply are no sufficient criteria at hand in order to specify the meaning content. Example: "special circumstances".[83]

In Finland as in many other countries the so-called general clauses (flexible norms) are more usual than some years ago. Even different kinds of resource laws have been given. They delegate the interpretation power to certain officials without giving any criteria for interpretation. In some cases the law only defines the goals of the procedure. The definition of the details has been left on the interpreter.

(b) If an expression has several meanings it is *ambiguous*.[84] One knows (all) the possible alternatives that fit in the denotation of the expression but he cannot identify which one of the alternatives is the *proper* one. This can be illustrated, for example, by the term "signed".[85] The Finnish Code of Inheritance, Sec. 23 Art. 9 includes a provision about the form of distribution of inheritance. It is possible to list more than 15 alternative meanings for the concept "signed document": a full and recognisable signing of one's name, an illegible signature, one's "mark" and so on. On the other hand the document can be a signed document without witnesses, a witnessed document, a document witnessed by unchallengeable persons etc. The provision itself does not give any criteria to make a choice between those alternatives.[86] Therefore this type of ambiguity is one of the genuine origins of interpretational issues.[87]

Syntactical ambiguity is involved when the location of an expression in a sentence or clause determines the way in which it should be interpreted. For example: "He lives in a house in Finland which is beautiful" as compared to "He lives in Finland in a house which is beautiful".[88]

(c) If a term is *evaluatively open* the identification of the meaning content presupposes evaluation as an extra-legal interpretation bases. The criteria of the interpretation is thus partially found in the value Code of society. In Finland several rules of equity have become quite general especially in family-law but also e.g. in the law of contracts. Example: According to the Act of contracts Sec. 36 the judge has a possibility to consider the equity of the contract *ex post* taking into account the circumstances of the case. The statute does not include any criteria for conciliation.

Also the so-called flexible norms often include evaluatively open terms. For instance, a statute may refer to "reasonable consequences". What is reasonable cannot be defined independently of taking stand on social or cultural values.

4.2.3. One logical drawback of the system that can be mentioned is *conflict*: Law text L_i connects consequence C_i to a set of legal facts, F, while law text L_j gives consequence C_j to the same set of facts. Thus, two contradictory norm statements can be formed.

It has been observed that in deontic logic it apparently can not be justified to speak of a conflict within the same system of norms.[89] One and the same norm authority cannot have a contradictory will. It is more natural to assume that in a case of conflict there are two conflicting sets of norms in force.

Even in practice, the possibility of conflict has not been ruled out, no matter how the concept of conflict is interpreted from the deontic point of view. A conflict can enter legislation for example in cases where the basic framework of regulation is old, and the norm system has been amended many times. One conflict which can be mentioned is that between Section 103 of the Finnish Marriage Act and Chapter 23 of the Decedent's Estate Act. According to the Finnish system, the net value of the assets of both spouses are to be calculated together. The total sum is then to be divided in half in order to determine the legal portion coming to both sides. Section 103 of the Marriage Act gives the person who owns more the right to decide, when the property of the spouses is being divided, what he is to yield to the other party in order to equalize the distribution. In Chapter 23 of the Decedent's Estate Act, this power is given to the executor of the estate when such an executor has been appointed. As it is possible to have an executor arrange the division of the property of the spouses, we are faced with the question of which provision is to be followed, and under what circumstances it is to be done. As such, both provisions cannot be applied at the same time. One must yield, at least in part.

The idea of the absence of conflict in regulation, which has at times been presented in the theory of law, is based, in my view, on a certain type of generalization. We speak without being more specific about the rational legislator and his non-conflicting activity almost as if it were possible to define him unambiguously as an agent working at a certain time.[90] This is not the case in practice. Instead, the fiction of the legislator (if such terminology can be used) covers many types of activity which differ not only in location but also in time. For this reason also the possibility of conflict in legislation should be recognized as a real possibility.

With an eye on justification, the conflict causes the problem already referred to in passing, which of the conflicting law texts should be applied or, from a slightly different point of view, how the provisions should be interpreted so that the conflict can be eliminated.

(d) Traditionally, a distinction has been made in the literature on the philosophy of law between a gap in law and a gap in the legal order.[91] It is said that there can be a gap in law but there cannot be a gap in the legal order. In looking for a point of departure for argumentation, attention is drawn specifically to gaps in law.[92] These Alchourrón and Bulygin have called, from a certain point of view, a normative gap.[93] These writers have set out by asking in what situations a lack of knowledge prevents the formulation of an individual decision. This is the case in subsumption: either there is a lack of information on the facts of the case (a gap in knowledge) or there is semantic uncertainty about the texts to be applied (a gap in recognition). The latter has already been dealt with in the foregoing. Gaps in knowledge, in turn, do not come up in legal dogmatics, as legal dogmatics does not deal with concrete individual cases.

On the other hand, Alchourrón and Bulygin believe that lack of knowledge can also be due to defects in the system itself. As has just been observed, there can be a conflict in the system or there simply may be no decision on the matter. This the writers call a normative gap. With an eye on the distinction between a gap in law and a gap in the legal order, a normative gap can be understood as the absence of a provision (norm) on the case in question. It is known (with certainty) that no provision regulating the matter can be found,[94] not even after a careful interpretation.

In such a situation, the task of argumentation becomes the filling of this gap. It is true that one can think, in a case of gap, that legal dogmatics must satisfy itself with just noting that there is a gap. It is noted with justification that the law does not answer such-and-such a question. Already Hans Kelsen saw the task of legal dogmatics in this light.[95] Apparently also Alchourrón and Bulygin would tend to think in this way.[96] If, however, we look at the matter from the point of view of the judge and ask him what he expects from legal dogmatics, the answer would doubtless be a different one. The interest of the judge in receiving knowledge presupposes that legal dogmatics presents a justified answer to the question of the normative gap. In my view this interest in knowledge corresponds also in general to those expectations that are placed on a study of the content of the legal order by society. Following Wittgenstein, we can say that the argumentation game in cases of gap belongs to those language games played in legal language. It is thus natural and, from the point of society, justified to interpret the filling of the gap as one of the normal tasks of the everyday legal dogmatics.

This also applies to the so-called axiological gap and the logical gap. Alchourrón and Bulygin define an axiological gap as follows: the model of behaviour defined by the norms is unsatisfactory with due consideration to the axiological points of departure.[97] A logical gap is dealt with more rarely in the literature on theory of law. Doubtless also such gaps burden the legal order. It is possible to deal with two situations as logical gaps. One can be involved when legislation requires certain acts of a procedure which are dependent on each other. If, in this, part A of the procedure is dependent on part B, but there are no provisions on part B, a *technical* gap exists.[98] In the case that a provision requires that other provisions be given, but for some reason this has not been done, then we can speak of a *legislative* gap in the strict sense of the word.

(e) It is a question of *excessive regulation* (redundancy) when more than one law text deals with the same matter. Excessive regulation cannot be considered typical of a "good" legal order. From the point of view of justification, however, it does not have the same significance as the other cases mentioned, and so it will not be analyzed in this study in any greater detail.

4.3. *The Procedure of Discourse*

The problems of legal interpretation result from the character of the legal *procedure*. For instance, in the civil cases the plaintiff makes a claim and the defendant tries to resist this level giving reasons against the claim. The reasons may refer to the facts of the case or to another interpretation of the statutes. The difference of the opinions may thus be either classificatory or legal.

This procedural setting can be transformed into a legal dogmatical one. In the procedure of justification, the interpreter attempts to *strengthen* the alternative interpretation he has chosen, I_1; and on the other hand, he attempts to *eliminate* the counter-arguments.[99] These counter-arguments, in turn, shall be dealt with as arguments in favor of the alternative interpretation I_2. In this way of thinking, then, there is thus a constant "competition" in discourse between two alternatives, and at the same time between two groups of arguments, pro and con. As in the following the matter will be analyzed from the point of view of alternative interpretation I_1, the pro arguments will be considered as arguments that justify *this* interpretation, and the counter arguments will be considered as arguments opposing it. As far as the alternative I_2 is concerned, the role of the arguments is the reverse. The elimination of the counter-arguments to a certain interpretation (in this case, to I_1), therefore, is part of the presentation of justification in support of this interpretation.

The arguments themselves can be arranged in a hierarchy. Arguments on the first level may require further justification. This is the case when we doubt the strength of the pro arguments. The further arguments that are then marched forth can be called second level arguments. At this stage there is no reason to analyze the structure and role of these arguments in any greater detail. Second level arguments, in turn, may require further support, and thus we come to third level arguments, and so on.

An argument may prove to be semantically (or terminologically) ambiguous. It may be that in the form presented, the argument is too general, and as such indefinite or ambiguous. On the basis of counter-questions, the interpreter must establish what the argument means.

On this basis, we can illustrate the general structure of argumentation in the following manner. To begin with, we shall denote the pro arguments with the letter p and the counter arguments with the letter c. A statement that clarifies the meaning of such an argument (an analytical statement) can be expressed by adding a prime to the basic letter as follows: p' and c'. A statement that analyzes a pro argument can consequently be written as follows: $p'p$. The level of the argument can be expressed with a number. The hierarchy of pro arguments would thus be $p_1, p_2 \ldots p_n$ (a first level pro argument, a second level pro argument and so on). In addition, we can assume that an argument which counters a certain pro argument (for example which counters p_1) will be written on the same line. A counter argument which is only intended to seek clarification of an analytical argument can be denoted simply as "?". In some cases, the presentation of a counter argument forces the interpreter to present an argument in support of a previously presented argument. Depending on the level of argumentation, the additional argument receives its own index. For example, p_1p_2 can be understood to denote "argument p_1 which is supported by argument p_2."

If we denote, as before, the alternative interpretation of law text L_i supported by the interpreter as I_1, and the opposing interpretation alternative as I_2, we can obtain two schemes of arguments as presented in Diagram 20.[100]

L_i

I_1	(I_2)
p_1	?
$p'\ p_1$	c_1
p_2	c_2
$p_2\ p_3$	c_3
p_4	
--	

Diagram 20

In the diagram, alternative I_2 has been marked in parentheses because, according to our point of departure, the recipient of the interpretation need not himself represent a particular alternative interpretation. It is enough that there is disagreement over interpretation I_1, which is being defended. Even so, the counter arguments presented by the recipient of the interpretation can be pro arguments for interpretation I_2. If so, the scheme of interpretation is, as noted, the reverse; whatever supports alternative I_2 opposes interpretation I_1.

The dashes after the last pro argument describe the situation in which the chain of reasoning is cut off.

It is indirectly apparent from the scheme that *within* the pro arguments there are various relationships between the arguments in respect of interpretation I_1. Some of the arguments directly support I_1. Hence, they can simply be called direct arguments. Other arguments, for example p'_2 and the additional argument p'_1 on line four, only offer indirect support to the interpretation result itself. Their significance lies in the support of a certain part of the chain of reasoning. Arguments that speak for the alternative interpretation can be placed very schematically in the following diagram, which demonstrates in a somewhat better way the internal relation of pro arguments (Diagram 21).

Naturally, the chain of argumentation can be continued on one side or

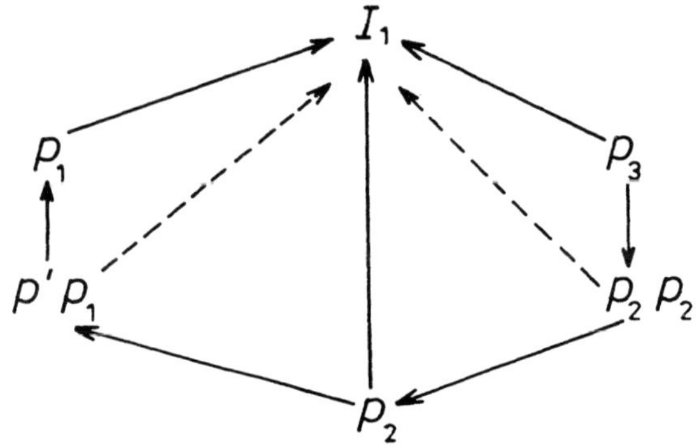

Diagram 21

another beyond what is assumed in the example, and its form can vary according to the case. Again, there is not one common structure for everything that we call argumentation, even though the above assumptions have been limited to certain types of language games. We can observe that even within this framework a functioning argumentation language is an enormous sum of individual games with family resemblance.

But no matter what the combination of moves is, and no matter how we describe the combinations, a question that is critical for all argumentation in legal dogmatics is left open: when can a chain of argumentation be cut off? At what stage are there enough pro arguments to make the justification sufficient? And on a more general level: does such a limit exist at all, or would it be possible that such a limit cannot be identified even in principle. We have thus come around to the ontological, epistemological and methodological questions outlined at the beginning.

The answer to those questions which is defended in this study is clear, although it may at the same time appear to be both radical and problematic. The position at this stage can be formulated as follows: even in principle it is not possible to demonstrate with general terms an exact limit at which justification can always be cut off. Cutting off the chain of arguments depends on what stage the conditions for achieving the acceptability of the statement I_1/I_2 have been created. This in turn is connected with the recipient of the interpretation. In more general terms, the interpretation is directed at a certain interpretation community or, in other words, an audience. Hence, the "final point" of justification is fixed in the audience or, in the terms introduced by Peczenik, it is contextually bound.[101]

Justification of this theoretical conception requires a clarification of not only some general features of the justification procedure, but also some examples from actual legal dogmatics. Let us begin by taking up some general points of view. Then the time has come to invite the reader to follow an example concerning a practical interpretation in legal dogmatics.

4.4 *Internal and External Justification*

Jerzy Wróblewski and, following him, also Robert Alexy have distinguished between the internal and the external justification of an interpretative proposition (or in general of a legal decision).[102] An internal justification (*IN*-justification), according to Wróblewski, means the deriving of the interpretation from the premises in accordance with accepted rules of inference. "The condition of *IN*-justification is the existence of the rule with which one can test the internal rationality of a decision. The validity of the premises is taken for granted", he writes. For example, according to Wróblewski the interpretative proposition "Norm N_i has meaning I_i in language L_i" is true on certain premises, $MP_1 \ldots MP_n$, if there are standards of inference $DI_1 \ldots DI_n$ and if the interpretation is based on values $V_1 \ldots V_n$ and the rules $DI_1 \ldots DI_n$ are used in the appropriate manner. Schematically presented, the following simple and, from the syllogistic point of view incomplete, formula shows the structure of the interal justification:

$$\frac{\begin{array}{c} MP_1 \ldots MP_n \\ DI_1 \ldots DI_n \\ V_1 \ldots V_n \end{array}}{I_1}$$

An external justification (*EX*-justification), in turn, receives the following characterization according to Wróblewski: "A decision is *EX*-justified if its premises are qualified as good according to the standards used by the person who makes the qualification. It is evident that legal decision could be *IN*-justified but have no *EX*-justification". In external justification, in other words, it is a question of the validity of the premises and the rules of inference. According to Wróblweski, they are dependent on the standards by which validity is evaluated. One can also say that an external justification ultimately depends on the norms and values to which one binds oneself in the justification.

In the following, an attempt will be made to demonstrate that the central problems of legal justification are connected with the external justification. The question of whether or not the interpretation result follows logically, i.e. internally upon some material premises and some rules of inference and values is trivial in itself. Such a background of premises, rules and values can always be constructed *ex post*. On the other hand, the difficulty that divides interpreters into different camps is tied, on one hand, to the choice and content of the premises, and, on the other hand, to the way in which the suitable principles of inference or basic values are chosen. The problem of legal discourse is thus concentrated upon the external justification.

4.5. *The Structure of the Ex-Justification Procedure*

The procedure of external justification – legal discourse as a form of general practical discourse – can be described in terms of internal and external justification as follows.[103] Let us take an example. The statute L_i expresses the norm: "If F_1, then ought to be G_1". A legal scholar A has put his opinion (standpoint) concerning the statute L_i in the form: in the case of f, there ought to be G_1. Let us call this standpoint interpretation I_1 (cf. Diagram 20). A natural question in this situation is as follows: *why* consequence G_1 ought to be connected just to fact f? Scholar A may answer that the term "F_1" in the law text means "f" and only this. Hence, A has given the first level argument in his justification. This part of reasoning can *ex post* be written in the form of a syllogism:

SYLLOGISM I	PR_1:	The law text L_i says: if F_1, then ought to be G_1
	PR_2:	$f \varepsilon F_1$
	C :	In the case of f there ought to be G_1

Premise PR_2 connects text L_i to its interpretation I_1. Therefore, the second premise (PR_2) has in this syllogism the role of the first level argument (p_1 in Diagram 20). The addressee B can, however, put the question: why just $f \varepsilon F_1$ why not e.g. $f' \varepsilon F_1$? In order to answer this question, A has to add his arguments giving a supporting ground for the statement "$f \varepsilon F_1$". It is again possible to put this stage of reasoning in a syllogistic form:

SYLLOGISM II	PR_1:	If the *travaux préparatoires* say "$f \varepsilon F_1$" in the case of L_i, then the proper interpretation of L_i is I_1, i.e. "if f, then ought to be G_1"
	PR_2:	The *travaux préparatoires* say "$f \varepsilon F_1$"
	C :	According to *travaux préparatoires* the interpretation of L_i is: if f then ought to be G_1

In the everyday practice of legal dogmatics the conclusion C has often the role of an independent argument. A scholar simply refers to the legislative history of the statute. However, the basis of this argument is a syllogism referred to above. In other words, there is always an internal justification for every step in the chain of arguments. In order to be precise one must therefore describe the syllogism II itself as a second level argument (p_2 in Diagram 22).

In the same way, arguments supporting a certain argument (e.g. p_1p_2) can be written in the form of a syllogism. Internal and external justification are, in this sense, interrelated with each other. Diagram 21 may thus be put also in the form presented below:

L_i

I_1	I_2
Syllogism I	?
Analysis of the terms	c_1
Syllogism II	c_2
Syllogism III	c_3
Supporting of an argument	
(Syllogism IV)	–
Syllogism V	–
–	–

Diagram 22

The standards of rationality (in general) and the traditional standards of legal interpretation point out how a certain individual syllogism can be formulated. The rules of syllogistic logic define the form of the inference and the standards of legal interpretation say e.g. that customary law must be used as an argument on certain conditions. Hence, each single transformation, i.e. each giving a pro argument (or an argument for an argument) is guided by this type of standards.

On the other hand, the complex totality of arguments (p_1, p_2, p_1p_2 etc.) does not deductively result in the interpretation I_1. Legal interpretation is not only syllogistic as to its nature. One cannot identify any rules accepted by the legal community by means of which the final conclusion (I_1) could be deduced just from the totality of *certain* syllogisms (cf. Diagram 22). In this sense, there are no syllogistic internal connections between different syllogisms in the chain of arguments. Here lies the kernel of the whole legal interpretation. The external justification is not syllogistic at all. It is a matter of convincing the other part, the addressee of the interpretation (B). This is done simply so that the interpreter adds new syllogisms supporting his interpretation or his arguments, but every step is guided only in a "loose" way by the standards of rationality or by the standards of legal interpretation. There are no exact criteria on the basis of which one could say that just this argument (syllogism) is the proper one. The interpreter will succeed if the totality of arguments (the chain of syllogisms) is convincing enough for the other part.

In this regard, it seems to be justified to say that the internal and external justification are interrelated to each other. External justification is the same as adding new syllogisms to the chain of arguments in order to support the former premise as is the case in Diagram 22.

4.6. *An Example of the Justification Procedure*

Very different views can be presented on the form of the transfer of one's share in an inheritance. Let us assume that interpreter *A* defends the position according to which the transfer must take place through a signed document that is witnessed by two persons.[104] I shall denote this interpretation with I_1. It is not enough to solely refer in this case to the law text (L_i), as the problem lies precisely in the fact that we do not know the content of the law text.[105]

If it were a question of a law text with a precise and unambiguous meaning content, no further justification would be necessary. A grammatical interpretation would be enough. In such a case, from the point of view of the application of the law one could speak of routine decisions. The law text is clear, the case has been proven and the application of the law does not create any difficulties. But, as has been said, our case at present is not like this. We must continue the chain of arguments.

4.6.1. *Travaux préparatoires.* In practice, the first warrant that comes up is almost always a reference to the *travaux préparatoires.*[106] Lying behind this is therefore the so-called principle of subjective interpretation.[107] In other words, the assumption (backing) is that when the grammatical meaning of the statute is not clear, it should be interpreted in accordance with its purpose.

In the foregoing, however, it has been pointed out that in the Finnish legal system *travaux préparatoires* are not strongly binding sources of law. Disregarding them leads only to an argumentative obligation to justify why this material was not used. Thus, in Finland the principle of subjective interpretation is not legally binding.[108]

What is most important is that the application criteria of that principle are open. What does it mean to say that the intention (will) of the legislator is clear? When is an intention clear? The difficulties are easy to understand if we were to analyse for a moment the notion of "clear intention".[109] In many cases the *travaux préparatoires* are full of gaps. Mention is certainly made of the need for regulation in a certain sector of life, as is the framework and basic structure of the regulation, but nothing is mentioned of individual interpretation problems of individual law texts. This is due in part to economy in the use of labor and in part to the fact that it is not even possible to anticipate all problems of interpretation. It is especially common that development (for example technical development) in society goes beyond the scope of the *travaux préparatoires*. It is simply not possible to consider everything that, at the time of the interpretation, is important.

And this is not all. *Travaux préparatoires* consist of language. Thus, expressions in the *travaux préparatoires* suffer from the same openness to interpretation as do law texts themselves.[110] At times interpretation calls for the interpretation of the arguments themselves. So it is not enough to refer to the *travaux préparatoires* in order to clarify the problematic law text. We need at least additional warrants. The additional warrants at times have been such matters as the personal careers of the legislators, at times the "spirit of the day" or at times the general legal discussion on the matter at the time of the legistlation. In practice, such additional warrants, however, do not lock an interpretation of the *travaux préparatoires* into the genuine interpretation. On the contrary, despite the additional warrants, the clarification of the statute calls for additional justification to the *travaux préparatoires*.

We can scarcely pass without mentioning the fact that in practical interpretation the identification of *travaux préparatoires* is also a difficult problem.[111] What *material* adequately expresses the will of the "legislator"? There are no clear guidelines for making a decision on this.[112] At times committee reports are used, at times Government Bills or the minutes of the meetings of Parliamentary committees. The following order of priority seems to be adequate as far as the prevalent practice in Finland is concerned.

If there is a clear expression concerning the problem in the minutes of the meetings of Parliamentary committees, they express the subjective intention, which can be taken as the basis for the interpretation. If this is not the case, the reasoning in the Government Bill may be used. One must depart from the assumption that the Government Bill with its reasoning has met with the approval of Parliament unless a specific amendment has been made. When other types of material are silent on the subject, one can turn to (non-Parliamentary) committee reports or similar data. It is only a question, however, of *presumptive* principles of rational discourse. Thus, no sanction is attached to the bypassing of Parliamentary material. The interpreter, however, has the obligation of presenting justification for why he has bypassed an explicit mention in the minutes of the meeting of a Parliamentary committee and has, shall we say, justified his interpretation with a statement taken from a (non-Parliamentary) committee report.

In most cases there is not one particular type of material in the *travaux préparatoires* that provides an answer to the interpretation problem. On the contrary, it is common that the interpreter attempts to construct an interpretative whole out of the *travaux préparatoires*. The result is a *reconstruction*, where statements in different materials are brought together to form a whole. Depending on the coherence and the extent of the reconstruction, its justificatory power varies greatly. At the best, such a reconstruction is a source which only in a weak way supports the interpretation. It does not conclusively justify the interpretation statement.

In our example the *travaux préparatoires* have relatively limited significance. It is true that the Decedent's Estate Act was in preparation for almost 30 years, and that as a result of this preparation a large number of committee reports, statements and other *travaux préparatoires* were produced. Nothing in these *travaux préparatoires*, however, takes a definite position on the interpretation of Chapter 17, Section 3 of the Act. For this reason the *travaux préparatoires* leave the problem unanswered to the extent that it is unanswered on the basis of the statute itself. In this case there simply is no historical intention of the legislator.

In such a situation, at times *ratio legis*, i.e. the objective intention that justifies the content of a statute being referred to. In this, two directions can be taken into account.[113]

The objective intention may have significance as the hypothetical intention of the legislator: if the matter in question had come up during the legislative stage, it would have been decided in such-and-such a way. In other words, the hypothetical intention is also a reconstructed intention.[114] At no stage any instance has represented this intention, to say nothing of having publicly stated it. Perelman writes, "Wenn man in einem solche Fall auf den Willen des Gesetzgebers zurückgreifen will, dann ruft man einen rein willkürlich vorausgesetzten, oft gänzlich fiktiven Willen zu hilfe, welchen man dem redlichen Gesetzgeber zu schreiben möchte."[115] Since it is a question of reconstruction *ex post*, the hypothetical intention as such will not serve as justification for the interpretation of the law. Thus, if the hypothetical intention is to have some justificatory value in general, it depends on matters other than the *travaux préparatoires*. It is not the historical intention. At the most, the *travaux préparatoires* can be an indication on the basis of which other justificatory material receives its proper significance in the reconstruction of the hypothetical intention.

The nature of justification becomes even clearer when we analyze the objective intention in another sense. By the objective intention one can also mean *ratio legis* here and now. It is the totality of meanings that is formed with due consideration to all of the factors.

In this very sense, it is a question of the meaning content of a statute at the time of the interpretation.[116] It is neither subjective nor historical. It is not subjective, as the *ratio* or the intention of the law is reconstructed on the basis of many factors, not just on the basis of the *travaux préparatoires*. This latter source does not have a preferred position in the justification. On the other hand, the *ratio* is connected specifically to the time of the interpretation. For this reason it is not correct to speak of the historical intention, in other words of the true intention that existed at some previous time.

However, in the theory of interpretation the concept of the objective interpretation is just a superfluous addition. Using it is a way of indirectly saying the same things as is said directly on the basis of the sources of law, using a generally accepted interpretation rule. If we again were to denote the sources of law with the letter S, the result of the interpretation with the letter I and we use the letters OI to refer to the objective intention, then the theory of the objective intention would seem to be saying something like the following:

$$S_1 \ldots S_n \xrightarrow[D_i]{} OI \xrightarrow[D_j]{} I$$

In this formula the sources of law and the objective intention are connected to each other with the interpretation rule D_i which defines *how* the sources of law are to be used. The interpretation result, in turn, is connected to the objective intention with rule D_j. This says, for example, "the law must always be interpreted in accordance with the objective intention".

As a matter of fact, however, the reasoning is more direct. Our point of departure is that due to certain rules, the sources of law support interpretation I. The interpretation is a "consequence" of the appropriate use of the sources of law. Schematically presented, the chain of reasoning is thus as follows:

$$S_1 \ldots S_n \xrightarrow[D_j]{} I$$

4.6.2. *Systemic interpretation.* It is usual in legal dogmatics to argue as follows: "The text of law L_i has to be interpreted in a way I_1 because the legal system is such that non-I_1 would make the system inconsistent". These types of arguments will later be called systemic reasons and the way to use them, systemic interpretation.

In referring to systemic reasons, an attempt is made to fit the statute at issue into its "natural" systemic context. As is well known, this kind of reasoning was adopted by e.g. the so-called conceptual legal dogmatics (*Begriffsjurisprudenz*). An example of this is also the explicit content of Article 6 in the ABGB. In commenting on the provision,

Heinrich Klang and Franz Gschnitzler observe that a word in a statute must not be interpreted against the background of the statute alone (on the basis of *travaux préparatoires* etc.). Its meaning should be sought by means of all other statutes that are connected to the provision to be interpreted.[117]

The ideology of systemic interpretation assumes that the sector of the legal order being dealt with, for example that of the Decedent's Estate Act, is internally consistent.[118] Within the framework of this totality, each provision has its "own place". This means that e.g. the following rules of interpretation are assumed to be followed:

(i). Norm N_2 may be complementary to norm N_1 or make norm N_1 more precise. A good example of the completing effect is the so-called *lex imperfecta*. It is a statute that only expresses general principles without giving any sanctions for violation of the principles. For instance, in the Finnish Marriage Act there is a statute (Article 37) that obliges a spouse to take good care of his (or her) property so that it does not unjustifiably grow less. Elsewhere in the same Act there are provisions that give a precise meaning content to this principle, e.g. in Article 94 according to which a spouse has a right to get a compensation in the division of the property if the other part has violated the principle expressed in Article 37.

Different statutes, e.g. the articles in a certain Act, may also form a hierarchy, where the "lower" statutes make the "higher" ones more precise. For instance, a norm of conduct N_1 uses the term "contract" and another norm N_2 gives the criteria what the notion "contract" in this context means.

(ii) Norm analogy mentioned above is also based on the assumption that the legal order is a systemic unit. In analogous cases a certain norm gives support to an interpretation of another norm. The same holds true of *argumentum a fortiori*-inference.

(iii) Legal order is supposed to be logically consistent. If a norm N_1 commands and norm N_2 prohibits the same behaviour, the norms are contrary to each other. On the other hand, if norm N_1 prohibits and norm N_2 permits the same behaviour there is a contradictory relation between the norms.

In addition to the logical inconsistency, there may also be *physical* inconsistencies in the legal order. If norm N_1 obliges the employee to work from 1 PM to 8 PM and the other norm N_2 gives the working obligation from 8 PM until 1 AM, it is physically impossible to follow both norms although there are no logical inconsistencies in such a norm giving.

In all these cases the same basic idea can be identified: the complex totality of legal norms is a systemic unity. The purpose of the interpretation is to find out the systemic connections between the norms and to "place" every norm in the proper way as a part of this whole. According to this idea, legal order is like a net, where every norm "finds its place" in a certain mesh of that net.

However, the criteria of the formation of the systemic whole have a key position in this type of interpretation.[119] Only if we truly know that the system is as it is said to be, and that the norm being interpreted fits into the systemic whole in a proper manner, our justification has strength from the point of view of the conclusion. This strength is in practice often lessened by the fact that the norm being interpreted in itself shapes the systemic unit. In part specifically because of this, the system is as it is said to be. In other words, the result of the interpretation depends on the systemic whole, and the systemic whole depends on the content that the norm being interpreted receives. The system is not given in advance (once for all) but is partially formulated on the basis of the interpretation. This reciprocity will be, from one point of view, analysed in a more detailed way in Section 4.7.

4.6.3 *Court decisions as reasons.* In our example, the systemic whole does not conclusively decide the interpretation in favour of alternative I_1. Further justification is needed. Here, it is in accordance with normal justification practice to refer to court decisions. In the present example, especially Supreme court decisions have a great value as arguments, as in the cases of inheritance, the normal avenue of appeal is open all the way to the Supreme court.

Let us take an example where there are three Supreme court decisions, *A*, *B* and *C*. The first two support interpretation I_1, while decision *C* gives support to another interpretation, say I_2. Let us also assume that the decisions were given in the order listed, i.e. decision *A* was given first. In practical legal reasoning, one can imagine that the decisions in our example can be utilized in at least the following two ways:

(a) It can be said that decisions *A* and *B* represent a certain *policy* (tendency), from which *C* marks an exception. Thus, "legal praxis" would support interpretation I_1.

(b) On the contrary, the decision *C* represents a shift of policy, as it is the most recent decision, and as the results of it depart from the previous decisions. Thus, interpretation I_1 *no longer* receives support from legal praxis.

Both approaches assume a certain position on the analogy between the decisions. Approach (a) contains the assumption that decisions *A* and *B* are analogous – which explains interpretation I_1 – while the facts in decision *C* differ in some relevant way from those in the previous cases. For this reason the interpretation is different. The exceptionality of decision *C* is thus due to the distinctive features of the facts of the case, not to the fact that the Supreme Court would have acted in an inconsistent way.

The second approach to legal praxis assumes that the facts in each case are regarded as analogous. Only on this assumption decision *C* can mark a departure from the court policy.

Thus, our example shows that the use of legal praxis as the justification for an interpretation demands careful analysis of the facts in the cases. The cases must be broken down into their basic elements, and a usable analogy key must be found in order to verify the similarity of the cases. A mere reference to the "policy" in praxis or to a "departure in policy" rests on air unless justification is given for the analogous relationships on which these forms of speech rest. This ultimately means that we must be able to justify why certain elements among the facts are regarded as relevant and why they were assigned weights in the way referred to in the selected analogy key. The differences between approaches (a) and (b) are thus to be explained as differences in the criteria of relevance and in the analogy keys used. And as this is the case, a reference to legal praxis does not "lock in" the justification of the interpretative alternative in a way which would shuts out possible disagreement. On the contrary, the chain of arguments must be continued.

4.6.4 *On the doctrinal opinion.* In such a situation the interpreter may turn to a new, additional warrant, a reference to the legal literature. As has been noted before, legal dogmatics can be regarded as a factual source of law. There is no obligation to use it, but its use is permitted.[120]

Legal dogmatics in itself is normally composed of a number of opinions. Only rarely we can recognize a clear direction in, or weight of, opinions. Hence, it is practically impossible to speak of "the prevailing opinion" concerning certain individual legal interpretations. However, in everyday scholarly practice such opinions are quite often referred to.

In this, the prevailing opinion is normally used more as a means of influencing the addressee than as a rational justification of the proposed interpretation. This is due to a number of reasons.

First of all, in practice it is often difficult to ascertain what the content of the prevailing opinion is. For it to be possible, the totality of different views must be analyzed into a prevailing opinion. We have to demonstrate what the interpretations taken as part of the sample contain; what does writer *X* ultimately say about the provision we are dealing with. But this is not all. There remains a difficult problem: the identification of the representatives of the prevailing opinion. We must be able to decide what opinions actually represent the prevailing opinion. What *is* the "prevailing opinion"? Is it the dominance of a position when measured in the number of scholars who support it? Does the length of time it has been accepted have a role? Should we take into consideration the authority of the scholars defending interpretation I_i in the community of science? Apparently not one factor alone is enough to determine what is "prevailing".[121] This depends on the research tradition of the field in question, the type of problem and so on. In practice, as has been noted, reference to the prevailing opinion is based more on a "sense of feel", on intuition, than on a thoroughly analyzed choice of criteria.

From the point of view of our subject it is not essential that we make proposals on how one should discern what the prevailing opinion is. What is important is that we ask what significance a position in legal dogmatics, ultimately the prevailing opinion, has in the legal justification.

(*a*) If opinions in legal dogmatics have an authoritative position in the list of sources of law, there is no problem. This is the case for example in Jewish law. In such a tradition, a certain interpretative standpoint receives the same status as a statute or the customary law in accordance with Chapter 1, Section 11 of the Code of Judicial Procedure. There are, however, no standards in the Finnish legal order which would grant legal dogmatics this status. If, therefore, a view in legal dogmatics is used as an authoritative argument it is truly a question only of an attempt to influence the recipient's interpretation. An attempt is being made to give the proposal regarding the alternative interpretation a greater weight than what it would have otherwise on the basis of its rational justification. In such a case legal dogmatics should be called a persuasive argument.

(*b*) The interpreter, however, can also use legal dogmatics for, for example, a reference to the prevailing opinion, in another way. Reference to it may demonstrate an attempt to justify the intersubjectiveness of the proposed interpretation, in other words its objectiveness in this regard. The prevailing opinion, as it were, acts as a type of control mechanism. It demonstrates that the interpreter's view is not just the result of his own subjective preferences. In this, reference is not made to the prevailing opinion as an authority, either as an official or a factual authority. The separation of cases (a) and (b), however, is very difficult to realize in scholarly practice.

(*c*) Closely following the above we can imagine that the prevailing opinion is seen to interpret the view that is generally accepted in the legal community. This idea is based on the awareness that legal dogmatics in fact has persuasive weight in the legal community. The interpretation represented by legal dogmatics is assumed to be accepted, for example, beyond the research community by legal educators and in the statements of experts. Usually the assumption of the degree to which the legal community accepts an opinion, however, depends only on a guess. For it to be possible to present such a proposition, it must be justified with certain empirical data. Just a reference to the prevailing opinion itself is not enough. Only when it is justified in an empirical way, it will become acceptable in rational argumentation.

In summary, we can say that in actual interpretation, legal dogmatics has more persuasive significance than what is referred to in (a). The assumption of the weight of an opinion in society, in turn, is usually based on pure guesswork. Thus, legal dogmatics can usually serve rational reasoning only in the sense referred to in (b). An individual opinion in legal dogmatics is no more a substantial reason than the prevailing opinion is.

The role of legal dogmatics lies in the fact that it brings intersubjective believability to the justification, thus eliminating, in part, the possibility that the proposed interpretation is merely the subjective fancy of the interpreter. Generally speaking, the significance of legal dogmatics in rational argumentation is relatively slight, in any case slighter than what actual interpretation praxis appears to believe.

4.6.5 *Practical reasons.* With an eye on our example, we are left with reference to the so-called practical reasons. It was noted in the foregoing that arguments of this kind are normally presented as the consideration of consequences. Let us call it practical reasoning. This type of reasoning involves two "steps": (1) the clarification of the possible consequences concerning the interpretative alternatives at hand and (2) placing these consequences in a certain order of preference. After the "best consequence" has been explicated, the reasoning turns around and goes back to the alternative interpretations. The interpretation which produces the best imaginable consequences is the "best justified".

The first step, the conception about the consequences, is either causal or noncausal. The belief is causal if there prevails a causal relationship between the alternative interpretations and the consequence candidates. An example of this is the case where the interpretation leads to the endangerment of the interests of trade, an economic loss to one of the parties, economic burdens on the courts or administrative organizations, and so on.

One may speak of noncausal (lateral) beliefs if the interpretation has a consequence in regard to the legal order (an internal, i.e. systemic consequence). If for example we adopt interpretation I_1, a consequence will be that certain other elements of the legal order have to be interpreted in quite another way.[121]

It is a question of practical reasoning in the proper sense of the term only if the consideration is based on causal beliefs. As a matter of fact the term "real" already refers to this aspect: the interpretation is weighed in the light of certain factors belonging to social reality.

The practical interpretation is not, however, an empirical way of reasoning as is e.g. the justification of sociological propositions. Interpretation is brought, it is true, into contact with reality, but at the same time one attempts to shape the constitution of reality by selecting a consequence worth furthering on the basis of nonempirical criteria. The interpretation is empirical *and* evaluative. Its structure is as follows. Let us assume that alternative I_1 causes consequences $C_1 \ldots C_n$ and that the consequences of alternative I_2 are $C'_1 \ldots C'_n$. On the other hand, consequences $C_1 \ldots C_n$ are considered to take preference over the consequences of the other alternative: the former are good, while the latter are bad, or both have a positive (or both negative) value but consequences $C_1 \ldots C_n$ are, on the whole, "better" than consequences of the second alternative. It does not matter what "better" means in this context.

In the American realist movement (in pragmatic instrumentalism) this model of reasoning is often discussed. One may speak of goal reasoning. Court decisions are instruments for the realization of certain goals. The same way of thinking has in the Finnish legal theory been called finalistic interpretation.[122] In the latter model, the finalistic reasoning can be either heuristic or have to do with the justification of the decisions. From the heuristic point of view, the theory explains how the interpretation was discovered. In justification the finalistic model offers a practical means to argue for the final choice of the interpretation alternative. In Finnish philosophy of law, Hannu Tapani Klami has presented this type of reasoning. According to this view, finalistic legal science defines the general conditions of goal justification and control. Mainly the finalistic approach has in Klami's model, however, been a heuristic tool to describe how the decision (or: interpretation in general) came about.[123]

As was noticed before, the heuristic point of view is not significant in this contribution. The focus of the analysis is solely on the justificatory procedure. On the other hand, the finalistic interpretation (goal reasoning) does not have a decisive role in legal justification. It cannot be called a genuine model of legal reasoning. Even so, goal reasoning is in many senses a relevant element of justification.

With an eye on praxis, it would appear to be well-founded to state that goal reasoning is often the ultimate (final) step of the justificatory procedure. In any case, our present example is construed in this way. Other sources of law create the legal framework within which the ultimate choice of the interpretation alternative has to be done. Statutes, *travaux préparatoires*, court decisions etc. define the legally possible interpretations among the semantically possible alternatives of the text to be interpreted. In this (preliminary) choice, the general rules of rationality and the directives of legal interpretation guide the justification procedure the whole time. After the decision has been delineated in this way, the *final* choice can be based on goal reasoning: the alternative that has the "best" (or "better") consequences has the priority in the order of preference.[124]

Hence, goal reasoning as such – separated from other sources of law – can never be a basis for legal justification. The interpretation receives its legality only (and specifically) because it is tied to the authoritative sources of law. In the statutory law system this means that legality is always dependent on valid statutes (law texts). The interpretation is a legal one if and only if at least one statute is referred to. Goal reasoning alone is just a form of social discourse. It may be useful, even necessary from the societal point of view but it has no special legal value. It gets legal "colour" only when it is connected to other legal sources, i.e. to the legal context. Understood in this way, goal reasoning is also in the statutory law system a form of legal reasoning.[125]

4.6.6 *Summary*. All in all, the justification of the interpretative standpoint can be cut off at this stage almost as a test. This measure may seem rather strained, but in so doing we will not only be able to summarize what has been said up to now, but we can also lay a better foundation for the problem that we have taken up. The problem was: are there general criteria on the basis of which it is possible to cut off the chain of reasons so that the interpretative standpoint can be regarded as justified? The problem is understandably important, if we consider the justification of an interpretative standpoint from the general point of view. If it is not possible to point out such general criteria, we have a fall-back question: Does all justification in legal dogmatics break down into opinions that scatter into different directions, and are these opinions in an important sense subjective? If, on the other hand, we believe that it is possible to demonstrate such a set of general criteria, we come to the classical problem of the one right answer. In the concluding part of this study we shall deal with these questions. For this purpose, it is time to draft a summarizing table.

In Diagram 23 a collection of reasons for an interpretation (I_1) of the contents of Chapter 17, Section 3 of the Finnish Decedent's Estate Act, as well as against it (and thus for interpretation I_2) is presented.

The column to the extreme left of the diagram characterizes the type of reasons (the sources of law). In the example, the custom of the land is not mentioned, as it does role in this example. The customary law is a mandatory source of law only when there is no written law. Thus, Chapter 17, Section 3 shuts out the use of customary law as a source.

The other two columns give, in an abridged form the reasons that can be imagined in such an interpretation game. The dashed line on the right shows that the chain of reasons has been cut off. In Diagram 24, our summary is presented in another way. In this diagram, the arrows show the progress of the reasoning. When one stops at grammatical interpretation, it is a question of routine decisions. The further the reasoning goes, the first matter to enter the question is subjective interpretation, in other words the clarification of the intention of the

L_i

	I_1	I_2
1. *Law text*	the wording of text L_i	the wording of text L_i
2. *The intention of the legislator*	committee report R_1 supports view I_1	committee report R_2 supports view I_2, or at least makes I_1 impossible
3. *The ratio of the law*	systematically, L_i must be interpreted in connection with law text L_j, from which analogous support can be derived for I_1	there is not sufficient justification for this analogy
4. *Court decisions*	Supreme Court decisions A and *B* support view I_1	Supreme Court decision C shows that the policy has changed in favour of I_2
5. *Legal dogmatics*	Scholar A advocates I_1	Scholar B advocates I_2
6. *Real arguments*	the consequence C_i of I_1 are more defensible than consequences C_i of I_2. For this reason I_1 is to be preferred over I_2.	

Diagram 23

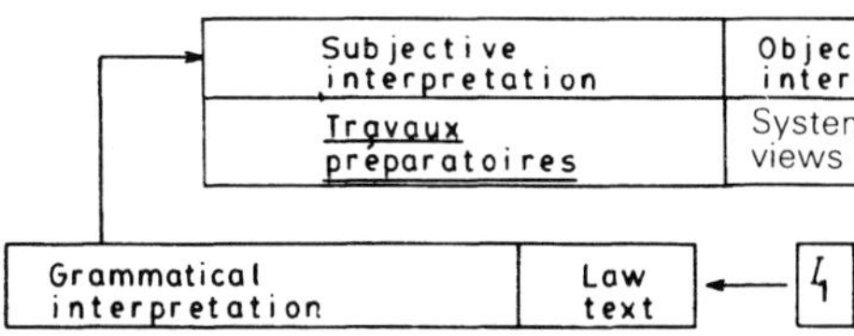

Diagram 24

legislator. If this cannot be ascertained, or if the indications provided by subjective interpretation are not enough, we come to the area of objective interpretation. By objective interpretation, in this, no reference is being made to the clarification of the hypothetical or objective intention, but to the justification of the interpretative standpoint in legal dogmatics taking all the sources of law available into consideration.[126]

The combination of justification that is formed depends on the type of problem and on the sources of law available. Theory cannot give a general form for the combination of justifications.

4.7 *The Relation Between the Systematization and the Interpretation of Legal Norms*

4.7.1 *The concept of systematization.* In their classical work "Normative Systems", Carlos Alchourrón and Eugenio Bulygin characterize legal systems as normative systems whose basis is composed of legal sentences.[127] The authors use the term "legal sentence" instead of the expressions "legal norm" or "legal rule" because of its neutrality as far as e.g. the definition of the concept of norm is concerned. Characterized in this way, the notion of legal system is more general than the concept of legal order. The last mentioned consists of a set of all legal sentences (norms) valid according to certain criteria of identification. In this respect, legal order as a complex totality of legal norms is the result of using societal power. Legal order is, as Otto Brusiin called it, a power-order.[128]

Legal system, on the other hand, is a product of a cognitive activity by means of which the elements of the legal order (norms) have been put in a certain relation with each other. This activity will be later on called systematization. In this regard, systematization is a counterpart of interpretation. From the point of view of legal justification, the kernel of the problem lies in the distinction between interpretation and systematization. As is the case with scientific approach in general, we meet here a question how the practical and theoretical elements are interweaved in human thinking. The systematizing activity in legal dogmatics can be called theoretical research, whereas interpretation is the core of the practical legal dogmatics. As to the main thesis of the present study, the theoretical and practical elements, systematization and interpretation, have reciprocal relations with each other. The systematization of (legal) norms cannot be carried out regardless of the (detailed) knowledge of the norms, and *vice versa*. In regard to the change and dynamics in law and the growth of legal knowledge in general, the systematization gives a framework for legal interpretation and every interpretation must be realized within a certain systematization.

The product of this joint activity (systematization/interpretation) is a legal system, i.e. a systematized conception about legal order. Furthermore, every change of legal systematizations also changes our view of legal order which is the subject-matter of the systematizing activity. For us, legal order *is* such as the systematization presents it because a legal system – as a result of systematizing activity – is like a "lens" through which we are doomed to look at the legal order.

According to Alchourrón and Bulygin this kind of change may happen and also happens quite often in society. All legal systems are relative to a particular time, i.e. they are momentary systems. As an example, Alchourrón and Bulygin refer to French law. It is not "one legal order, but a temporary and discrete succession of (momentary) legal orders". The dynamics of the legal order is, in the end, producted by practical jurists. From this point of view, the most important "creator" of the system is – besides the legislator – the judge, especially the judges of the Supreme Court. The scientific (legal dogmatical) systematization is, according to these authors, of quite another type. It means substituting a different basis for a certain legal system so that the normative consequences of the system remain the same. The scientific system is always axiomatic as to its nature. Therefore, the reformulation of the system lies in the fact that the original extensive basis of the legal system will be replaced by another that is more restricted but deontically equivalent. The system becomes simpler and more general.

This very characterization of legal systematization will be brought into question later in this contribution. To begin with, let us recall certain main viewpoints presented by Alchourrón and Bulygin.[129] In their opinion, an important part of what is called "interpretation" can be understood "as a determination of the normative consequences of a set of legal sentences for a certain problem or topic". Jurists simply attempt to make explicit what already is hidden in the legal order. This means, for Alchourrón and Bulygin, the same as the construction of an axiomatic system. Here the systematizing activity finds its corner stone. The precondition of systematization is the identification of the system. "This presupposes the existence of certain elements which are the starting points for the systematization. These elements are: (1) a problem or a group of problems (a topic) whose regulation by the law is of interest to the jurist; (2) a set of legal sentences relevant to the topic in question; (3) a set of rules of inference used by the jurist in the derivation of the consequences".

Alchourrón and Bulygin use concepts with sharpness that is typical of logicians. The following concepts will help to understand the three groups of problems mentioned above.[130]

UD (Universe of Discourse)
UD is the set of all states of affairs or situations, which defines the issues to be decided on. For instance: a situation in which a certain person *A* has transferred to another person *B* the possession of real estate that is owned by a third person *C*.

UC (Universe of Cases)
A particular case is defined by certain criteria or properties within the framework mentioned above. Let the properties be *F*, *G*, and *H*. Whether a given property is present or not (e.g. *F*), we obtain 2^n different combinations of properties. Alchourrón and Bulygin present the Universe of Cases (*UC*) as follows:

		UP (Universe of Properties)		
		F	*G*	*H*
UC (Universe of Cases)	1	+	+	+
	2	–	+	+
	3	+	–	+
	4	–	–	+
	5	+	+	–
	6	–	+	–
	7	+	–	–
	8	–	–	–

In the table, "+" signifies the presence of a property, and "–" signifies the absence of a property.

UA (Universe of Actions)
After having pointed out the relevant cases within the Universe of Discourse, it is natural to ask how one ought to act in a given situation. In other words, one would like to know whether a particular kind of action is obligatory, prohibited, or permitted. The Universe of Actions consists of that kind of actions. They can be signified generally with the letter *R* (in the example above: return of real estate to the proper owner).

R has a so-called deontic content in Alchourrón's and Bulygin's conceptual apparatus. The deontic character of an action may be either obligatory, prohibited, or permitted. If we signify the obligatory character of an action with "*O*", prohibited character with "*Ph*", and permitted character with "*P*", we may present the universe of actions with the symbols, *OR*, *PhR*, and *PR*.

US max (min)
A solution is an action with deontic character, which is related as a correlate to a certain case; e.g. *OR* (real estate is to be returned to its owner).

The concept of a normative system, too, can be characterized with these background concepts. Since it has a special meaning in Alchourrón's and Bulygin's conceptual network, an introduction of some additional concepts is needed.

Let (a) be a set of sentences. Each such ordered pair of sentences (e.g. p and q) of which the latter one (q) follows deductively from the former one (p), when p is combined with the set of sentences (a), constitutes a deductive correlate for the set of sentences (a). When a deductive correlate from the set of sentences (a) is such that the former of the two elements of a pair of sentences (p) is a case and the latter one (q) is a solution, the correlate is named a normative one by Alchourrón and Bulygin. If there exists at least one normative correlate among the deductive correlates of (a), the set of sentences (a) is said to have normative consequences.[131]

Having defined the concepts needed, it is now simple to define the concept of a normative system. A normative system is a set of sentences which has at least one normative consequence. Quite roughly one could state that a normative system in the sense meant by Alchourrón and Bulygin is such a set of sentences from which one can *deductively* derive solutions to cases. In this regard, a normative system is a deductive system, as well; and, when the basic sentences have been chosen, a normative system is equally an axiomatic one, too.

A solution (e.g. S_i) may follow deductively from a case (e.g. c_i) if and only if there exists a conditional clause (e.g. "If C_i, then S_i") which connects the case and the solution. Such conditional clauses may be obtained from the law text, judicial decisions, and other kind of official material. Independent of their origin, the set of conditional clauses (a) forms the systemic basis.

Alchourrón and Bulygin characterize the forming of the systemic basis as a two-phased process. In the first phase, the sets of relevant cases (UC) and solutions (US) are defined. In the second phase, solutions are derived deductively for the cases that belong to (UC). Thus we have obtained all the (possible) normative consequences of the system.[132]

In Alchourrón's and Bulygin's conceptual usage, systematization is equal with the remoulding of the systemic basis, or – in other words – its reformulation. The original systemic basis is replaced with another, which includes concepts (terms) that are of a higher level of abstraction. The clarity and demonstrativeness can thus be improved. Systematization is not, however, expected to alter the contents of the system. In other words, the normative consequences of the old and the new systems are to be the same. Alchourrón and Bulygin express this by stating that the two systems are to be identical.[133]

In all, the formulation of a system and its reformulation are thoroughly rational activities. The only accepted rules of inference are the rules of logic.

Slightly in other words, the systematizing activity does not modify the system at all; it only provides us with a new mode of presentation of the system. As regards the scholarly work, this means that the (genuine) modification of the system is outside of its framework. The creation of a new systemic basis belongs to the legislator – and in everyday practice – to the judge.

Hence, in order to be scientific the work of the legal dogmatician has to be logically coloured. The derivation of the consequences from the basic sentences is a problem of logical inference because the rules of inference are logical rules. On the other hand, the relation of the original basis to the new one is a matter of logical implication. The scholar gets the general principles belonging to the new basis by means of deductive inference using the original basis as starting point. Yet, for Alchourrón and Bulygin systematization is not a mere mechanical activity. The discovery of the general principles requires "a considerable degree of creative activity" as does also the discovery of the logical or mathematical conclusion from a given set of sentences as premises. This kind of activity presupposes creative imagination, too. The same holds true of the proof which shows that the new basis is deducible from the sentences of the original basis. The authors add, however, that the creative feature of legal dogmatics does not involve the creation of totally new basic norms. This societal function is not involved in legal science.

In terms of legal philosophy the viewpoint presented by Alchourrón and Bulygin can be called formalistic. Part of what is meant by formalism in this context is this: all sound normative consequences can be derived from the basis by means of valid deductive operations. The only task of legal dogmatics (as scientific approach) is to find out what is hidden in the legal system and, in addition to that, to present the results in a simple and general language.

This is not only important but also acceptable in many respects. However, this kind of characterization does not refer to all essential features of everyday legal dogmatics. Let us begin with some concepts introduced by Thomas Kuhn.[134]

For Kuhn, science is essentially the use of conceptual instruments. In the concrete scientific work, scholars learn how to use these instruments in practice. As a product of that learning procedure, scientists adopt a certain uniting framework which are called, as we noted, paradigms or matrixes. Every matrix is articulated in scientific theories. In legal dogmatical practice, however, the current usage of the concept of theory is ambiguous in many respects. The ambiguity reveals, for example in civil law, where the concept "theory" may sometimes refer to general (legal) principles, sometimes to a certain way to solve individual problems and sometimes to a doctrine, like a doctrine of ownership, doctrine of authorization etc. On the basis of the foregoing, the loose concept of theory is applicable neither to the paradigmatic analysis of legal dogmatics nor to the analysis of the change of legal systems. Therefore, an attempt for conceptual specification is needed. In the following, the concept of theory *in* legal dogmatics is defined by means of the notion of systematization.

> *Def*: A theory in legal dogmatics is a set of concepts and statements used for systematizing legal norms.

From slightly another point of view, a theory in legal dogmatics is a result of the systematizing activity. A conceptual network (theory) is used as instrument to arrange legal norms in a certain way. In other words, legal systematization (theory) is a partial articulation of the legal dogmatical paradigm. The theories in legal dogmatics can in this respect easily be compared with the theories in other sciences. As was pointed out, the systematizing activity is the theoretical part of legal dogmatics whereas the interpretative activity fulfills the practical function in the scholarly work.

Every legal interpretation is formulated within the framework of a certain systematization. In this very respect, systematizations (theories in legal dogmatics) lock the limits of legal interpretations. This means, furthermore, that legal dogmatical interpretations, coloured by the systematizations, produce the (scientific) legal *systems*. This side of the problem can be elucidated as follows.

As an example of a theory in legal dogmatics I shall take the theory of ownership. According to Alf Ross and Simo Zitting[135] the concept of ownership – among other concepts comparable with it – is a (practical) instrument in presenting a very complex totality of legal norms. Instead of describing a vast number of different norms one can communicate by means of a few general concepts. An abstract scheme of that kind of theory is presented in Diagram 25.

	Theory T_i	
Theoretical part of the theory	C C_1 $\quad C_2$ $C'_1 \quad C''_1 \quad C'_2 \quad C''_2$	Theoretical concepts (and propositions)
Interpretative part of the theory	$P_{n_1} \ldots P_{nn}$	Norm statements (norm standpoints)
Normative part of the theory	$N_1 \ldots N_n$	Norms (norm formulations)
Factual part of the theory	$S_1 \ldots S_n$	Situations dealt with in the norms

Diagram 25

Let us accept the theory T_i as an illustration of a theory (system) in legal dogmatics. The concept C may refer to any kind of legal concepts: ownership, authorization, guardianship etc. What does it mean, in accordance with this, that a legal system is changed or will be changed? What is the reformulation of a legal system?

Behind every legislative act there is a many-shaded group of various elements:[136]

(a) *Generalizations*, formed on the basis of everyday experience, on the prevailing states of affairs, for example on the existence and the nature of a phenomenon in society. For instance, beliefs, based on everyday experience or systematized knowledge, on the effects of the use of a certain legislative measure. Such beliefs include, for example, causal estimates of changes in the amount of criminality when put in relation to certain punishment scales.

(b) *Theory-like totalities* of propositions regarding the reasons for and the consequences of phenomena, the structure of institutions and so on. A good example of this is the economic theory "behind" the theories of commercial law analyzed to a great extent by Juha Tolonen.[137] Various legal doctrines and theories, such as the doctrines of authorization and of contracts, also belong to this group.

(c) *Normative and axiological views* of how things should be in society. In this connection, reference is often made to ideology. Also in legal context it is specifically through such ideological factors that one outlines a picture of society. These factors give the measure for evaluating what is a defect in or wrong with societal relationships, and how these negative states of affairs must be corrected through legislation. Such matters can only be recognized when the prevailing situation is compared with the hoped-for state of affairs. Legislation is a means of improving society by amending faults or at least by lessening their significance. Here lies the instrumental value of legal norms.

The list is not exhaustive. Even so, it gives a first indication of the background material on which every legislative act is based. I shall call this totality the *pre-theory of legislation* (*PT*). The term can be defended on two grounds. The views which formulate legislation are not in spurious contact with each other; instead, they form a whole that is systematized to some extent. This whole also includes factors which can be regarded pure theory. On the other hand, the views do not form a theory which would be based on scientific criteria. The systematization is sufficient from the *legislative point of view* in general, but it is only a "pre-theory" for example from the point of view of legal dogmatics. It is in this and specifically in this sense that we say that the legal system is a (pre-)systematized power order. Legislation is the use of power based on a certain systematized preconception.

A normal societal situation, however, is marked by ties to tradition. The reform of legislation does not start from nothing. The new legislation either changes, supplements or clarifies the old. It is never the case that the societal institution which is the focus of the legislation in question changes completely. The matters dealt with by the provisions form a totality where a change on one or some parts does not change the totality. The legislator, in other words, does not create the system *in toto*. He only transforms and reproduces it. Legal tradition consists of normative structures that are independent of each individual, and also of the law giver.

An example would be the reform of the law on inheritance in Finland in 1965. Many individual institutions changed at this time, for example the statutory share in an inheritance and the administration of the estate. On the other hand, totally new institutions were created in the legislation, for example the right of the spouse to inherit from the deceased spouse. Despite the changes, many basic matters that belong to the structure of inheritance remained the same: it is still possible to transfer one's inheritance through a will, the estate must be settled, the inheritance must be distributed in some way, and so on. Thus, the new legislation has many points of contact with the old. As a matter of fact, the basic systematization of the new set of norms took place on the basis of the old, with some development. The system in the law of inheritance is like a cluster of normative solutions. Some individual elements of this cluster may be changed or repealed, while the main structure of the system remains the same. Thus, one must add one more element to the above list:

(d) Previous legislation and its systematics give the framework for new legislation. Special mention must be made of the systemic analysis that legal dogmatics has directed at the then prevailing legislation. The drafters of the new legislation normally receive their basic concepts for their legal thought from the ways of thinking prevailing at the time. I shall denote the system with these concepts with S_i.

All in all, the use of legislative power is based on pre-theoretical thought. It has many elements and its general task is described above. An important role is played by normative and axiological points of view, but no factor mentioned in the list lacks significance. The results of the wielding of power are law texts. As linguistic expressions they carry certain meanings. These meanings form a system which is in accordance with the pre-theoretical systematization. This can be called the *basic system*. I shall denote this with S_b. What exactly is this basic system?

The natural point of departure of all legal thought is the everyday meaning of law texts. As has been shown, this does not, however, offer a sufficient basis for decision-making. We must turn to other reasons in addition to everyday usage. With an eye on the content of the basic system, the historical intention of the legislator then receives a decisive position. It expresses the pre-theoretical view adopted in the legislative stage. Ahti. E. Saarenpää has used the apt term "intended system" in this connection.[138] This is true. The basic system is the system of intended meanings, or the intended system. One function of the application of law is to adapt the intended system to the prevailing social situation. The task of legal dogmatics, in turn, is to shapen and enrichen the basic system. Then the adaptation can take place with as much justification as possible. In this task, legal dogmatics must further develop the basic system.

As has quite correctly been observed by Otto Brusiin, it is this that is meant when one distinguishes between a legal order and scientific system. The goal of legal dogmatics is specifically the formulation of a *scientific* system. To this end, legal norms are rearranged or reformulated. The result of this procedure, scientific system, will be denoted as S_j.

Theoretically, systematization has been regarded as the replacement of the basic system with an identical (scientific) system. This is how the matter has been presented by Alchourrón and Bulygin. They see as the benefits of systematization, for example, the reaching of a more general view and, in addition, the fact that the increase in the level of abstraction makes the system simpler. There are fewer basic terms. Their scope, in addition, is larger.

There are strong legal positivist features hidden in this view. Its particular problem is the concept of identity. It would appear that research praxis shows the result of systematization not to be identical to the basic system. On the contrary, systematization is, in the true sense, a creative process. System S_j is something "more" than basic system S_b. There is a need for further clarification of this statement.

Man arranges his social relations through legal norms, i.e. through the legal order. According to Aleksander Peczenik, legal norms qualify social states of affairs.[139] Norms reflect the view of those who decide on legislation, and the basic system expresses, therefore, the way in which it is intended that societal states of affairs are to be qualified. The basic system is a way of intervening in and systematizing society. The basis of the systematization is a pre-theoretical view with various elements. When the basic system is resystematized (reformulated), we have another basis for systematization. As a matter of fact the entire key to reformulation lies in the change in the *basis* of systematization. In the foregoing, this basis was called the theory (in legal dogmatics). Let us denote this theory with *ST*; it means systematization theory.[140] The change from the pre-theoretical basis to the scientific systematization gives the framework for practical legal dogmatics. An example of such a theory is the systematization of ownership. That conceptual framework defines our conception what ownership means according to the (Finnish) legal order.

A view on the philosophy of science which has been much repeated and referred to is that every observational statement (to a certain extent) is laden by theories. There is no pure observation, in the sense that it would be possible to shut out in advance all theoretical understanding. We speak of theory-laden observations. In legal dogmatics, this corresponds to the concept of theory-laden interpretations. The concept calls for a preliminary clarification. Systematization theory provides a set of basic concepts within the limits of which every problem regarding the content of legal norms must be set. Systematization theory defines the limits of interpretation. But is also locked in something more. Systematization theory organizes legal norms in a certain way in relation to each other. The realization of norm N_i within a systemic connection created by norms N_j and N_k affects the way in which the content of norm N_i is understood. It is not merely a question of their relative order; it is a question at the same time of the content of every element which enters the question. In other words, we are dealing with an example of the way in which the whole affects its parts. We must, however, remember the feed-back: the reinterpretation of the content of the norms may force us to test and rectify the systematization theory. This re-examination in time has an effect on the interpretation of the norms, and so on.

The meaning interpreted on the basis of the systematization theory forms replacement system S_j referred to above. Already the term "interpreted meaning" shows that the system is not identical with the intended system. The intended system is based on subjective interpretation and, through this, with a pre-theoretical view. Even though the pre-theoretical view may, and often does, have a connection with the systematization theory, systematization according to this theory is not identical with pre-theoretical systematization. It is not merely a question of the raising of the level of abstraction, or something similar. The systematization theory changes our view of the relationship between norms, and as a consequence it is possible to pose new questions, and these in turn make it possible to give new kinds of answers.

It is important to note that within the framework of system S_j one cannot pose problems which were not known under the basic system S_b or under the previous reformulation of the basic system. Every systematization gives new possibilities of interpretation. Some principles cannot come up even in principle in a certain system, as the set of terms necessary to present the problem is lacking.

The relations between pre-theory and the systematization theory, the relation between the basic system and the replacing system, and the creating role of interpretation can be presented as in Diagram 26, where PT = pre-theoretical systematization, ST = the systematization theory, S_i = the scientific systematization presented before legislation L, S_b = the basic system or the system of the intended meanings expressed by

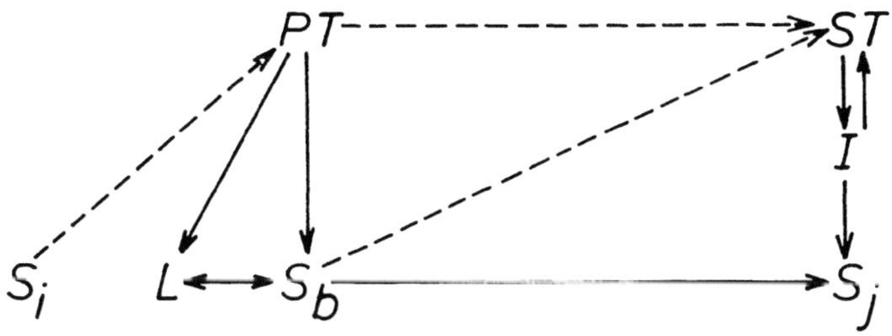

Diagram 26

the law text (L), I = interpretation in legal dogmatics, S_j = the replacing system or the scientific systematization.

The diagram can be read as follows. The pre-theoretical systematization (*PT*) and the former scientific systematization (S_i) give the systemic framework to the legislation (L). Norms belonging to L form a systemic unity called basic system (S_b). The task of legal dogmatics is to reformulate this basic system in a way that is, for instance, more general. For the reformulation one needs a systematizing theory, i.e. a network of theoretical concepts by means of which the norms of L can be interpreted and rearranged. The result of this activity is a new system (systematization of norms). It is called S_j. Norm standpoints concerning L are now formulated in the system S_j. Furthermore, *ST* is the new theoretical basis, a "lens" through which one interprets the legal order.

On the other hand, it is important to emphasize that at the same time or at different times there can be given two or more replacing systematizations of the same basic system (S_b), for example S_j and S_k. They each involve their own systematization theory. For this reason, two replacing systematizations can never be identical. S_j and S_k form two separate (non-identical) pictures of the legal order interpreted on theoretical grounds.

This observation entitles us to return once again to the concept of *identity*. As noted, the point of departure of Alchourrón and Bulygin is that the basic systematization and the replacing system are identical. If the basic system is defined as the intended system, as presented above, the view of Alchourrón and Bulygin is not correct. The pre-theoretical view (*PT*) and the systematization theory (*ST*) are two different ways of systematizing the legal order. When we add to this the interaction between the systematization theory and interpretation, the replacing system (S_j) of necessity receives a different content than does the basic system (S_b). Despite this, we can speak of a "weak" identity. The replacing system attempts to present an interpretation which is in accordance with the law. It "describes" the valid legal order. Even though it is not identical with the intended system, it still represents the meanings expressed by law. Finnish law (Finnish law texts) has the content shown by S_j. The same applies also to other replacing systems, for example to system S_k. Also it does not give the same solutions as does the original intended system, but even so, it gives a valid interpretation of the given law text. Both S_j and S_k involve a creative element: the replacing system shapes the intended system so that the content of the law becomes rational and acceptable at the time of the systematization.

On the other hand, Alchourrón's and Bulygin's view is only in an apparent contradiction to the idea described in Diagram 26. To some extent, the contradiction is terminological as to its nature. The problem is connected to the way one uses the terms "system formulation" and "system reformulation" ("systematization"). For Alchourrón and Bulygin, the procedure that results in S_j can be called system formulation. Hence, the reformulation of the system is based on S_j. In this regard, Diagram 26 does not deal at all with the systematization procedure that results in an identical system (in the sense that Alchourrón and Bulygin define the notion). Systematization "begins" after the formulation of S_j. Alchourrón and Bulygin can thus easily claim that Diagram 26 describes the system formulation but not systematization.

However, from the point of view of practical legal dogmatics just the procedure dealt with in Diagram 26 has a key role. Furthermore, the procedure that results in S_j also contains elements that – according to the normal vocabulary of legal dogmatics – have been called systematization. In order to formulate S_j we need certain systematizing activities, such as those which are elucidated e.g. in the theory of ownership presented by Ross and Zitting. This activity is "creative" in a more profound sense than Alchourrón and Bulygin allow.

The significance of Diagram 26 lies just in the fact that it fits together with the practice of everyday legal dogmatics. The "move" from the basic system (S_b) to the replacing system (S_j) normally occurs as it is expressed in the diagram. Naturally, the thoroughly rational way of system building defended by Alchourrón and Bulygin is one possibility for legal dogmatical research practice. However, it is not adequate as far as this practice is concerned. What is more important, it makes the whole terminology confusing. If one restricts the meaning content of the term "systematization" to the "logical" reformulation only, one also cuts off the possibility to analyse the very complex procedure of system formulation. The result of this procedure is dependent on the systematization we use in arranging the legal material. Here we also meet the problem of theory-ladenness. From the point of view of this work, the concept of theory-ladenness is, on the other hand, the mediating link that makes understandable the reciprocity of systematization and interpretation. On the basis of Alchourrón's and Bulygin's theory this interrelation cannot be described in a proper way. They do not have any conceptual apparatus for that purpose. And here lies the kernel of the criticism presented above.

Summing up, we can also say that system formulation presupposes a certain kind of conceptual framework. This framework is based on the way that the legal material at issue is systematized. In other words, systematization is a precondition for system formulation. The result of system formulation can, naturally, be a subject matter of further reformulations. One type of this reformulation is the view of systematization defended by Alchourrón and Bulygin. In order to avoid this confusing ambiguity of the term "systematization" one may suggest the following clarification:

(a) The systematization dealt with in Diagram 26 may be called *systematization*$_1$. This is the concept normally used in the theoretical legal dogmatics. When a scholar speaks about systematization he actually refers to this activity.

(b) The "logical" reformulation of the system – described by Alchourrón and Bulygin – is purely a theoretical construction. Let us call it *systematization*$_2$. The possibility is open for this activity after the system is formulated by means of systematization$_1$.

The systematization theory described above is graphically illustrated in many examples taken from everyday praxis in legal dogmatics. In the following, one such example will be presented, taken from the systematization of the norms of inheritance law.[141] The example is not intended to be complete in that it would completely represent the network of systematization in legal dogmatics. Even so, it offers sufficient material for the concretization of the above theoretical sketch.

4.7.2. *An example of systematization: an analysis of the position of the heir.* A classical basic question in the continental law of succession has been the following: at what time is the inheritance transferred from the decedent to the heir? Continental European, and in this connection also Scandinavian legal thought has developed two answers to this question. They can be called the *ipso iure* and the *aditio* principles. According to the former, the inheritance is transferred to the heir *in toto* at the time of the death of the decedent, and so at this moment the heir replaces the decedent as owner and, with some reservations, as the person responsible for debts. The *aditio* principle assumes that the heir undertakes specific legal acts in order to receive a legally protected position in relation to the inheritance. The inheritance is not transferred from the decedent to the heir until that moment.

An aspect that is essential to both lines of thought is that they regard the inheritance as being transferred at one certain moment. It is a question of a momentary event. There is an apparent analogy to the transfer of ownership. As is well known, according to the classical Continental theory, the ownership is transferred from the transfer or to the recipient as a whole and at one certain moment.

An either/or way of thinking limited to these two alternatives is unsatisfactory, especially when we must be able to deal with complicated special cases. The set of concepts is simply too rough to enable us to give a satisfactory answer. Argumentation that limits itself to two alternatives leaves itself open to criticism, and in a complicated case the result of the argumentation can easily be toppled. For this reason another approach has long been represented in Scandinavia. The first to suggest this approach in the law of succession were O. A. Borum in Denmark and Ake Malmström in Sweden. In the general theory of ownership, this way of thinking has been developed the furthest by Alf Ross.[142] In the field of property rights, in turn, the Rossian view has been applied in Finland by Simo Zitting in a way that has also received considerable international attention.[143]

Without going into further details, it can be said that the basic idea is the demonstration of the fact that ownership is a successive series of events. At every stage in the series, certain legal consequences are connected to certain separately discernible legal facts. For example, in an installment purchase, certain elements of ownership may at moment t belong to A and certain elements may belong to B without there being any justification for saying that either would, in some true and unambiguous sense, be the genuine owner. The same applies to inheritance. According to this way of thinking, inheritance is a successive series of events that begins with the death of the decedent, and ends with the distribution of the inheritance. Different types of legal consequences are connected with the different stages, and loosely speaking, we can say that it is possible to regard the rights of the owner to be increasing gradually with the progression in the chain of events.

Behind this way of thinking there are certain views which, in philosophy of law, are *a priori* assumptions. Perhaps the most important one is the idea that all rights are manifested in certain personal relations.[144] A legal norm is a matter that arranges a relationship between persons in a certain way. For example, it entitles a person to do something while it obliges another person to do something else. When, in this respect, one speaks of, for example, the legal position of the owner, reference is being made to the legally protected position of one person in relation to others. In this way of thinking, the legal position is a complex of personal relationships which is typified by the fact that this complex is regulated by legal norms.

From the point of view of ownership this means that at moment t person A has a legally regulated relationship to persons B, C . . . N. At moment t_1, when a different set of legal facts exists, for example due to a transfer, the complex of personal relationships is different. The relationship of A to the other parties is arranged in a different way. Speaking of the successive transfer of ownership becomes a more precise description of the changing complex of personal relationships. Every configuration of states of affairs (legal facts) is connected with a certain arrangement of personal relationships. The so-called legal consequence is just the way of arranging a relationship between two or more persons. This way of organizing matters changes during the successive transfer of ownership. The successive transfer is the same as a gradual change in the legally regulated personal relationships.

As far as the inheritance is concerned, this means that when the decedent dies, the relations of the heirs to those mentioned in the will, to the widow, to the debtors and so on, are arranged in a certain way, locked in by the provisions regulating the problem. After the heir has expressed his intention to receive the inheritance, the situation changes somewhat. Finally, the distribution of the inheritance shapes a stage where the position of the heir as the owner of the estate receives its final form. At this stage he has reached the same legal position in respect of the property apportioned him as the decedent had before him. In the full sense of the word, there has been a change in the subject.

When compared with the normal transfer of ownership, the situation is more complicated in the law of succession as there may be many heirs: for example, two or more heirs from the same generation, or a heir and a general legatee, or two general legatees, and so on. In this sort of situation there is an intermediate stage between the death of the decedent and the distribution of the inheritance; during this intermediate stage the property has "several owners" and no one has received ownership to the extent that the decedent had it.

The legal state referred to has been terminologically described in different ways. In the Germanic legal culture it has often been called a "Gesamthand" relation.[145] In the Scandinavian countries, the usual way of speaking of the matter is by saying that the heirs have joint ownership. The legal nature of the community of the heirs is linked to this same conceptual basis. The question is, do the persons succeeding the decedent together form an independent juridical person (subject) – comparable to a company – during the intermediate stage or not? And if we can speak of an independent juridical person, what is the extent of the independence of this legal formation?

In Finnish literature, the views have been divided into two opposing camps until the end of the 1960's. These camps have sharply criticized each other. On the one hand, there were those who believed that the joint ownership of the heirs was indivisible, i.e. the ownership had many subjects without any of them being the sole owner of the property. The second camp rather ironically referred to such a situation by saying that, instead of there being the heirs Tom and Jerry, the first camp believed that there was an indivisible whole, Tomjerry. The second theory has been labelled the theory of "ownership of fixed portions". It started out from the view that the ownership of the property of the decedent was divided upon his death into imagined fixed portions. Each successor was the owner of such an imagined portion. He "owned" this fraction.

These approaches, which both had their forbears in Germanic Law, and above all in the German theory of inheritance as it was at the end of the 1800's and the beginning of the 1900's appeared to be decisively opposing. Let us call them theory T_1 and theory T_2. In this connection there is no possibility of dealing with the details of the theories. It is enough, in order to demonstrate the problem of systematization, to mention one feature which can be considered the key problem in the discussion on the legal position of the heir. The problem may be stated as follows: "How can the heir, during the intermediate stage before the distribution of the inheritance, mandate over his right to the inheritance?" In various legal orders, this has usually been called the problem of the transfer of one's share in an inheritance.

According to theory T_1, the transfer of a share is and it involves the transfer of the whole subjective right belonging to the heir. The heir transfers his right to the recipient in the same way as a partner in a company transfers his rights to be a partner. A change of subjects takes place, a total transfer of the right to the inheritance. Theory T_2 states that such a total transfer is not possible, as the heir has no subjective right to the entire state; he has only a group of imagined fixed portions. According to this theory, then, the transfer of a share is really the transfer of the imagined fixed portions belonging to the heir. Nothing prevents the heir from transferring all his fixed portions to the different objects in the estate, but even so, he is transferring only all his portions and not some "mystical" subjective right.

The difference of opinion is heightened by the question of the form of transfer. According to the Finnish (and Swedish) system, the transfer of real estate must always be done according to a special procedure. According to theory T_1, even if real estate belongs to the decedent's estate, the transfer can still take place in any form as the focus of the transfer is an independent subjective right (the "membership" in the estate) itself, not specifically the right directly to real estate. The heir does not transfer real estate but a "membership right". Theory T_2 represents an opposite view. According to it, the proper object of the transfer is the imagined portion of ownership concerning real estate. Therefore also the parties of the transfer have to follow the special formalities given for the transfer of real estate.

The picture is disturbed by the fact that also according to T_1 the heir can conditionally transfer his share in an object that belongs to the decedent's estate. This, the theory calls "dealing with a future object" (*res futura*). If we try to see how this act differs from "dealing with an imagined portion", we meet with a surprise: there is no essential difference between the two. The difference between the two is reduced to the fact that theory T_2 does not approve of the transfer taking place in any form whatsoever.

In 1965, the Finnish Decedent's Estate Act brought a partial solution. According to the new Act, the transfer of a share can take place without any of the formalities concerning the transfer of real estate. But even so, the contrapositioning of the two theories seems to be lacking in justification. It is based on the idea that there is one ownership that as such is transferred from the decedent to the heirs. According to one theory, this right is an indivisible whole, while according to the other, it breaks down into parts, albeit imagined portions. Neither theory asks what the said transfer means, and what it means to say that the ownership goes from one subject to another as one whole, in the same way as a physical object. On the basis of what has been said above about Scandinavian theories on ownership, it is easy to observe that criticism of the traditional views of ownership is as adaptable as such to the traditional theory of joint ownership. If the view that ownership is an indivisible whole is in general open to criticism, then there is also room for criticism of the traditional view on inheritance.

Instead of choosing between the two alternatives, we must go beyond these alternatives. We should not ask whether the inheritance is transferred from the decedent to the heirs at death or at a later time. The problem must be formulated so that we ask what different legal consequences, manifested in the various personal relationships, are connected to different stages in the successive transfer of inheritance. There is no reason to stop weighing the eternal question of the indivisibility or divisibility of joint ownership. Instead, our question should be as follows: how can we describe the complex of personal relationships in which the heir stands legally, not only in relation to third parties, but also in relation to his coheirs? The problem of joint ownership opens up into a number of legal relationship problems regarding the position of the heir. They can and must be solved with the normal legal tools, by utilizing sources of law and legal argumentation techniques. Briefly speaking: the question of the indivisibility or divisibility of joint ownership, as such, is posed incorrectly, and is an *unnecessary problem*. Consideration of such a problem is at most an academic play. By changing the point of departure we can enter directly into the interpretation of the legal norms to be applied in the various situations. Metaphorically speaking, the conceptual material preventing the understanding of legal norms is removed.

Thus we come to the core statement in this study. The analysis of the legal position of the heir is a new way of systematizing legal norms. Also theories T_1 and T_2 were competing theories, but their conceptual equipment were systematizations of a rougher nature. In complicated legal relationships they do not offer a satisfactory basis for rational discourse. We need a new way of systematizing the norms of the law of succession; a way that will present this set of norms in a more adequate way than before.

As a summary, this systematization can be presented in the form of the following conceptual elements. The position of the heir can be compared to a "conceptual tree" with branches as shown in Diagram 27.

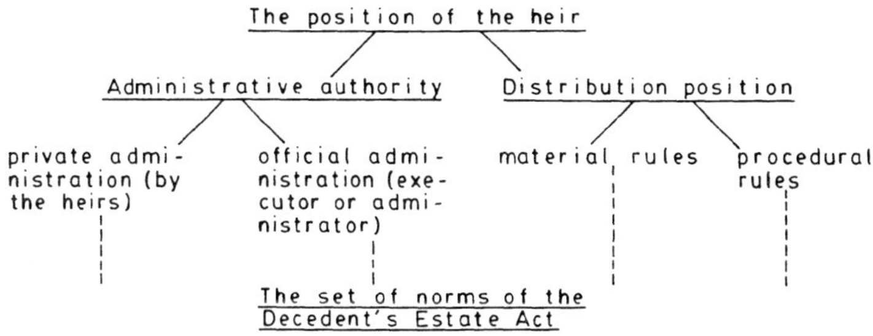

Diagram 27

Each of these three main branches can be broken down to subelements, which can again be broken down to other elements, and so on. Ultimately everything is reduced to the set of norms in the Decedent's Estate Act and its interpretations. In other words, the above conceptual tree describes valid law. The concepts are "tied to" the legal provisions: they are not just an arbitrary collection of arbitrary images.

This model of systematization can be generalized by using symbols instead of the literal descriptions of the concepts. This kind of generalization is presented in Diagram 28.

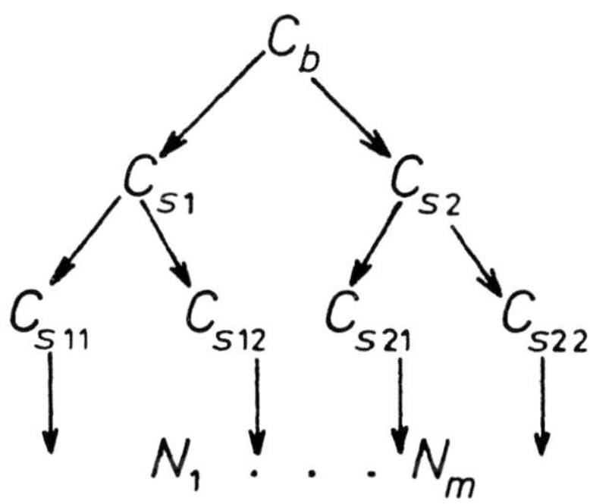

Diagram 28

The way of arranging the concepts is called, in this study, the systematizing theory (*ST*). In the end, the systematized set of concepts is connected with the legal order. The goal of *ST* is to present, in an adequate manner, a certain complex of valid legal norms. The result of this activity (application of *ST*) is a new system marked in this contribution by S_j.

From another point of view, every conceptual element presents a complex of personal relationships which are legally regulated and which come up in some connection. Let us consider the example of the right to participate in the joint administration of the estate. Here, the heir is in a relationship with his co-heirs. This relationship is closely regulated in Finland and Sweden by Chapter 18 of the Decedent's Estate Act. At the same time, the heir is in a relationship with third parties. The problematics, on the other hand, are regulated by both the norms of the Act and by the general norms of ownership. By presenting the contents of these norms ($N_1 \ldots N_m$) precisely, we also obtain a picture of what the right to participate in the joint administration of an estate, as one of the basic elements of the position of the heir, means. In other words: what is the content of this element in accordance with the valid law in Finland?

The "description" of the norms which regulate the problem in question, in turn, depends on the set of concepts which is being used in the systematization of the norms, i.e. on the *ST*. The description is theory-laden. We receive exactly the picture of the valid legal order that our set of concepts allows. Systematization theory may be compared to a lens which limits and sharpens our view. Thus, *ST* is a legal framework that defines our conception about the legal order, in this case about the law of inheritance. It is impossible to pose other questions than this framework allows us. Hence, the framework also locks the type of the answers we can get to those questions. On the other hand, the interest in knowledge in society defines which kind of information concerning legal order is important (and relevant). The interest to put questions thus grows up in society. The societal practice is thus a continuous test for the conceptual framework and this test is realized by legal interpretation (legal reasoning). At times the situation demands an improvement in our descriptive tools, possibly even a change in them. Thus is born the dynamic interaction of systematization and interpretation, a phenomenon which is continuously in progress in legal life. Only as a result of this interaction is the conception which shapes the answer given at each time to the legal problems in society formulated. Thus, also the question of whether or not legal dogmatics is able to fulfill its task in satisfying our common interest in interpretative knowledge receives an answer.[146]

CHAPTER IV

THE ACCEPTABILITY OF AN INTERPRETATIVE STATEMENT

1. THE PRINCIPLE OF THE ONE RIGHT ANSWER

1.1. *A Terminological Clarification*

Even after we have gone through all the legal material, two possibilities may remain: either the interpretation is the right one or in principle there are more than one alternative interpretations. The latter possibility would seem to drop the bottom out of the idea of justification. What sense is there in justification in general, if even at its best it only produces a number of equally valid interpretative proposals? We are also close to the idea that the justification leaves room for arbitrariness. There is no rational basis for the justification of an interpretative standpoint in legal dogmatics.

It is thus no wonder that the question of the one right answer has troubled legal philosophers and legal theorists for a long time. The matter has been approached from a number of directions, without any unanimity being reached on how we should regard this idea. In the following, we shall mainly bypass the historical aspect of the study of the problem. The focus will be on some special questions concerning the principle of the one right answer in legal dogmatical interpretation.

According to Jerzy Wróblewski, the discussion on the idea of the one right answer has touched upon at least three matters:

(a) The principle of the one right answer has been connected to the tripartite division of power in society. It is common knowledge that Montesquieu distinguished between legislative, judicial and executive power.[1] Perelman, in turn, reminds us that the doctrine of the division of power is based, as a matter of fact, on a certain view of man: the separation of will ("Wille") and reason ("ratio").[2] The passing of legislation belongs to the realm of will, actually to the related use of societal power, while the application of law is more a matter for reason. Furthermore, as law and legal order were equated with each other, the result was a thoroughly rationalist view on the interpretation of law. The interpretation is, on the one hand, clarification of the statutes (legal dogmatics) and, on the other hand, the application of the statutes, through subsumption, to verified facts (decision-making). From this point of view, therefore, the doctrine of the one right answer is an expression of a certain image of man and of a certain social ideology. According to this doctrine, the act of application is not creative human work. It is a mechanical act.

(b) The principle of the one right answer also has an ideological feature in another respect. Some authors have especially emphasized that legal certainty implies that every legal problem will be decided only in one way. If it is possible to point out two or more "equally right" decisions to the same case, legal praxis would become imbued with randomness and arbitrariness. The equality of citizens would be endangered, and it would not be possible to anticipate future activity with sufficient precision.

When formulated in this way, however, the principle of the one right answer has two meanings: either the one right answer exists for every case or there is an actual possibility of finding a right answer for each individual case. Thus, for the doctrine of the one right answer, we obtain three meanings with varying strengths:

(1) If we say that there exists one right answer and that it also will always be found, the doctrine has been adopted in its strong sense. This view implicates that every interpreter endowed with the appropriate professional expertise will reach the one right answer through the use of the sources of law according to the directives of legal interpretation.

(2) In a weaker sense, the doctrine adopts the view that there always exists one right answer and that it is possible to find it, although in practice it may be that we do not always succeed in finding it.

(3) If we admit the existence of the one right answer at the same time as we deny also the principal possibility of finding it we have adopted the doctrine in its weak sense. In this, the one right answer is an ideal that can never be reached but which forms the regulative goal of all legal interpretation.

The above means that the denial of the doctrine of the one right answer assumes also the denial of it in the weak sense: there is not one right answer, nor can such an answer actually be found.

From the epistemic point of view, the doctrine of the one right answer comes up in an interesting light if, on the one hand, we accept the idea that it is possible to find the one right answer and, on the other, we question whether the interpreter can know that he has found that answer.[3]

According to a traditional definition, subject *S* knows something if *S* presents a justified and true belief of the matter. In this case the definition contains the condition that *S* has a justified and true belief according to which he has found the one right answer to an interpretation problem in legal dogmatics.

If we adopt the position that it is always possible to find the right answer, and at the same time we accept the view that the interpreter always also knows that he has found the right answer, we have adopted a very strong version of the doctrine of the one right answer. A more moderate view is represented by the view that it is possible (in principle) to know that one has found the right interpretation, but in practice such knowledge cannot always be reached.

A similar distinction can be made if we admit the possibility of finding the one right answer but we deny that that answer can always be found (Case 2). The weakest point of this is the view that even if the one right answer is (at times) to be found, we can never be sure that we know we have found that answer. The answer, as it were, may be found by accident quite independently of our awareness that we have found it.

(c) Possibly the most common way to understand the doctrine of the one right answer is to tie it to problems concerning the form of legal reasoning. Here, the interpretation is analyzed from the internal point of view, in other words as a syllogistic operation. The connection of the inferior sentence to the superior sentence through subsumption leads to the "right" interpretation. In this, the syllogistic form can be seen to be applied to the (heuristic) description of the bringing about of the interpretation result or to the (justificatory) *ex post facto* rationalization of the decision.

In the following, the doctrine of the one right answer will be considered primarily in the sense of (b), above. This naturally ties the doctrine of the one right answer to the thematics of this contribution. One can pose the question whether or not the chain of reasoning can be completely cut off at some stage. *If* the doctrine of the one right answer holds true the answer must simply be as follows: the justification can be cut off when the interpreter is able to verify the truthfulness of the interpretative statement. In other words, according to this doctrine the justification is directed at the presentation of true interpretative statements.[4]

In order for us to grasp the problem we shall first examine some applications of the doctrine of the one right answer. No attempt has been made to make the following sample representative of the various historical versions. The choice only implies that the approaches reviewed reflect, in an important way, the central ideas in the doctrine of the one right answer, and reflect these precisely from the point of view of the problematics of truth.

1.2. *Examples of the Doctrines of the One Right Answer*

1.2.1. *Ronald Dworkin's Theory*

The title of Dworkin's exposition on the subject is quite apt: "Taking Rights Seriously". The title anticipates criticism in two directions. On one hand, Dworkin takes issue with legal positivism, which according to him would grant individuals only those rights which law (the positive legal order) gives to them. On the other hand, he is opposed to any version of utilitarianism. According to utilitarianism, law should attempt to bring the greatest good to the greatest number. According to Dworkin, this goes against the rights of the minority, as the minority is not to be found among the "greatest number".[5]

Dworkin divides rights into two categories, institutional rights and basic rights (background rights). Both categories are political rights. A legal right, in turn, is an institutional right, the right to get a favorable decision from the courts. For example, ownership as a right is the right to receive protection from the court against certain violations. From this point of view, individual rights are much the same as the counterpoint of the activity (use of power) of the courts. What is essential in Dworkin's theory in our point of view is that rights belong to citizens *ex ante*. The individual has rights regardless of whether or not the authorities uphold them. In a way, rights "exist" already before the decision of the courts in the matter. They "exist" as the right to a favorable decision. This is one reason why Dworkin believes that we must take rights seriously.

In the following, the problematics will be dealt with only to the extent that it concerns the idea of the one right answer, and, in particular, to the extent that they deal with this idea from the point of view outlined in case (b), in Section 1.1. above. First, a few words on Dworkin's thoughts on the application of law.

According to Dworkin, a problem of rights must primarily be decided in the way that law requires. If the wording of the law is ambiguous, the decision must be given in accordance with the intention of the law. On the other hand, the decision-maker must take into consideration the demand of equitable treatment: similar cases must be dealt with in a similar manner. According to Dworkin, this principle, however, does not receive its meaning from positive law until it is applied in the individual case. Apparently one could say that to Dworkin the rules of positive law that materialize this principle form the ultimate justification for the decision.[6] Actually, it is precisely this feature which interests us in Dworkin's theory. Let us take a closer look at it.

Dworkin starts from a case which he calls, in accordance with traditional terminology, a "hard case".[7] Such a case is typified by the fact that not one provision gives a clear answer to it, the intention of the law cannot be recognized, and court precedents as well as other interpretative material point in different directions ("pull both ways"). As an example Dworkin uses a case where an employee of *X* accidently cuts a power line leading to *Y*'s factory, and thus causes damage to *Y*.

Yet, is the person *X* responsible for the damage. There may be cause to note that from the point of view of the law of Finland, this case is relatively unproblematic. It would fall within the sector where so-called "master's liability" would be applied: the employer is responsible for the actions of his employees. This, however, is not significant when we are dealing with the question of Dworkin's reasoning.

One of Dworkin's basic ideas is, as said, the argument that in such a case both sides have their own rights. Both have rights in respect of each other ("primary rights") and both have rights in respect of the authorities ("secondary rights"). In the decision, the rights of one will have to yield, and for this reason it is important to be able to justify the decision in the best possible way. Through this, Dworkin's problematics twist around the idea of the one right answer.

It is true that Dworkin does not argue that in each case there exists one right answer, but he believes that in principle one right answer is possible and in most cases there is such a solution. In this connection it is enough to refer to the following. Dworkin admits that there are situations ("tie judgements") where the rights of the plaintiff can be justified just as well as the rights of the defendant. In such a situation it is impossible to say what the right answer to the problem is. But there are also cases where the idea of the one right answer can clearly be defended. How should such decision-making situations be characterized? Dworkin suggests the following answer.

When we solve a legal conflict in favor of, shall we say, the rights of *Y*, the decision can justifiably be made on the assumption that there is a theory of law. I shall call this the basic legal theory. In his examination of Dworkin's ideas, Neil MacCormick emphasizes that this is not a descriptive theory about law but specifically a justifying theory of law.[8]

According to Dworkin, such a theory has a very decisive role. It renders understandable and gives sense to legal provisions and court decisions as a system which, on one hand, protects the rights of individuals and on the other hand takes collective interests into consideration. The basic legal theory includes the principles which give content to the abstract theory of equality. It is through this that we can say that the basic legal theory is the theory that justifies legal decisions.

In the sense used by Dworkin, however, the basic legal theory does not only express principles protecting the rights of individuals or goals related to collective interests ("policies"). It also gives them an order of priority, "an order of priority by assessing weights to them", as MacCormick formulates this view.[9]

From the point of view of legal reasoning, the significance of the basic theory lies in the fact that it enables us to justify the decision in "the best possible way". This is the case when the standpoint that states something about the rights of an individual – for example the right of *Y* to compensation – is coherent with everything that has previously been said about rights. In other words, the best possible justification will be achieved when the proposition in question is *coherent* with the basic legal theory. Dworkin, however, does not say that we can always be sure of the contents of this theory. Legal scholars as well as judges can err. On the other hand, Dworkin emphasizes that finding "the best possible theory" should be the goal of the judge and the scholar. Such a theory can be constructed even if in practice we do not know how it should be constructed.

It is also important to note that for Dworkin, the basic legal theory is not something which can be found for example through intuition or the like. For him, the basic theory is always a constructed theory or, preferably speaking, a theory which can be constructed. As it is still the "best possible", Dworkin's theory runs into difficulties.

These difficulties are aptly described in the parallel of the semi-god "Hercules J" who, with his superhuman abilities, is able to create a theory which brings the different elements of the legal order into harmony with each other. No single person can be a Hercules, but everybody can, no doubt, intelligibly postulate such a superhuman being. Therefore every judge can and should try to get as close to Herculean competence as he can.[10]

Let us accept this description. We still have to face the basic problem in Dworkin's theory. In his examination of Dworkin's theory, Max Oker-Blom has set into opposition with each other in a rather interesting way the ideas of Dworkin and Kaarle Makkonen. Some of the key questions in this opposition should also be dealt with here, as they can suitably be used in an evaluation not only of Dworkin's theory but also of the doctrine of the one right answer in general.[11]

One of Makkonen's main arguments is that legal interpretation is not based on so-called dual value logic. It is completely possible to demonstrate more that one right answer without our being able to demonstrate any of them to be false. Not only is this the case in decisions regarding penal scales in criminal law, a matter that also Dworkin has dealt with, but also for example when we apply so-called open texture situations (flexible norms). They adopt as the criteria of the decision such matters as reasonableness, expediency, the circumstances of the case, and so on.

Dworkin would apparently be ready to admit the existence of several alternative decisions in such cases. Only one of them, however, is the right one. Let us take an example. *A* represents view T_1 and *B* represents view T_2. Logically, there are three possibilities: T_1 is the right one, T_2 is the right one, and both T_1 and T_2 are right. Dworkin's point of departure is that only one of them is the right one. For example, a will is valid or invalid. The matter is no different when there are several alternatives, as is the case with flexible norms. In all cases one of the alternatives is the right one, even if we do not know it.

Presumably such a critic as Makkonen would reply to this that in "tie judgement" cases Dworkin's theory is based on the idealistic assumption that the one right decision is hidden in law and only needs to be uncovered. This is hinted at by Dworkin's idea of the "existence" of rights *ex ante* regardless of the decisions of the authorities. This idea is not tenable – so Makkonen would think – since legislation is an act of will, where there is no way of taking into advance consideration all the practical situations possible. Dworkin, however, would scarcely admit that such criticism is justified. He might possibly say that the criticism ignores something that is essential to the entire legal order. Legislation is certainly not based on the actual impression of the legislators (the different instances) regarding what cases the provisions deal with. In legislation, one operates with terms and typical situations, and a term can cover a number of situations which the legislator did not actually take into consideration or allow for.

Even if we were to accept the counterarguments suggested by Dworkin, there are still two problems that Dworkin clearly does not deal with. Furthermore, his semantics would not allow him to analyse these problems. He does not deal at all with the possibility that an expression is *genuinely ambiguous*, in other words that several alternative meanings of equal value can be presented for it. It is this that Makkonen apparently means when he speaks of flexible norms. An even more difficult question is connected to the assumption of the one right answer itself. Let us return to the example of the last will and testament. Dworkin apparently assumes that the will is either valid or invalid. This is the case in all conceivable circumstances. But what if one has to decide an individual case T_i: is the last will of *A* valid *or* invalid? In such a case, the decision is always tied to a value basis, and neither decision is right over and beyond these evaluations (in the entire society). This possibility must seriously be taken into consideration completely regardless of whether this can be the case with the will in question. The doctrine of the one right answer in Dworkinian justification is too rough to be suitable for different types of situations. Dworkin postulates something that in practice one perhaps can never reach. The "best possible theory" is a postulated ideal which entitles us to say that a certain decision is the right one, as it corresponds to the ideal. At the same time, however, it is only a postulated ideal.

Thus, in a way, we have come to the crucial point in the Dworkinian idea of the one right answer. The basic theory that justifies decisions may contain evaluations, and these evaluations must at least in some sense be assumed to be absolute. Only on this assumption we can, even in general, regard the construction of "the best possible theory" as possible. The assumption of absolute values is, however, a very strong point of departure. If one does not accept this kind of value theory, the whole idea of one right answer looses its basis. "The best possible theory" is only an unjustifiable philosophical postulate. Furthermore, our (Western) legal culture is not based on such absolute ideas. Therefore, the Dworkinian theory of one right answer does not fulfill the needs of the actual legal dogmatics, either.

1.2.2. *Norms Statements as Norm Propositions*

1.2.2.1. *Norm Statements as Predictions*

1.2.2.1.1. *The specific nature of legal predictions*. In the discussion about the possibility of prediction in legal science the focus of attention has traditionally been restricted to the activities of the courts of law (or other authorities). Prèdicting the behaviour of the courts has been regarded as natural because – among other things – it is closely connected with the principle of legal certainty. The legal certainty of individuals requires that action taken by the authorities can be anticipated at least within a given certainty margin. This again is connected with the demand for equal treatment. If a certain case is solved in way *A* at one time and in way *B* at another there is no equality among the members of society. On the other hand, it is evident that if it is impossible to anticipate the application of the law, activities cannot be planned in a sensible way either.

If we start from the idea that we really can observe invariances in the authorities' behaviour and that these invariances in themselves create a basis for prediction, the scheme according to which a prediction could be drawn up seems relatively simple. It would run: in every decision belonging to the series of decisions $A_1 \ldots A_n$, given in the past, fact f_1 has been established and legal consequence g_1 been confirmed: therefore it is extremely probable that legal consequence g_1 will also be confirmed in future decision A_{n+1} where the facts of the case are of the same type. At least two kinds of fundamental problems are connected with such a prediction:

(a). Is it possible to find in legal life the invariances, prediction requires and (b) is it possible to foresee future actions on the basis of these invariances? Before we answer these questions we should notice that one can conceive the prediction itself to be of two main types.

(1) A researcher has established that the following law prevails in the legal community: "Always when *X* has the quality f_1 quality g_1 is connected with it". Such a 'law' would be of the same type as the classical statement "All ravens are black". Now a prediction would state that if a state of affairs prevails where characteristic f_1 can be found, consequence g_1 is always connected with this state of affairs in juridical practice.

It is easy to subject this kind of prediction to the same criticism which generally applies to the verifiability of all-clauses. If we want to verify the 'law' meant above, we must actually examine all the cases it covers. A single case (A_{n+l}) which would be solved in another way falsifies the law in the same way as a single white raven falsifies the statement that all ravens are black. It is clear that a 'law' representing this kind of certainty is out of the question when we try to predict the behaviour of the authorities. The presumed invariance is based on the examination of decisions given in the past; it is obvious that these do not enable us to state anything certain about future cases. We should indeed try to find the theoretical ground of prediction elsewhere.

The "all-proposition" described above may of course also be analytic as to its nature. One may for instance regard the sentence to give a definition of the raven. In other words, the black colour is per definitionem a characteristic of the raven. It is clear that as an analytic proposition the sentence does not tell anything about reality: no evidence whatever can substantiate or refute the sentence. According to the definition for example a white bird which looks like a raven is not a "raven" but something else.

This type of all-proposition cannot be used in juridical predictions. Indeed, an analytic sentence would only state some kind of truth having the nature of a definition.

(2) The conception according to which prediction only involves inductive probability offers a natural starting point. It seems useful to distinguish between two cases.[12]

(a) First, one could think that prediction is based on statistical probability. The so-called case of the black and the white balls has often been mentioned as a trivial example of this. If nine balls out of ten are white and one is black the probability that the black ball will appear is one in ten. In the same way one could affirm on the basis of judicial decisions one has examined that there is a 90 % probability that case A_i will occur. We should notice that in this kind of case a prediction concerning the probability of occurrence may be quite truthful though a prediction concerning the characteristics of an individual case proves to be false. It is also natural that not even a high probability allows us to generalize that "all cases are A_i".

(b) We may indeed tentatively characterize a juridical prediction in the following way. Such a prediction says: if state of affairs f_i occurs, which has these and these characteristics, the authority will presumably confirm consequence g_i.

Here probability does not mean a statistical estimation of the probability of occurrence of consequence g_i but credibility, which is on a more modest level of certainty and which cannot be reduced to numerical quantities. In this respect juridical prediction is of the same type as the forecasts we frequently run across in everyday life. As an example of such an everday prediction we may mention the statement "I shall probably be able to manage this task alone". This may merely imply that the person speaking has good reason to believe that he will be able to manage the task alone.

On the other hand one should notice that we are not concerned with a prediction relating to an individual event. Legal research does not deal with individual cases as for instance a barrister does who presents an estimate of the final result of a law suit to his client. A prediction put forward in legal research is always general as to its nature and, therefore, it does not tell anything about, for example, a judge's individual attitude to an individual matter. As we pointed out above, a prediction states only that if a state of affairs belonging to class *F* occurs the court will (presumably) confirm a legal consequence belonging to class *G*. Even in this clarified form juridical prediction is ambiguous in many respects. Most problems are associated with the opposition between regularities and rules mentioned above. Let us first briefly examine this side of the matter.

When we compare juridical prediction with prediction carried out, for example, in natural science we may observe that the types of material they are based upon respectively are in many respects different. First, it is typical of legal research that the cases serving as a basis for prediction appear always in verbal form. Consequently, they need interpretation: in other words, a jurist putting forward a 'generalization' is always obliged to give a meaning-content also to the facts appearing in the judicial decisions concerned before he can draw up any prediction. To this a natural scientist may object, it is true, that for instance in physics of microbiology facts do not manifest themselves to the researcher in 'pure' form either. They appear as readings of various measurement devices and contrivances or otherwise as messages which should be interpreted further. Undoubtedly this is true, but in spite of this there remains a fundamental difference between those sciences: the material a legal researcher deals with is always expressed in everyday language. It is presented to him in a language the meaning of which he, being a member of a certain cultural community, has already beforehand learnt in a certain way. This point is significant in many respects.

The cases are often based on very complicated facts. If one, referring to these facts, claims that there is invariancy to be found in the behaviour of the court he has to simplify the cases in order to establish a regularity. The similarity between different cases that the regularity implies can be established by means of only relatively few characteristics. A researcher tries to find the essential features of the cases he examines. As I have remarked before, comparison aiming at establishing similarity requires two things: dissolving cases into elementary parts and establishing the correspondence of these elementary parts to each other in reference to a key. Precisely the key is in a crucial position. As was emphasized before, the analogy key is value loaded, i.e. it is intertwined with the axiological basis of society. The relationship of analogy prevails if and only if the similarity between the cases is relevant from the legal point of view. This means that the criteria of relevancy are continuously changing in the court praxis.

Let us suppose that in some field of life a very uniform practice of the courts has been established. The court has given n decisions ($A_1 \ldots A_n$) in all of which legal consequence g_i has been connected with state of affairs f_i. This invariance does not express, as would be the case in natural science, a causal law between two sets of states of affairs – the legal facts and the legal consequences. One could, on the contrary, think that the uniformity is due to the fact that the court has considered every previous decision (e.g. A_1) binding when giving a subsequent decision (e.g. A_2); the previous decisions are precedents for the subsequent ones. Such a conception is quite usual, which is clearly indicated by the theoretical discussion on the binding force of precedents. When we present the conception in this way it also seems, however, to overlook a fact which is characteristic of the whole construction relating to precedents.

In a system of codified law, like the legal system of Finland, the court, when making its decision, cannot directly adduce a given previous decision as the (only) criterion of decision. A good example is formed by the case where there exists no provision of written law, where there is a so-called gap in the law. The court, however, solves the problem in a certain way. If later a similar case comes up for decision in court and the court regards the previous decision as binding, this does not result from a ideological precept according to which previous decisions always commit the judge, but from the fact that the previous decision is considered to express a rule the judge feels obliged to comply with. Just because of these rules the cases are the way they are. On the other hand these rules make the given decisions understandable, because before one can grasp why consequence g_i has been repeatedly attached to a given configuration of states of affairs f_i one should know the legal rule which has guided the solution.

In any case it is clear that even accurate knowledge of the rules to be applied at the moment the prediction is made (t_n) is not enough. These rules enable us to understand decisions which have already been given, it is true, but a predictor should also be able to prognosticate which rules will be applied at the moment t_{n+1}, or in other words: will certain rules still be regarded as binding at the moment t_{n+1}. If he can be (nearly) certain about this he has an obviously good basis for his prediction. New information the judge becomes acquainted with in connection with case A_{n+1} acquires a very important position in the foresight. It may prove the previous practice of the courts to be inadequate or even opposite to the purpose of the statute under consideration. New information is usually presented to the judge in the counsels' written statements or in jurists' authoritative opinions. It is also flowing continually from society.

A change in the social structure often creates situations where traditional interpretation of a legal provision leads to inappropriate results. In a new decision this contradiction between the former interpretation and the demands arising from structural changes in society may be eliminated. All in all the change in the legal material to be applied may take place in many different ways and a prediction should be capable of determining precisely this change.

This is shown in an interesting way in the studies Alf Ross has written on jurisprudence and in particular on prediction in legal science. By incorporating Alf Ross's views in our discussion we can at the same time elucidate in an important way the notion of prediction itself. As far as the background philosophy is concerned, only some rough points will be dealt with here, because the theory of valid norms has already been discussed in the foregoing.

1.2.2.1.2. *On Alf Ross' predictive theory.* According to the Rossian philosophically basic assumption, legal norms can be investigated following the general principles of empirical sciences. Every scientific statement in legal research mus be empirically verified. As was noticed before, Alf Ross was in this regard a genuine logical empiricist. On the other hand, Ross had also to define the object of legal research. Here we meet the legal philosophical background assumption accepted by Ross. It is formulated as a theory of valid law.[13]

On this basis one gets an appropriate theoretical status for legal norm statements: the task of legal research is to predict the authorities' future behaviour. A prediction again means that a statement affirms: a given legal norm will be included in the reasons for a future judgement. However, this way of expressing the kernel of the prediction theory leaves certain central problems open. First of all, a legal norm included in the reasons for a decision may either direct the decision, legitimate it or make the decision understandable. Let us briefly deal with all these alternatives:[14]

(a). The researcher tries to predict the normative ideology (rule) the court actually regards as binding. In this case the object of prediction are the circumstances directing the decision. The form of a prediction may thus be, e.g., as follows:

> P_1 It is probable that the valid norm N_i will actually affect the court's decision.

(b). The researcher puts forward the evaluation that legal norm N_i will (probably) be included in the legal reasons corroborating the decision:

> P_2 It is probable that the court will quote N_i as a part of justification of its decision, although the justification may be a mere rationalization, a facade designed to support a belief in the objectivity of the decision.

If one tries to give a rationalist form to the prediction, the following formulation seems to be quite adequate:

> P'_2 Given the background B, the probability is P that the courts *would* have quoted N_i as a part of justification of cases $C_n - C_{n'}$, had the courts acted in an optimal, rational, socially adequate, etc. manner.

(c) The prediction merely states that the future decision of the court can be made understandable if and only if the explanation is based on norm N_i. This means that the prediction does not bear at all upon how the decision will *de facto* be justified or in which way it will possibly be legitimated. The purpose of this prediction is only to indicate that no sensible connection of meaning between legal phenomena will come about if the future decision, which will be given when state of affairs f_i will occur, is not 'explained' by norm N_i.

As far as Ross' prediction theory is concerned, the alternative (b) seems to be quite problematic. If the idea is to predict the future behaviour of the judge, the focus must be on the actual relation between arguments and the conclusion. The norm at issue belongs to the normative ideology relevant in the case if and only if the judge commits himself to follow the norm. In other words, if and only if the norm is a part of the motivation background that directs the behaviour of the judge. From this point of view, it does not matter how the judge legitimates the decision. The outer shell of the decision is another matter than the reasons of the behaviour. Hence, the alternative (b) cannot be the basis for a genuine Rossian prediction.

A statement conforming to alternative (c) again can hardly at all be called a prediction in the proper sense of the word. It does not foretell any future event or state of affairs on the basics of present knowledge. One might rather say that it entails the claim that whatever happens, this happening can only be understood by referring to a certain group of rules.

The first of the alternative mentioned above seems, on the other hand, to conform the demands of a Rossian forecast. In that case, the form of the prediction is: because the margin of decision-making, the judge's motives and his causal beliefs are (presumably) these and these and because it is probable that they will not change, the court will at moment t_{n+1} confirm consequence g_i when state of affairs f_i occurs. It is clear that if all premises are right the issue will correspond to the prediction. Yet, the prediction does not state this – no more than for example a prediction relating to natural science would state this about its own object.

On the other hand, this kind of legal prediction does not clearly differ from a normal interpretative standpoint presented in legal dogmatics. In many situations where a prediction should be made the predictor should, above all, have knowledge of the normative ideology the judge feels himself committed to. One can elucidate this ideology by examining the wording of the legal text concerned, the various manners of interpretation of the law and the material to be utilized in interpretation, like legislative drafts and precedents. To the material elucidating normative ideology belong also customary law and a large number of so-called real arguments like the interests of different sides, and so on. To put it short, the predictor should as well as possible know the system of rules prevailing in society, the presumable purport of the rules and also the criteria of application of these rules.

Yet, a legal dogmatician proceeds in exactly the same way. He also obtains his results 'directly' from different sources of law. In other words, a methodological corollary of the analysis carried out above is that the predictor and the scholar applying common legal dogmatics act to a great extent according to the same principles.

In practice this easily leads to a kind of pseudo-predictions. This concept has been introduced e.g. by Hans Albert.[15] In some cases a researcher may imagine that he puts forward a prediction or he expresses himself in this way, though he actually presents only his own evaluation telling how things ought to be. Maybe he has abstracted a certain margin of decision-making from the common sources of law, but he has no evidence concerning the decision-maker's goals and beliefs nor concerning the invariability of the frame of the prediction. Precisely in such a case we are concerned with a pseudo-prediction. According to Albert it is characteristic of such pseudo-predictions that they are hidden evaluations and in fact do not contain actual information about future events.

When we consider prevailing legal research it seems that many 'predictions' prove to be more pseudo-predictions. Usually this results from the fact that it is difficult to obtain information on the frame of the prediction and its invariability. On the other hand, at least in Finnish law an "unwritten rule" obtains according to which a researcher should do more than put forward a mere margin of decision-making (or alternative decisions): research should present views substantiated by arguments. Now, if such a view is cloaked in the form of a prediction this is definitely a pseudo-prediction.

What has been said does not mean that it would not be possible at all in legal research to put forward predictions in the actual sense of the word. When doing this, one, however, encounters a difficulty. Indeed, when in an intricate situation the margin of decision-making has to be inferred "directly" from the sources of law, it is possible that evaluations intermingle with the inference already made at this stage. This means that at least in some cases knowledge of the frame is merely non-positivistic certainty. In hermeneutics this knowledge would be called knowledge pertaining to meaning. Consequently, even if one could adduce evidence concerning the invariability of the frame in the sense meant by Albert, the question of the content of the frame may remain partly independent of the evidence. This again implies that in fact we should know the methodology of legal dogmatics in general before we can learn to know the methodology of drawing up predictions. Thus we ultimately, also in the field of prediction, end up at the far-reaching and difficult question whether it is possible to methodically control in some way the process where an interpretative standpoint is inferred from certain sources of law.

In any case it is clear that the use in legal research of the model of prediction found in the natural science is misleading. This applies, e.g., to the conception conforming to logical positivism represented by Alf Ross. All these positivistic conceptions or the conceptions related to them fail to attach necessary attention to the importance of rules. Indeed: rules ultimately give a meaning to the things also in the social reality. Besides, these conceptions omit – or in any case attach too little importance to – the analysis of the agent's purposive behaviour. The agent's purposes and his reasons (these of the court or another authority) may only in certain cases and to a relatively small extent be inferred from features of his behaviour. Such 'behaviourism' cannot be completely carried through for example when there is no practice of the courts whatever in the field the prediction touches. In this case an analysis of the reasons used by the judge may be based, for example, on how matters are generally viewed in the legal community concerned; both the predictor and the court belong to this community.

All in all the predictor needs also information he cannot obtain from previous judicial decisions. Drawing up a prediction is not entirely a matter of empirical research. When we take this into account and when we bear in mind that the difference between drawing up a prediction and putting forward a view relating to legal dogmatics is problematic, we are once more driven back to the question about what knowledge is in the field of legal thinking.

1.2.2.2. *Ilkka Niiniluoto's approach.* In different contexts Ilkka Niiniluoto has defended a viewpoint that in general can be called realistic,[16] even though, Niiniluoto's analysis has succeeded in avoiding many of the classical errors of traditional realistic doctrines. Therefore this view calls for more serious attention not only on the basis of its originality but also on the basis of the fact that it reveals two important features: a connection with legal realism and an attempt to formulate the doctrine of the one right answer from the point of view of correspondence theory.

Niiniluoto's point of departure is that a statement regarding a norm can always be a proposition. It is true or false depending on whether or not, in a Tarskian sense, it corresponds to reality. The concept of truth depends on the correspondence between the statement and the external reality. According to Niiniluoto, this correspondence is intertwined with the validity of legal norms.

In his first proposal, Ilkka Niiniluoto has distinguished between two concepts of validity, which can be denoted with the abbreviations VO_1 and VO_2. Validity in the first sense (VO_1) can be defined with three propositions:

(i) Norm *N* is valid in society *C*.
(ii) Norm *N* is part of the legal order of society *C*.
(iii) The legal community in society *C* accepts norm *N* as part of the legal order.

The content of validity VO_1 can thus be obtained from proposition (iii). In other words, norm *N* is valid if the legal community has accepted it. Thus, a norm proposition always states something about an empirical fact, i.e. the acceptance given be the members of the community in *C*. Niiniluoto defines, furthermore, the legal community as follows: the legal community consists of the legal profession together with the agents acting in legally relevant positions (e.g. in legislation, administration, as members of a jury, etc.).

Acceptance means much the same as "reasonable consensus". Most of the members of the legal community accept norm *N* and believe that also most of the others accept *N* and believe that these others act as if *N* is valid.[17]

In clarifying validity VO_2 Niiniluoto takes an example from scientific knowledge. If proposition *p* is part of scientific knowledge at moment *t*, and if proposition *q* can be deduced from *p*, then *q* is also part of scientific knowledge. In a similar manner we can think that also all of those norms which have not actually been accepted in a legal community but which can be derived from accepted interpretations (norms) are valid in the community in question. We thus receive the following definition of VO_2:

(i′) Norm *N* is valid in society *C* if the legal community has committed itself to accepting *N* as valid.

One is "committed to" something when one is committed to certain legal norms and principles from which it can be deduced.

Later, in his second answer, Niiniluoto has developed and clarified his idea of the truth of norm propositions by drawing a parallel between propositions regarding a legal order and language (for example, Finnish). His point of departure is that the valid legal order (in Finland) is the result of a complicated historical process. The same applies to language. "The system of syntactic and semantic principles governing the correct use of Finnish is a historically changing social product of the Finnish community." Both the legal order and language are contingent social matters.

Thus, Niiniluoto suggests that it is justified to define the truth of a proposition regarding language in a way corresponding to the truth of a proposition regarding legal order. The statement "Norm *N* is valid in Finnish" is true if and only if the linguistic community accepts the norm as a principle of the appropriate use of language.[18]

As also within the sphere of language we cannot think that each member of the linguistic community has actually accepted every language norm, Niiniluoto makes the same reservation regarding the acceptance of linguistic norms which we have just dealt with in regard to legal norms. The statement concerning the validity of norm *N* in Finnish is true if and only if this norm is a consequence of other linguistic norms accepted by the Finnish linguistic community.

Niiniluoto admits that the norms of language cannot be compared without reservation to legal norms. There is no societal norm authority for language that would correspond to the legislator. Also, the sanctions for violating a norm are different, and the linquistic community does not have the type of official interpretation organization that the legal community does. Despite these differences, Niiniluoto is prepared to compare language norms to legal norms in regard to the truth problematics of norm propositions. According to Niiniluoto, both seem to belong to Popper's World 3. Both language norms and legal norms "exist" in this sense. As acceptance is a contingent societal fact, it can also be studied (for example) with the methods of empirical social science. In other words, propositions regarding acceptance can be verified on an experiential basis. In this respect, Niiniluoto's way of thinking resembles those versions of legal realism which connect existence to the behavior of the norm addressees. Niiniluoto, however, does not interpret acceptance through the concept of legal conviction, nor does he use the concept of the behavior of authorities, as does Alf Ross. In Niiniluoto's model, the legal community is something essentially more than a community of judges. It includes all those who have a "juridical role" in that community.

Despite its many great benefits and the noticeable degree of originality, the approach denoted by Niiniluoto is beset with difficulties which make it vulnerable. First of all, drawing a parallel between legal norms and language norms in considerably more problematic than what Niiniluoto appears to believe. As a matter of fact he brings up these problems when he observes that there is no legislator, interpretation institution or coercive sanction for norm violation in the field of language. It is these aspects that demonstrate the essential feature of law, the use of power. The legal order is, in an important sense, a power order, something which language is not. Language is a means of and basis for communication. In this point of view, language is also the pre-condition for the use of power. The same thematics is brought up when we observe that the legal order and the moral code are closely connected to each other.

When we speak of the acceptance of legal norms in a legal community, we cannot bypass the fact that the norms are accepted on the basis of a certain value system. Acceptance is a process of evaluation. The acceptance of a language norm is not – at least not in the same sense and to the same extent – a value-based choice. As a matter of fact, a legal norm is a moral norm, from a certain point of view. It is an officially ossified section of the moral code of society. Thus, even though we would speak on one hand of the acceptance of a legal norm and, on the other hand, of the acceptance of a language norm, this acceptance signifies different things. It is problematic to state that language norms become valid if accepted, or in other words that a certain language norm becomes valid if and only if it is accepted in the linguistic community or it can be (deductively) derived from accepted norms.

In order for it to be possible to accept a language norm (N_i), we must already have *a* language. Thus, language is the necessary precondition of acceptance. In this sense, language is "outside" of individuals, it is an inherited background that is independent of them, to use an expression of Ludwig Wittgenstein. In Niiniluoto's conception, the traditional nature of language becomes in a way confusing.[19] It is true that for example in Finnish, the language is constantly being renewed on the basis of new recommendations open to "acceptance". But even so, it would be audacious to state that the rules of Finnish are valid because the Finns have accepted those rules. The difficulty lies in the concept of "acceptance". How do we control the claim that norm N_i is accepted by the (Finnish) linguistic community? It is not enough to refer to e.g. interviews or to actual ways of using this norm. People may also, even consequently, violate the proper norms of the language at issue. In other words, one always can ask if people speak in a correct way or not. The correct use of linguistic norms cannot thus be legitimated on a basis of acceptance only. Every new acceptance of a norm must already be in accordance with the valid set of norms of (Finnish) language. If we do not assume this, then the concept of "acceptance" receives something that does not correspond to the normal use of that concept. Norm *N* can be accepted because it is in accordance with the valid set of norm of language but it is not valid only therefore that it is based on the acceptance. Validity precedes the "acceptance", not *vice versa*.

As for the acceptance of a legal norm in particular, there is reason to refer to the following details. First, let us assume a new norm which is not yet accepted in the legal community. Possibly the norm has not even come to the attention of the legal community. Under what circumstances can we say that the norm is valid in the first application? The same is true of gap cases. According to this concept, there are no generally accepted norms for such cases. Apparently, Niiniluoto would answer this by saying that we must turn to validity concept VO_2.

If the legal community must commit itself to this norm on the basis of the material already accepted, then the new norm is valid in respect of the first authority to deal with the matter. Actual acceptance is not presupposed. However, the legal community never accepts so unambiguous a norm foundation that a new norm or a solution to a gap can deductively be derived from it. The source material is insufficient, the rules of inference are very loose, and so on. Even at their best they only give the framework for the decision. On the other hand, Niiniluoto does not seem to accept the possibility that the majority of the legal community has erred in accepting a certain point of departure. This may be the case, for instance, in a very authoritative community where the majority is "manipulated" by a few strong opinions. If those opinions are not in accordance with the valid norms there prevails a "total error" in that community. Let us illustrate this with a simplified example.

A hiker must choose between two paths, T_1 and T_2. He knows that the majority of hikers have accepted facts X, and deduces from these facts that the majority of necessity must also accept path T_1. He may furthermore see that quite many people take this path. Deduction and observation, however, do not shut out the possibility that path T_2 is the (only) right one, if he intends to reach his destination. This is a classical situation. It would not be extending matters too far to refer to the discussion between Galileo Galilei and the scholars of the time. When Galilei told the scholars to look through his telescope and verify the existence of the satellites of Jupiter, they retorted that every significant textbook on the subject demonstrated that there could be no such satellites. Thus, what is seen through the telescope cannot be used to deduce that what has been seen, also exists, as it is against what is generally accepted in the scientific community.

The analogy is apparent between the case of the hiker and the problem of the validity of legal norms. As far as the validity is concerned, it may be interesting, even important to know what the general common view on the matter actually is. This view may have importance as circumstantial evidence, i.e. as a criterion of validity. The ultimate question, however, is whether or not this evidence is enough. We can ask: "Is the chosen alternative the right one?"

There is also reason to remember that the intention of legal dogmatics is not the presentation of statements regarding what is (generally) accepted. In other words practical legal dogmatics does not work in accordance with Niiniluoto's suggestion. For this reason this suggestion should be regarded as normative, at least in the weak sense of the term. Niiniluoto's view could be condensed into a sentence: legal dogmatics should function in this way in order to be a science that presents empirically verifiable propositions.

The connection with the idea of the one right answer can be found in the fact that the legal community in society C can, on the basis of the conditions suggested by Niiniluoto, accept one and only one norm N as valid at moment t_1. As was noted, acceptance is defined according to the point of view of the majority. In turn, it would appear to be logically impossible to defend the view that there can be two or more legal norms regulating the same matter in the same way in force at the same time in the same legal order. This implies the possibility of a contradiction, which in turn would mean that the concept of acceptance is open to contradiction.

Niiniluoto's suggestion is considerably different from the doctrine of the one right answer suggested by Ronald Dworkin. The latter is constructed on certain postulates, "the best possible theory" and the concept of Hercules J. The position on the one right answer defended by Niiniluoto does not rest on postulates, but instead on an empirical element. On the other hand, it is precisely here that we find the weakness in Niiniluoto's way of thinking.

Our legal ideology does not unconditionally accept the idea that everything that is generally accepted is also right. As we have noticed, acceptance may be based on mere persuasion and authority, or even on pressure or coercion. But the possibility of manipulation is foreign to the idea of legal certainty. Validity VO_1, however, is based on the idea of actual acceptance: a norm is valid if it has in fact become accepted by the legal community. The point of departure of validity VO_2, in turn, is the deductive inference made on basis of the accepted norm foundation. Thus, Niiniluoto's theory allows both validity which is based on external coercion or the use of persuasion, and validity which is based entirely on error. This means that Niiniluoto's concept of validity opens itself up to random factors in a way that is foreign to our inherited concept of law.

It would be in accordance with legal ideology to base the concept of validity not on actual acceptance but on rational acceptability.[20] In this sense, law which would become generally accepted on the basis of the prevailing system of values if matters were considered rationally, is valid.[21] The acceptability is the measure for the legitimacy of the legal order. It is an ideal to evaluate and to criticise the formally valid as well as effective legal norms.

1.2.2.3. *Norm propositions as technical norms.*

1.2.2.3.1. *General remarks.* Let us assume that expression L may mean two ideas I_1 and I_2. The scholar may, without actually taking a position on the "order of superiority" of the alternative meanings, present assessments on where the choice of either alternative would lead. According to him C_1 follows from I_1, and C_2 follows from the choice of I_2. On basis of this the scholar may now form a so-called technical norm: If you desire consequence C_1, you must act in manner I_1. A pure analysis of the alternative interpretations has thus been altered in its nature.[22]

To characterize technical norms one can recall the figure of the so-called practical syllogism in verbal form. It may be phrased as follows:[23]

A aims at *E*
A considers that he will not achieve *E* unless he does *T*
A undertakes to do (does) *T*

Here the interesting premise is the latter one, "*A* considers that he will not achieve *E* unless he does *T*." That, after all, means that if the person wants to achieve goal *E*, he actually has to do *T*. In other words: doing for him is a necessity for reaching the goal. It is exactly a sentence expressing a "must" ("ought to") that we call a technical norm or, by another term, a teleological norm. Von Wright writes about this type of norm as follows: 'The third main class of norms are rules or instructions which express that something ought to, may or may not be done in order to achieve certain goals. Technical norms are often expressed in the form "For the case to be this, do this or that"; for example, "If you want to relax, go to the movies . . ."'.[24]

No element of command is associated with the technical norm. It is not a prescription, but a norm which is based on a practical necessity touched upon above. It is exactly for this reason that the concept of technical norm would seem to offer an appropriate possibility to understand the quality of "has" (norm *N* has to be interpreted in manner *I*) often contained in interpretation sentences. Here we actually may have the simple comment "in order to achieve goal *E*, interpretation *I* has to be chosen". Such an interpretation is, in other words, in the situation on hand a practical necessity.

However, two different types of technical norms can be identified: the primary technical norm meant for the authorities and the secondary norm directed at individual citizens. In doing this distinction I have found an analogy in Alf Ross's discussions of norms. Ross holds that the norms of behaviour (conduct) have always been directed at the judge and the norms meant for private citizens are a kind of reflections of the former. This, however, is still only an analogy. Technical norms, after all, are not prescriptions and they are not "directed" at any private parties in the manner of "proper norms". The intention is simply to show what, on the one hand, a private citizen and, on the other, the judge have to do to achieve a certain goal.

1.2.2.3.2. *Secondary technical norms.* According to the Finnish law, the sale of real estate ought to be in writing. Referring to this regulation, the scholar or the barrister may state: "The transaction of real estate has to be in writing". This is not a prescription but a technical norm, quite typical in the legal context. It is based on a practical necessity: if you want to make a valid sale, you have to act in accordance with what has been stipulated in the text of law". The statement tells thus something about the content of the legal order. It is obligatory to follow certain formalities.

This "if-so"-statement can be interpreted at least in two different ways. "If you want to make a valid sale" may mean roughly the same as the sentence "if you want to make a sale on the basis of which you will get legal protection both towards the vendor and towards other parties you have to . . .". The getting of legal protection may, in the realistic sense, mean that the authorities are going to react in a manner which protects the buyer against disturbance from outside. If the forecast is justified (plausible), the technical norm, too, is true. As was noticed in the foregoing, the nature of this kind of forecasts is problematic. The distinction between a forecast and a norm standpoint is like a line in the water. Therefore, the "if-so"-statement can normally be understood as an interpretative standpoint concerning the valid law.[25]

Several preconditions for applying the norms of conduct can be expressed by means of technical norms. A good example is the stipulation of the Finnish Marriage Act concerning the spouse's right to transfer certain realty without the other spouse's approval. A doctrinal statement "The sale requires the other spouse's consent" turns out to be a technical norm which states what is necessary to do to make the sale valid. Underlying we find again the statement of how the authorities have to behave unless the approval stipulated by the law is acquired. It will depend on the truthfulness of the statement if the technical norm is true or not.

1.2.2.3.3. *Primary technical norms.* As noted above, in this type of norms can be included also such technical norms as are "directed" at the authorities, such as the judge and the administrative official. Structurally they satisfy all the requirements mentioned at the beginning. An example would be, for instance, a technical norm within criminal law stating "If, by your decision, you want to achieve a preventive effect *E*, you must interpret the law in manner *I*".[26]

If we think of the interpretation statement as similar to a technical norm in its logical status, it would seem permissible also to discuss its validity. This is clearly revealed if we analyze what aspects of the matter scholar *B* may point to if he doubts the validity of a technical norm presented by scholar *A*. Let this be the sentence "The text of law must be interpreted in manner I_1". *B*'s doubts may be specifically directed at the practical necessity between interpretation I_1 and goal *E*. *B* claims that it is not contradictory to act in manner I_2 even when the goal is still *E*. In other words: it is not necessary to arrive at interpretation I_1 in order to achieve goal *E*.

A statement of this kind naturally requires a careful analysis of the cause-effect relation, or, in the case of systemic relationship, the analysis of the legal system itself.

The scholar may in a case like this even claim that interpretation I_1 is the only right one. This he can do when he means that I_1 is necessary in practice for achieving goal *E*, and there is no other means that leads to this goal. But we cannot generally claim that one interpretation is the only one possible unless we, at the same time, also present a claim to the effect that it is possible only to strive to reach one goal, which is *E*. In that case however, we do not merely present a technical norm we also say something about the goal itself. We put forward an evaluation the validity of which is not verifiable in the same way as that of the causality assumption.

It follows from what was said above that several alternative interpretations can be suggested to one passage of law due to the fact that it is possible to strive for different goals and the fact that several means may, perhaps, lead to one and the same goal. Thus it may be necessary to interpret an expression in manner I_1 in order to achieve E_1, and further in the manners $I_2 \ldots I_n$ in order to achieve $E_2 \ldots E_n$. Several technical norms can thus be simultaneously true (or correspondingly false). From this point of view, then, there cannot be any universal truth in such legal dogmatics, which presents technical norms. It cannot offer one single right interpretation. The truth of technical norms put forward by legal dogmatics is always relative; it is in a certain relationship to certain goals and to the means to be chosen.

If the interpreter is satisfied with offering practical necessities, his activity cannot be claimed to merely recommendative or "influencing" or "unscientific". The analysis of the goal-setting (*E*) and of the means (*I*) can be carried out, in a Weberian sense, with a value-freedom of the same degree as, for instance, in any positivist sociological analysis. In actual fact, it is important to notice that the methodololgy of interpretation understood in this way is essentially a methodology of the study of social problems. The traditionally considered rigid borderline between legal dogmatics and legal sociology on this point virtually disappears. The prevalent doctrine according to which legal dogmatics only studies norms, sociology on the other hand empirical reality, turns out to be untenable when we think of how technical norms are set.

In practice, interpretation works mainly so that it relies on the interpreter's everyday experience and intuition. But note: information based on everyday experience is information concerning reality as well. It is empirical knowledge. The difference with regard to knowledge acquired by methods of legal sociology is, above all, to be found in the fact that everyday experience produces knowledge in an unsystematic form whereas sociology amounts to a deliberate systematization of experience.[27] No one can, however, completely evade taking empirical reality into consideration when he is trying to present practical necessities.

Interpretation practice indicates that only juridico-technical consequences are generally taken into consideration when technical norms are formed; they are interpretative advantages or disadvantages, the difficulty of obtaining evidence, advantages connected with registration etc. The interests of various parties are also often stressed in a significant way. On the other hand, it seems that the social consequences of different alternative decisions have seldom been taken into consideration in legal dogmatic interpretation. Thus no attention has normally been paid e.g. to the effects of different interpretations on the position of various social groups and classes. The interpretation setting technical norms has thus in this respect, too, remained "purely juridical".

It is, however, important to notice that the structure of these statements – their status as technical norms – does not change if the nature of the consequences is not legal-systematic in nature but socially coloured. In both cases the interpretation can express a practical necessity: if you want this, you must do that.[28]

If we pay attention to legal research as it is actually being carried out, it seems evident that it is not possible to describe exhaustively the whole area of interpretation by means of technical norms either. This goes both for socially neutral interpretation and the kind of interpretation that takes social consequences into consideration. At most it can be said that expressions like the sentence "The text of law must be interpreted in a way *I*" can in certain circumstances be understood as technical norms. However, the main content of legal dogmatics, in any case, consists of interpretative standpoints, i.e. standpoints concerning the meaning contents of the law in "hard case"-type situations. As has been noted, the goal of legal dogmatics is not in these cases to reach acceptance but rational acceptability. Hence, the focus of the final remarks in this contribution is just on the concept of rational acceptability.

2. ACCEPTABILITY AND RATIONALITY

2.1 *The General Preconditions of the Justification of an Interpretative Standpoint*

An interpretative standpoint is always connected to a so-called hard-case situation. The interpreter has at least two alternatives to choose. For it to be a question, however, of a standpoint and not merely of a recommendation based on authority, it must be justified. Whosoever is able to make a mere choice without any reasons and – perhaps – to recommend it for other people. This kind of a random choice can not, however, be a basis for rational acceptability. It is precisely this that we have been discussing when describing the interpretation from the procedural point of view. Justification is a procedure of rational practical discourse. In a way, the justification of an interpretative standpoint is the same as to follow that procedure.

The final point of the justification has been left open until now. The question was: when can the chain of reasons be cut off? In other words, what does it mean to present a justified interpretative standpoint?

A preliminary characterization of a justified interpretative standpoint might, on this basis, be as follows:

(*P*) Taking into consideration all sources of law (*S*), interpretation I_i of law text L_i is the best justified.

Let us assume that, in accordance with the earlier point of departure, the hard case-situation includes two competing interpretation alternatives, I_1 and I_2. Interpreter *A* presents a standpoint concerning the content I_1. In order to be "the best justified" the interpretation I_1 has to fulfill at least the following preconditions:[29]

(a) The sources of law (*S*) have been used in the way presupposed in the rules of legal interpretation. This means, for example, that the categorization standards of the sources of law have not been broken, the priority standards of the sources of law have been followed and that, for example, the prohibition against analogy has not been violated.[30] The interpretation standards lock the framework within which the sources of law should, can, or cannot be used. Following the interpretation standards only does not ensure, however, the sufficiency of the justification, as has been pointed out. The reason for that is quite obvious. The fulfillment of these general preconditions only demonstrates the interpretation to be legally possible.[31] By means of the sources of law and the standards of legal interpretation the interpreter can choose from the semantically possible interpretative alternatives those that are legally possible and legally relevant.

(*b*) As also was discussed before, all the standards of legal interpretation are contentually open. These standards are of the principle type, not of the rule type. Hence every hard-case situation and every choice of interpretative alternatives in legal dogmatics is open to evaluative criteria. Already the order of preference of the sources of law presupposes reference to evaluations.

On the other hand, if one disagrees with the cognitivist value theories, one also has to admit that there may be at the same time more than one well founded interpretation for a hard case and more than one possible standpoint in legal dogmatics when the scholar has to make a choice between different meaning possibilities. What does it mean, then, that a solution or a standpoint is "the best justified"?

In order to single out the kernel of the story, the cluster of statements, *Q*, shall be defined so that it is composed of statements *S* describing the sources of law and of value judgements *V* based on a certain value-system. In addition, these statements have been arranged in a coherent manner *M* into a connection with an interpretative standpoint *P*. This standpoint concerns the interpretative alternative *I*.

Let us assume that there are two standpoints, P_i and P_j referring to corresponding interpretative alternatives. In this case, we get two clusters of statements:

$$Q_i\ M_i\ (S_1 \ldots S_n \ \&\ V^i_1 \ldots V^i_n)$$
$$Q_j\ M_j\ (S_1 \ldots S_n \ \&\ V^j_1 \ldots V^j_n)$$

Clusters Q_i and Q_j "compete" with each other as the proper justification of an interpretation concerning a certain statute. As can be noticed, the coherence characterizing the cluster is not a sufficient criterion for preferring a certain standpoint to another. On the contrary, both cluster Q_i and cluster Q_j fulfill the criteria of coherence. The justification of a standpoint, for instance P_i, depends also upon three other matters:

(i) What statements are accepted as part of *Q*, i.e. which kind of catalogue of the sources of law and what value judgements can replace *S* and *V*,
(ii) what is the material content of the statements that cluster *Q* is composed of, and
(iii) in which way do the statements describing the sources of law relate to each other, in other words, what is the respective order and weight of the statements *S*?

The answer to the first two questions depends on three matters: (1) the standards of classification of the sources of law, (2) the value system accepted as the basis of justification and (3) the subject matter of the justification, i.e. the legal problem to be solved. The order and weight of different statements – question (iii) – depend, in turn, on the standards of legal reasoning as a part of practical reasoning and on the value-system mentioned above.

There are good reasons to repeat in this phase that the justification procedure is essentially a dialogue. It is a succession of questions and answers on the basis of which different *pro* and *contra* arguments will be presented. In this way, the interpreter finally finds out a combination of pro-arguments needed for the justification. The addressee can rationally accept the interpretation only if the justification results in a coherent cluster of statements and if this cluster fulfills criteria (i)-(iii). This means, that the procedure of the discourse must be acceptable and that the interpreter shares the arguments with the addressee. This is so, because the standards of legal reasoning alone do not guarantee the coherence of the justificatory material. All reasons must also be used in a rational way. Hence, if the general preconditions for the rationality are fulfilled and the special standards of legal interpretation have not been violated the recipient can assure himself of the justification if he binds himself to the same system of reasons as the interpreter.

In this regard, the decisive point as far as the "the best justified" interpretation is concerned is, no doubt, the difference in value judgements. This can also be expressed as follows: on the basis of a certain value-system V_s^i the largest imaginable coherence within the set of statements at issue gives maximal rational acceptability. From a slightly different point of view, one could say that this feature makes it sensible to speak of more than one right answer in legal reasoning. The problem of two (or more) clusters Q in legal interpretation is, in other words, the problem of value relativism and its role in the justification procedure.

We are thus left with two questions to answer: (1) how to define the concept of rationality so that it will be adequate in legal justification and (2) is it impossible on the basis of value relativism thesis to speak about rational acceptability? In other words, what is the internal connection between rationality and the relativity of value-judgements.

2.2. *The Concept of Rational Acceptability*

A promising anchor seems to be offered by Chaim Perelman's pair of concepts, "rational" and "reasonable", which has been dealt with in many connections.[32] The expressions, especially the latter can be interpreted in several ways. As J. R. Lucas has pointed out "In contemporary English there is a slight difference in sense between the words "reasonable" and "rational", the former having a moral overtone suggesting some degrees of consideration for others, while the latter is austerely egoistic in connotation."[33] In the following, the same concepts will be referred to by speaking of "rational" and "acceptable". Both concepts would seem to call for some preliminary clarification.

The concept of rationality can be used in many different ways. First, it is possible to speak of legal rationality and rationality in general. The concept "legal rationality" refers here to the paradigm of legal dogmatics (and adjudication). Helmut Schelsky speaks about juridical-instrumental rationality, according to which, the legal justification must follow certain standards of interpretation and it must be based on certain sources of law.[34] Let us call this legal rationality. It is simply the same as proceeding according to the traditional paradigm of legal reasoning. Following the traditional model, one realizes the legal positivistic rationality. In this respect, this kind of rationality gives criteria to differ legal conclusions from, for instance, sociological ones.

There are, however, other types of rationality, too. One of them is the teleological, i.e. finalistic rationality. Teleological reasoning, that has been dealt with before, is based on different standards from the legal positivistic rationality. Therefore, depending on the structure of legal order the teleological rationality has different degrees of significance. If the system of legal norms consists of flexible (elastic) norms, the teleological model, goal reasoning, has more use than in the interpretation of well formulated norms.

The concept of institutional rationality refers to the rationality that is involved in the legal system itself. Every legal order has its own general principles, the systematic relations between norms etc. The system has "internal" sense. Werner Krawietz has in many contexts pointed out that the understanding of the functions, and functioning, of legal norms and legal order in general presupposes that one takes into account rationality in the system-theoretical sense.[35] The last mentioned type of rationality is – roughly speaking – a system-theoretical interpretation of institutional rationality.

As far as the basic assumptions of the present study are concerned, the institutional rationality is a societal precondition for all legal reasoning. Even more: the social role of legal dogmatics is just to interpret the content of this rationality ("the internal sense" of legal order). On the other hand, the system theoretical rationality may give valuable information for legal reasoning. It points out the functions of legal order. In this regard, the system theoretical rationality is not only a precondition for legal reasoning but a source of information – among other sources of that kind.

The concept of rational acceptability refers to quite a different phenomenon than the ones described above. Rational acceptability is a property of the final result of the procedure of legal justification. Therefore one speaks of the rational acceptability of the interpretative standpoints. Legal interpretation is, in turn, a dialogue as to its nature, i.e. it is, in this sense, a form of human communication. Following Jürgen Habermas one can thus call this kind of rationality communicative rationality.[36] It is connected with argumentation and convincing. Hence, communicative rationality is the basis of human understanding and, furthermore, the basis of acceptability.

This very type of rationality can, on the other hand, be understood at least in two different ways. First, rationality may refer to the form of reasoning. In that view, logical (deductive) inference is always rational. This mode of reasoning follows certain rules, and it is tautological. Every chain of reasoning which goes in a deductive manner from premises to a conclusion is thus rational.[37] This means that the internal justification referred to by Wróblewski is always rational in this sense of the word. Let us call logical rationality simply *L*-rationality.

This is, however, only one side of communicative rationality. As noticed above, legal justification is a form of practical discourse. Here, it is not merely a question of the form of reasoning but also of a discoursive procedure bound by other than logical rules. On the basis of

Habermas' ideas Robert Alexy has pointed out that rational discourse in legal reasoning is always connected to the external justification. It deals with the procedure through which the premises are justified. The rationality in connection with discourse will be called *D*-rationality.[38]

We thus have two characterisations of rationality:

(1) rationality *sensu stricto* = *L*-rationality, and
(2) rationality *sensu largo* = *L*-rationality & *D*-rationality.

In the following, the focus is specifically on rationality in the sense of (2) above. It refers to both the logical form of reasoning and the discourse that justifies the premises. For the reasons noted later in the text, the main attention will be on rational discourse, i.e. on the external justification.

The concept of acceptability, in turn, is connected with the conclusion, in other words, with the material content of the interpretation and not with the form of the reasoning or with the properties of the justificatory procedure itself. We do not say that the process of reasoning is reasonable, but we speak about the reasonable result of the interpretation. In order to be acceptable, the result must correspond to the knowledge and value systems of the legal community. Often, mention is made of expectations (*Erwartungen*) in the receiving community. The specific role of the values and evaluations in the legal dogmatical interpretation (justification) has already been noted. For this reason, acceptability is examined here above all as axiological acceptability.

If we denote rationality (*sensu largo*) with the letter *R* and acceptability with the letter *A*, we obtain a result as shown in Diagram 29.

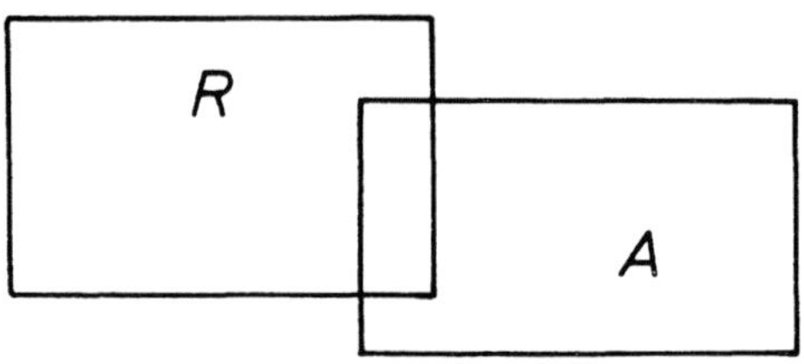

Diagram 29

The diagram allows for a total of four possibilities: (a) *R* & *A*, (b) *R* & ~ *A*, (*c*) ~ *R* & *A* and (*d*) ~ *R* & ~ *A*. In the first case, we are just in the core of the diagram. The interpretative standpoint is both the result of rational reasoning (rational discourse) and it is acceptable (reasonable). Due to the noncognitive property of value judgements, acceptability is not universal. Some part of the legal community may have values on the basis of which the rationally reached result is acceptable, while in another part the same result does not strike a chord. For this reason, especially alternative (b) is interesting. In it, it is true, the procedure of discourse is rational (*sensu largo*) but the result is still not acceptable. In other words, some addressee or a group of addressees could not accept the interpretation even if its members would act as rational as possible. Yet, alternative (a) is not shut out. On the contrary, in accordance with our relativism thesis, it always offers a possible alternative to situation (b). Some partial group in the recipient community can also achieve agreement on value judgements.

On the other hand, alternative (c) is problematic. Chaim Perelman has pointed out that interpretation can be reasonable (acceptable) even if it is nonrational.[39] In this, Perelman refers in part to *L*-rationality, and in part to a standpoint of actual acceptance in the recipient community. In fact, there is a possibility that the legal community accepts as reasonable also results that do not fulfill the criteria of *L*-rationality. On the other hand, Perelman's view does not appear to be convincing. If an interpretation is based on a random choice between several alternatives it is not in accordance with the standards of legal certainty. In this regard, an arbitrary interpretation can, in principle, be reasonable. Yet, only acceptability on the basis of *D*-rationality satisfies our expectations of legal certainty. It is thus a consequence of the concept of rational acceptability that alternative (c) will be left aside in the following analysis.

For the sake of simplicity, the problem will be approached only from the point of view alternative (a). The question is, on what preconditions can an interpretation receive the acceptance of a rationally acting legal community?

In order to answer this, two types of theories are assumed, a procedural theory of legal reasoning and a substantial theory concerning the material acceptability. The composition is as follows:

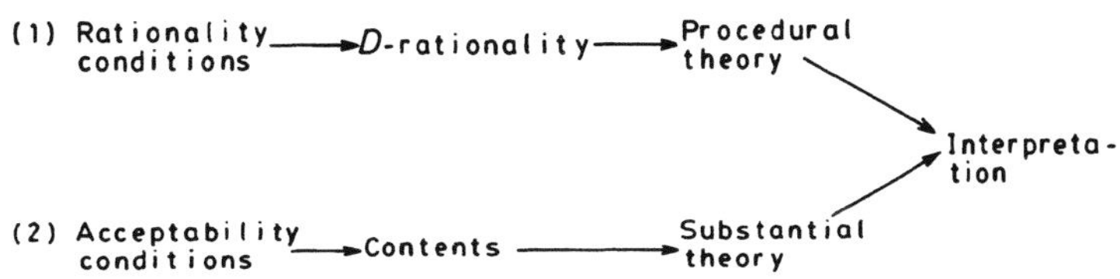

Diagram 30

The rules of rational discourse are hierarchically the highest basis binding the sources of law to the result of the interpretation. They form the framework of all interpretation, including interpretation in legal dogmatics. In a rough way, the role of rationality is like it is presented in Diagram 31.

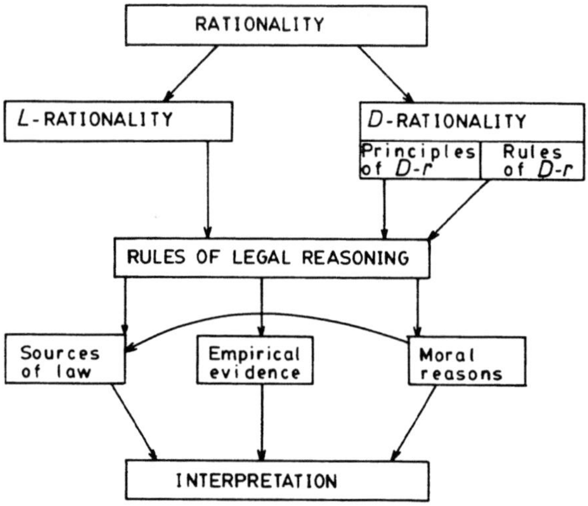

Diagram 31

In the scheme, all the possible interrelations between the "boxes" are not described. The idea of the presentation is merely to point out the place of rationality in the structure of reasoning, and, at the same time, to specify the different types of other factors in legal reasoning. Here, the heart of legal justification lies in a *mixture* of legal, empirical and moral arguments. This mixture cannot be avoided in hard case situations. The interpreter always has to find out a balanced combination of these distinct elements. Especially in this respect, it seems to be well-founded to speak about the reasonableness of the interpretation.

On the other hand, the contents of the interpretation is based on certain general principles of (D-)rationality and on certain specific standards legal reasoning, e.g. on the rules of grammatical interpretation and analogy. These principles and rules are the methodological core of all legal justification. They give the general guidelines (for the use of the sources of law and they show the place for empirical evidence as well as for the role of moral reasons in legal contexts.

2.3. *Why Be Rational?*

The normal question in the legal dogmatical practice is as follows: how can an interpretative standpoint I_i be justified? The answer to this question refers to the sources of law, to the standards of legal interpretation etc. In other words, one gives a contextually sufficient legal justification for the interpretative standpoint.[40] It is contextually sufficient because the answer gives the legal background on the basis of which the interpretation can be acceptable in the legal community.

As was pointed out in the foregoing, a legal philosopher often puts a question of quite another type: why is the (contextually sufficient) legal justification possible? What are the general preconditions for a sound legal justification? In other words, one has to justify the justification itself. Aleksander Peczenik calls this "the deep justification".[41] As far as rational acceptability is concerned the basic question could be formulated as follows: why be rational in legal justification? Or: why is *D*-rationality such an important background element in the theory of legal reasoning?

Let us follow, for a moment, a critic who claims that *D*-rationality is always and only a constructed concept, although very suitable for the purposes of legal justification. Yet, it is possible – according to this critic – to construe more than one *D*-rationality. In other words, he would say, if *D*-rationality is not merely logical, why in general can we speak of rationality? Maybe it would be better to use some other concept than just rationality in this context.

The critic is right in saying that the concept of rationality and thus also the concept of rational acceptability are reconstructions. They are ideal models for legal reasoning. Nevertheless, the reconstruction itself is not an abitrary one. It is not only a stipulative or lexical definition of what the term "rational" means, or what it should mean in a "correct use of the language". The purpose of the analysis is not to describe the prevalent linguistic usage.

The deep justification for *D*-rationality cannot be based merely on empirical facts either. The idea is not to claim that people are rational in their everyday life, or that people will, at some later stage of their development, be rational in their needs and thinking. People are, in many respect, human beings who are provided with a lot of irrational features.

The roots of rationality are in our culture, i.e. in the ways we use this concept in ordinary language. Our form of life is constructed in such a way that we expect people be rational in the human intercourse. In this regard, rationality is an intersubjective (supraindividual) given fact in our culture. Let us take an example. All interpretations presented by *A* are totally inconsequent and non-coherent in every respect. What do we think about *A*? We are inclined to say that either *A* is crazy, or that he belongs to a culture unknown to us. It is impossible for us to understand him. A consequent and coherent way of thinking is rooted so deeply in our culture that we use it as a measure when evaluating other peoples' behaviour. In this sense, e.g. the concept of consequency and coherency are necessary elements of our common concept of rationality. They belong to the basis of human communication. Our social life and our human communicative interaction will function only provided these preconditions are satisfied. Referring to these features, it seems to be correct to say that the reconstruction of rationality only makes explicit something deeply hidden in the common linguistic usage of the modern-minded Western people.[42]

In this sense, rationality is an idea that goes through the whole social life. Therefore, the mere *L*-rationality is too limited a form of rationality. An individual may make logically perfect inference and, at the same time, he can be quite unable to participate in a rational *societal* discourse. For such people, rationality – as a logical concept – does not necessarily belong to the field of societal life, legal thinking, moral discourse or politics. In all these areas, this person may accept arbitrariness in human intercourse although he highly evaluates the *L*-rationality. Here lies a deep and important line of demarcation between those who accept *L*-rationality as the only form of rationality and those – as the author of this work – who judge human communication also through *D*-rationality.

On the other hand, rationality (rational acceptability) is an ideal, only. It is a standard by means of which one can weigh the actual (legal) discourse. Rationality and rational acceptability are not, however, only transcendental concepts in the Kantian sense or concepts comparable to the basic ideas of natural law. The rules of *D*-rationality are not universally valid eternal rules governing the thinking procedure of man. In this regard, rational acceptability does not presuppose a metaphysical interpretation.

On the contrary, there is always a genuine possibility open that in certain, although for us very alien culture: people are rational in a different sense than is defined here. They are not rational *for us* – although they are rational for themselves. Yet, such a rational discourse is important for everyday practice both in (legal) scholarly work and in decision-making in both types of cultures. From that point of view one can say that rational acceptability (as a concept) – understood in the way presented by the author of this work – is a result of a cultural analysis. The result may be rough or there may be gaps in the concept but without this concept it is impossible to understand the idea of law and the idea of legal order.

However, it is impossible to give direct evidence for the following interpretation of the concept "rationality". We do not have any "empirical" means to testify the results of our analysis. The only test is indirect as to its nature. If our proposal is in accordance with the common use of the notion of rationality we have good reasons to say that the proposal functions in this culture. It makes explicit something that is implicitly accepted as the basis of the human communication.

2.4 *The General Conditions of Rational Discourse*

2.4.1. *The point of departure.* The rules which guide rational discourse form a whole that, using the terminology of Jürgen Habermas and Robert Alexy, we can call the procedural theory of rational discourse. For Alexy, these are the following principles of (practical) rationality: consistency, efficiency, coherence, generalisability and sincerity. According to Aleksander Peczenik the list of principles is, however, redundant. Minimal rationality, as Peczenik calls it, is a "practice fulfilling the demand of logical consistency and oriented towards the optimal combination of two regulative ideas: the idea that one should be able to express both description and evaluation generally and the idea that both description and evaluation should be supported by reasons".[43] One cannot grade consistency, says Peczenik, but one can grade support and generality, and thus rationality, too. Decreased generality sometimes accompanies increased mutual support, and *vice versa*. In such cases, rationality thus is optimal "mix" of generality and support. On the other hand, there are no universal criteria for that kind of optimality. One cannot know *in concreto* what is absolutely optimal, i.e. if the discourse at issue is rational or not in universal meaning. As far as the optimalization of rationality is concerned, Peczenik is right, I suppose. On the other hand, the very concept of rationality is, in Peczenik's analysis, "too minimal". Sincerity and efficacy cannot be reduced to generality and support only. For the sake of conceptual clarity, the necessary conditions for rational discourse can be listed, as Alexy does, in five elements: consistency, efficacy, sincerity, generality and support. However, in the Alexian catalogue of principles (and rules based on the principles) there is a mixture of different kinds of elements. Certain rules or principles have a character of natural law, the other ones may have an empirical colour. Therefore, the following list of rationality principles and rationality rules is not of "Alexian type" in the strict sense of the word. Only the basic idea of *D*-rationality is formulated according to the model presented by Habermas and Alexy. For our purposes it is important that we present the analysis in a way that as adequately as possible connects the concept *D*-rationality to ordinary legal dogmatical research practice. In this, it is possible to choose e.g. the following mode of presentation.

2.4.2. *The basic principles and rules of D-rationality.*

2.4.2.1. *Consistency-rules.* Every step in the rational procedure of discourse must fulfill, as is natural, the criteria of consistency. The rules of *L*-rationality are thus rules of consistency.

For the first, the principles of logical consistency covers, for example, the demand that there is no internal conflict, the third excluded law, and the transitiveness rule.[44] These have all been dealt with in brief above. The absence of inner conflict means that a statement and its negation cannot exist at the same time in the same justification configuration.

According to the third excluded law, a proposition is either true or false, there is no third possibility.[45] The same law can be stated in a number of other ways, for example by saying that if being *X* has property *P*, this property cannot at the same time be missing in being *X*. According to the transitiveness rule, the following is true: if a person accepts the statements, "if *p* then *q*" and "if *q* then *r*" he must also accept the statement "if *p* then *r*".

2.4.2.2. *Efficiency-rules.* In order to be rational, practical discourse presupposes effectiveness: the discourse must result in a conclusion. An ineffective discourse in an anomaly. This means, for instance, that people using language use the expressions in the same way. In other words, the participants (*A* and *B*) do not have any apparent linguistic disagreement. All linguistic differences in opinion must be eliminated before it is possible to discuss material disagreement on a reasonable basis. This can also be called the principle of similar meanings (similarity).[46]

Not only must the parties to the interpretation have a common language, they also must use each expression in a uniform manner. A party in the interpretation cannot change language games unexpectedly without justifying the change in the use of language. If an unexpected change of linguistic conventions is done, the whole discourse will be disturbed. Binding oneself to this kind of consistency-rule one prevents the possibility that during the interpretation a material disagreement will turn into a linguistic disagreement.

2.4.2.3. *Sincerity-rules.* Everyone who speaks the language in question has a right to participate in the discussion. We can speak of the principle of subjective openness.[47] This means, in addition, a prohibition against referring to authorities. The discussion loses its rational basis if one of the discussants is eliminated because he cannot rely on authority. Rational discourse always progresses on a material basis, not on the basis of the prestige of the participants.

The prohibition against coercion. Physical or mental coercion is not to be used against a discussant. In connection with the above point, we can also note that rationality assumes that authoritative persuasion is eliminated. Only within a framework which in all respects is free of coercion can a material basis come to bear with all its strength.

Every discussant has the right to question a presented statement. There can be no barred subjects in the discussion, no taboos. This can be called the principle of material openness.[48] It supplements the above criteria which make criticism possible.

The demand of honesty means that a discussant may not refer to justification that he knows is nonvalid. A person who consciously makes use of nonvalid justification is not attempting to influence the result on material grounds but through persuasion. In other words, a person who violates the demand for honesty violates a condition of rationality.

This group includes, albeit as a lesser form, activity where a person states that the justification is valid even though he is not sure of this. For example, in the discussion about the ingredient of our food a substance,

X, is said to be non-poisonous as food even though at the moment there is no possibility of ascertaining either its harmlessness or its danger.

If someone wishes to assure another person of his point of view on rational grounds, he must be impartial, in other words he must be objective specifically in this sense.[49] With an eye on justification, this means above all that the interpreter must present not only his own views but also arguments that speak against his reasons. In other words, he must follow the principle of *audiatur et altera pars*. Robert Alexy refers to this when he observes, "Diesem auf einem Sprecher bezogene Forderung der Unparteilichkeit entspricht die auf Diskussionen bezogene Forderung nach dem Recht eines jeden Sprechers, jedes Argument einzuführen."[50]

2.4.2.4. *Generalization-rules.* A discussant cannot refer to a value judgement that he is not prepared to generalize to cover other similar cases. Robert Alexy writes, "Wer alle überzeugen will, darf nur Normen vorschlagen, die jedermann akzeptieren kann".[51] Let us call this the rule of the generalizability of evaluations (and of normative standpoints). For example, in Perelman's opinion an attempt at universality is the basic foundation of all rational argumentation. Violation of the rule of generalizability leads to the use of grounds that are only connected to the situation in question. They are, so to speak, *ad hoc* arguments, the justificatory power of which does not go beyond a particular situation. For this reason, they also do not fulfill the requirement of rationality.

The rule of generalizability includes, among other, what follows: (i) One must accept the consequences of a norm one accepts even if they affect one's own position at the same time: and (ii) the consequences of a norm satisfying a person's interests must be acceptable to everybody else: you must behave so that your act can be generalized.

Naturally, the same holds true as far as empirical statements are concerned: one should be able to express the description of data in a general way.

2.4.2.5. *Support-rules.* The rule of the necessity of justification states that when so demanded, every proposition must be justified.[52] It is easy to see that this as well as some of the previous conditions is connected with the prohibition against authorities. If a discussant in the interpretation questions a statement that has been presented, the criticism cannot be avoided by referring to the prestige of the person who presented the statement – not without violating the rules of rationality. The questioning of the statement leads to there being an obligation to respond, and this, in turn, can only be done on material grounds.[53]

As far as the substantial support is concerned, the key concept is coherency. The interpretative statement (P_i) must be in the relation of coherency to all the material – sources of law – that has been used as reasons for P_i. On the other hand, the concept of coherence itself calls for a further analysis. Let us recall, for the sake of clarity, the two clusters of statements:

$$Q_i\ M_i\ (S_1 \ldots S_n\ \&\ V^i_1 \ldots V^i_n)$$
$$Q_j\ M_j\ (S_1 \ldots S_n\ \&\ V^j_1 \ldots V^j_n)$$

It is unnecessary to point out here the difficulties that are involved in the very concept of coherency. Here the only attempt is to point out that the concept of coherence is of special value for legal dogmatics. As was referred to in the introductory chapters, legal dogmatics is not an empirical science as far as the confirmation of the norm statements is concerned. It deals with language, with the meaning contents of the statutes. In this regard, legal dogmatics is interpretative as to its nature and it belongs to the same family of research as the human sciences (*Geisteswissenschaften*). All this is the reason why the concept of coherence is more closed to legal dogmatics than the very concept of correspondence. The problem lies in the fact, when and on what conditions it is possible to say that all the argumentative material gives a coherent support to the interpretation.

The relation between coherence and support is controversial. Justifying a standpoint is the same as to give support to that standpoint. On the other hand, support is connected with coherence. If p supports q then p is a good reason for q. In this regard, Peczenik writes as follows: If p is a good reason for q, then p and q are coherent with each other.[54] There seems to be, however, a *circulus vitiosus* in this kind of definition. The concept of support already includes coherency. Thus the concept of coherence cannot be defined by means of support. Here, coherence has been understood as a criterion for support: p is a good reason for q, if p and q are coherent with each other. On the other hand, the coherence-relation prevails if:

(a) The statements are not logically contradictory.[55] In addition, the statements must fulfill at least the following two requirements.

First, no individual source of law S_i can be both a *pro* and a counter argument.

Second, the source of law S_i and its opposite $\sim S_i$ cannot be used as justification. The condition that there is no contradiction, however, is rather loose as a criterion of coherence. It does not set any internal requirements on the justification statements. Whatsoever statement is coherent, as long as it is not logically contradictory and it fulfills the other conditions given.

(b) For this reason we must also require that the statements fit together. To repeat what Charles Taylor has pointed out, it is a question of a plausible but non-deductive connection between the interpretative standpoint and the justifying material.[56] In this view, sources of law S_1 and S_2 fit together with an interpretative alternative I_i, if those arguments bring further believability to the justification.

The real problem concerning coherency, however, lies just in the concept "fitting together". Here only a few outlines explaining the nature of the problem can be given. At least two additional conditions must be fulfilled if a set of S_i and the standpoint I_i can be said to be coherent with each other:

(i) Justification S_i must be relevant from the point of view of interpretation I_i One can also say that the justification must have certain justificatory force.[57] The condition of relevancy refers, first of all, only to situations where S_i and I_i are contingent. The validity of the justification must be capable of decision without regarding I_i as justified. In other words, a logical or conceptual relation between S_i and I_i is not part of the condition of relevance.

(ii) The relevancy itself can be defined as follows. If it is possible to justify I_i without reference to sources of law S_i, S_i is not relevant from the point of view of I_i. Loosely speaking, relevancy means that there is a factual connection between the justification and the alternative interpretation. The role of coherence can also be illustrated by recalling the idea of internal and external justification. As was pointed out, it is possible to put every interpretation *ex post* in the scheme:

SYLLOGISM I	Premise P_1 Premise P_2
	Conclusion I_i

The core of the legal justification lies in the *pro-* and *contra-*

argumentation by means of which one gives support to the premises (or one of them). Hence, the whole procedure can, from the external point of view, be written as follows:

	Conclusion I_i
Arguments:	Syllogism II
	Syllogism III
	.
	.
	Syllogism N

It is possible to write each single argument in a syllogistic (deductive) form, i.e. in the mode of the so-called internal justification. However, the chain of arguments, from the premise P_1 to the final syllogism (Syllogism *N*) is not deductive as to its nature. It is only guided by the rules and principles of rational discourse (in addition to the standards of legal interpretation).

Hence, the very concept of coherence is connected to the totality of arguments. The conclusion I_i is justified if and only if the chain of arguments fulfills the criteria of coherency, i.e. if and only if the arguments S_1–S_n together with I_i form a homogenous part-whole totality. This means, on the other hand, that the rules of rationality (*L*-rationality and *D*-rationality) do not guarantee the coherent set of arguments – coherency can also be reached by accident – but these rules do maximize the possibility in society at producing a coherent argumentation basis for legal interpretation. The goal of justification is to reach coherency, and by means of it, acceptability in the legal community. The means that serve this goal are just the rules of legal interpretation and the general rules of rationality.

2.4.3. *The Rules of the Burden of Proof*

The rules of the burden of proof can roughly be divided into two main groups. The first group includes the procedural rules of justification. In certain situations the person presenting the justification is obliged to present proof regardless of the type of justification. The second group, in turn, consists specifically of the rules concerning the content of the justification. They are the material rules of the burden of proof.

In connection with both groups there is reason to speak specifically of rules and not principles. There are only two alternatives for the rules of the burden of proof: either they will or they will not be followed. In this respect, they differ from norms having the character of principles.

2.4.3.1. *Procedural rules of the burden of proof.* (a) Following Chaim Perelman, we can say that the basis of intellectual and social life lies in continuity.[57] It is not sensible to give up without justification whatever has been adopted as prevailing. This is not an exhortation to conservatism to maintain the *status quo*. It is only a rule of the burden of proof: of necessity, a change in the prevailing situation must be justified. Robert Alexy formulates this principle as follows: "eine Auffassung, die einmal akzeptiert wurde, nicht ohne hinreichen den grund wieder aufgegeben werden darf".[58] The prevailing situation or the prevailing understanding has justification as it is. It is the point of departure. The burden of proof lies with the person who criticizes the prevailing situation and wants a change. But on the basis of this criticism, the burden of proof may change so that the prevailing situation has to be justified for it to remain as it is. The value of the burden of proof thus deals with social dynamics.

The rule referred to here has been derived from the general principle dealt with in the foregoing. According to this general principle, not everything that is possible demands justification. The necessity for justification does not come up until someone questions the presented view. We thus come to the second rule regarding the burden of proof.

(b) A person who presents justification for his proposition or standpoint is obliged to present additional justification only in the case that the justification is questioned.[59] According to this prohibition against unnecessary justification it is not rational to present further justification for the original justification if no one demands this. The question of justification, in turn, can lead either to the need for new justification or to the necessity for justifying the presented justification or for making it more exact.

(c) A person who refers to a proposition or a standpoint that is not relevant to the justification or that does not have any justificatory power has the burden of proof for saying why he used this justification. The principles of rational discourse will be violated if he uses as justification material that does not have any connection with the matter to be justified. At the least we can presuppose that the person presenting this justification gives reasons for his behaviour. In this way, the possibility can be eliminated that the discussion will be sidetracked by surprising reasons in order to manipulate the discussion.

2.4.3.2. *Material rules of the burden of proof.* (a) The principle of equitable treatment prescribes that similar cases must be dealt with in a similar way. In other words, the goal of the principle is to guarantee substantial equality. When written out as an a burden of proof rule, it states that a person who violates the principle of equitable treatment is obliged to present justification for his course of action.[60] It is not a question of a material obligation to deal with those in the same position in the same manner. The rule only pertains to the obligation of presenting proof. One has to reveal the (real) reasons why, for instance, *A* and *B* have been treated in similar situations in a non-equal way.

On the level of norm theory, the difference appears in the fact that the demand for materially equal treatment is something that belongs to the category of principles, not rules. The principle of equitable treatment may receive a number of different applications. None of them violates the principle itself. The obligation of presenting proof is defined by an ordinary rule-like norm. If it is violated, the interpreter is not acting rationally.

(b) The burden of proof rules in special branches of science are connected with the methodology of the branch in question. In legal dogmatics there are at least two rules that would belong in this category. They deal with so-called weakly binding sources of law.

— If *travaux préparatoires* are bypassed, the person who does this must justify his procedure, and

— if a person does not refer to the court praxis on the matter in question, he must justify his procedure.

2.4.4. *Summary.* It can be said on the basis of the above discussion that the dialogue between interpreter *A* and the recipient of interpretation *B* follows the criteria of rational discourse if it fulfills the general conditions of rationality and if the special burden of proof rules are not violated. The discourse is then in accordance with *D*-rationality. Following the rules of *D*-rationality and the standards of legal interpretation one transforms the institutional rationality of the legal order into the interpreted law. In other words, he gives an interpretation of what is the institutional rationality in society.

D-rationality, however, does not solely ensure that the interpretation

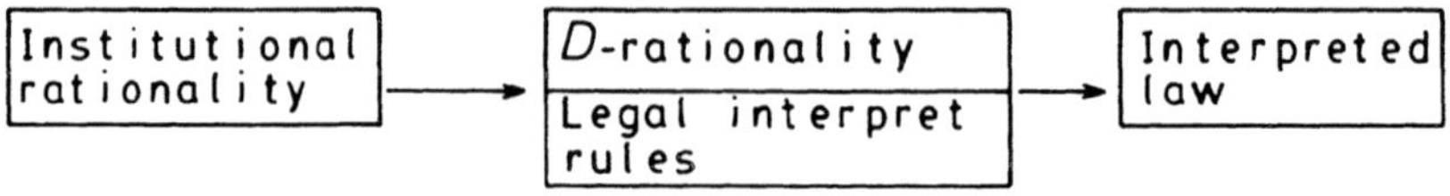

will be acceptable in the legal community. In addition to rational discourse, acceptability requires (to repeat what has been said above) the following conditions: (a) the parties in the dialogue have a common basis in knowledge, i.e., their evidence regarding reality is equally large, and (b) both parties must bind themselves to the same values. The accumulation of evidence leads to the removal of disagreement to the extent that it is a question of cognitive differences. As for values, this is not the case.

In the following, a moderate value-relativist position has been adopted in respect to values. This means that values are not interpreted objectively in that value judgements could be true or false in the strong sense of the word. One can only speak of truth on the precondition that the criteria of truth have been agreed upon. Thus, the sentence. "The scenery here is beautiful" is true if and only if the criteria of truth have been defined in advance. Criteria, in turn, are not universal in respect of time and place. On the contrary, the criteria are typified by historical relativity. This is not due solely to the fact that human knowledge of values varies with time and culture. The problem lies deeper. Values are not an ontological entity which would exist regardless of the subject. In this respect, there is a difference between physical reality and "value reality". It may be that also our knowledge of physical reality is very limited; it is still the case that the physical world is "there", outside of us. This is not the case with values.

This does not mean that values would not have objectivity in an intersubjective sense. Values do not vary with the individual to the extent that each of us would have our own autonomous value constitution. As it is precisely this aspect that is of decisive significance in responding to the criticism regarding the arbitrariness of legal interpretations, there is reason for further discussion about the question of the intersubjectivity of values and value judgements.

2.5. *Interpretations and Evaluations*

Values and evaluations may enter the interpretation procedure in various ways:

(a) When a legal interpreter has to make a choice among several legal sources which give support to quite different kind of interpretation alternatives, the legal sources have to be ranked into an order of preference according to their argumentative weight in legal justification. For instance, a precedent is considered to have more argumentative weight than a reference to the issue in a committee report or the like. The choice among the legal sources that are to be used in the justification of a legal decision is therefore partly value-laden.

(b) Legal analogy, which has a wide usage in the legal interpretation praxis, is by necessity value-laden, too. That is due to the key of similarity used in analogical inference. The existence of such similarity that legal analogy is justified cannot be defined with mere objective or cognitive criteria.

(c) Practical reasoning, i.e. the discretion of the consequences of a legal decision, is value-bound, as well. The consequences of a legal decision may be either causal (concerning the real world effects of the decision) or systemic (concerning the effects the decision has on the legal system) in nature. In both cases, the consequences of the decision are observable with the help of cognitive criteria. The choice among the different interpretation alternatives leading to the different kind of consequences, however, is partly value-laden, since the consequences have to be ranked into a preference order.

(d) There may be also a direct reference to a certain value or moral principle in the justification of a legal decision. Let us take the example of the Abortion Act in Finland. According to the law, abortion is legal only on the ground of the reasons mentioned in the enactment. One of the acceptable grounds for abortion is called "social reasons". The contents of this concept is determined by e.g. such considerations as the value of life itself, the value of the health of the mother, and the social well-being of both the mother and the child. Similar value-bound interpretations can be traced in other parts of family law, too; for instance, in the interpretation of the legal grounds for divorce. One could state quite generally that ethics and moral points of view enter legal justification so soon as a legal norm concerns man as a moral being.

The existence of the values inherent in legal interpretation does not, however, mean that the legal interpreter would always base the decision on his very own evaluations. If e.g. in the field of the contract law the interpretation outcome is based on a comparison of the interests held by the customer and the seller, the decision reached may as well reflect the prevailing social values, as conceived by the interpreter. That is the case e.g. in the interpretation of an agreement made by two ordinary citizens. The interpreter may thus approach the issue from the "external point of view". However, this interpretation standpoint is not a proper norm standpoint. It will become such only after the interpreter himself has made a choice in the sense meant in points (a) to (d). A norm standpoint is conceivable in the legal relation between a customer and a seller for instance when the one is a private citizen and the other a representative of the public administration. The outcome of the case may then depend on the attitude the interpreter has towards public administration. If he is inclined to systematically favor individual interests at the expense of collective interests, his interpretations will tend to protect the former's interests in conflict situations. In such a case, the interpreter does not confine himself to merely expressing "objectively" the currently prevailing social values, but makes a choice of his own. The same issue is illustrated also with the interpretations of family law referred to above. In what follows, it is just that kind of value compositions that will be treated.

We divide things into valuable and unvaluable. A value (and correspondingly a nonvalue), according to this, is thus a property of a state of affairs or an object. It is the property of being valuable. The object *X* has the property *Y*. An evaluation, in turn, is the belief of a subject that a certain matter has or does not have a value. An evaluation is thus always tied to the subject. *A* has his evaluations, *B* has his, and so on. Evaluation is of form: "*X* has the value (property) *Y*".[61]

A value is not an objective property in the same sense as for example hardness or softness can be properties of an object. It is not possible either to derive values from objective matters nor justify them with objective matters without something being left over. For example, it is not possible to demonstrate that the biological needs of a person objectively justify some value. Let us take an illustration. We can say that food is necessary for man in order to maintain his production of energy and, through this, the propagation of the human species. This is a biological fact, which does not need to be proved here. Even so, the ensurance of food for all persons is not an objective value. Biological necessity is something else than the value of nutrition. When we say that it is valuable to ensure food for everyone, we have given the matter this value. Whether we admit it or not, evaluations have become twisted around the biological proposition. The survival of every person is doubtless something which, in the name of humanity, should be given every support, but the biological need for food as a fact does not make survival a value in itself. If, for example, someone states that the conditions for survival should only be ensured for those who are the "best of the human species", we regard this person as inhuman and we are not prepared to support his views. But we cannot defend our own views (solely) on the basis of the biological need for food. Something more slips into our reasoning. It includes the respect for human life as a value in itself. It is true that this, in turn, can be justified with different empirical arguments, but at some stage the tie between values and matters belonging to reality is cut off.

The statement of "X is good" may, however, be of a technical nature only. For instance, a knife can be good for cutting a branch of a tree. Here, a certain thing is a proper means for a certain end (or goal). The statement "X is good" is true or false dependent on the existing state of affairs. This kind of goodness is not interesting from the actual point of view of this approach. The special problematics is connected with the so-called intrinsic values. There one cannot find out a means-end-relation.

It follows from the above that for example such intrinsic value as "good" is not, in a sense, objectively controllable. Therefore, I do not deal with the problem "What is the nature of values?" at all. Instead of this, an attempt has been made to analyse the structure of the evaluations and, especially, the structure of their justification. The statement, "X is good" is not a mere description of the speaker's attitudes, standpoints of psychological state any more than of some special entity. It is not a question of a statement that would correspond a state of affairs. If *A* says that *X* is good, and *B* contradicts this statement, both can stick to their positions without it being possible to demonstrate on an objective basis that the position of one of them is wrong. In this respect, evaluations concerning intrinsic values differ from propositions of fact. If a statement of fact (p) is true its negation (statement$\sim p$) cannot also be true at the same time. If in turn statement q says that X is good as an intrinsic value, its negation, $\sim q$, can justifiably be valid at the same time. The negation of this kind of value judgement is something other than a negation of a statement of fact.

As Timothy Stroup puts it, there is no rational way to settle the dispute between *A* and *B*, because there are always various non-rational methods involved in the dispute.[62] Hence, if A or B really succeed in having the other one change his mind, this is due to the fact that the persuasion of the first has led to a result. If it is truly a question of factual and ultimate evaluations (intrinsic values), the joining of the opinions cannot be the consequence of the presentation of objective justification. This means, in a somewhat different point of view, that it is impossible to state on a universal level that something is good or good in itself.

When defined in this way, subjectivity and relativity do not, however, lead evaluations to arbitrariness, although the diversity of opinion is the rule in the moral realm. There are no reasons to subordinate ourselves to the naive relativism according to which the mere facts of moral disagreement show that no single moral principle can be absolutely right. The terms "subjectivity" and "relativity" do not say anything about whether it is possible to solidify evaluations somewhat. Above all, the following question is left open: is it possible to justify evaluations in a way that in at least some sense would allow us to speak of the control in their connections? Taking into consideration the bonds between evaluations and legal interpretation, this at the same time refers to the question of the rationality of argumentation and the philosophical conditions of rationality.

Let us take as the point of departure the following proposition: "*X* is good". If we do not agree, we must ask the following question: "Why?" Depending on the point of departure, the answer could be, for example, that *X* is good because it causes such-and-such consequences. Moral philosophers would call such justification teleological: it refers to the consequences of a matter or of an act. Hence, the problem lies in the means-end relation and the technical evaluation of this kind may be true or false depending on the facts. The other type of answers can be called deontological. In this case, the justification refers to a norm that gives support to the evaluation. The supporting norm that covers the case at issue may be e.g. teleological as to its nature. Even after these answers, however, it is possible to ask a new question: "Why is this so?" This question does not refer to the means-end relation but to the ends at issue. The chain of questions and answers can thus be continued, and every answer brings something new to the concept of "good" (or "the best") ends. But at some stage we reach a limit. At the end of the chain of answers, it is no longer possible to present further justification. *X* is simply regarded as good because it causes such-and-such good ends or, briefly, *X* is good because it *is* good.

This means that evaluations can be justified to a certain limit, but the last justification presented will not be fixed. If in this situation someone else presents different opinions as to the value of *X*, nothing can be done to remove the disagreement. The fact that the chain of justification has been revealed, however, is not meaningless. To the extent that it is at all possible, the parties have ascertained the opinions of each other, and have found the ultimate cause of disagreement.

Thus also discussion of rationality of evaluations is in some sense possible, and in another not. An ultimate evaluation can be understood as true in relation to a system of values. Hence, within the system of values chosen it is possible in the strong sense of the word to present, on a rational basis, arguments on behalf of an evaluation. On the other hand, the system of values itself is not something that can be justified on an objective basis, and with reference to this side of the matter there is reason to state that every evaluation is relative as to its nature.

Does this mean that value systems in themselves are arbitrary matters and evaluations, in the end, are depending on the "taste" of a person? My answer is negative. As Edward Westermarck pointed out, as far as differences of moral opinion depend on knowledge or ignorance of facts, on specific religious or superstitious beliefs, on different degrees of reflection, or on different conditions of social life or other external circumstances, they do not clash with that universality which is implied in the notion of the objective validity of moral judgements. This is so because there is substantial uniformity in the structure of human beings.[63] I share Westermarck's opinion as far as the cognitive causes for moral controversy are concerned but my reasons for this conclusion are of a different kind.

In societal praxis, value systems are not created autonomously by individuals or a group. In the logical sense it is only possible to "decide" on the adoption of a system of values. Why? My own view, which attempts to eliminate extreme conventionalism, is based on a certain interpretation of the concept "form of life". To get somewhat ahead of the discussion, I would argue that every evaluative statement is connected to a complex totality of other statements. Following Ludwig Wittgenstein one can speak about a nest of statements. This nest of statements is not, however, an arbitrary one. As a whole it is connected to a certain basis, i.e. to the form of life. This means that value systems are "bound to our life", they are connected to our "life practice". Thus, also the criteria of evaluations are locked outside of us.

This means roughly the same thing as what R. M. Hare refers to when he writes, ". . . in preferring what we prefer, morality compells us to accomodate ourselves to the preferences of others, and this has the effect that when we are thinking morally and doing it rationally we shall all prefer the same moral prescriptions about matters which affect other people."[64] On one hand, Hare calls his position non-descriptivism and on the other hand, he terms it rational universal prescriptivism. In this regard, my train of thought runs as follows.

As an individual, a person can hold any opinions he wishes, also in regards to values and moral principles. But if he wishes to take part in social interaction, he must take other persons into consideration. Morals is a way of generalizing, it is participation in social interaction and communication. In this context an individual cannot act autonomously in any way he wishes. We can also go one step further.

A social community is a cooperative community. Open and democratic social life cannot allow everyone his own code of values. It can also not allow each individual to rely merely on intuition in support of his value judgements. Social life requires participation in forms of joint activities. It must be possible to publicly control a person's value judgements. And what is the most important, the controlling of these value judgements must fulfill the criteria of rationality. Also it must submit to *D*-rationality. The value judgements must be supported with as rational a justification as possible. It is not, for example, rational to regard something which in principle surpasses the actual (physical) potential of people as valuable. The practical nature of rationality respects the capacity of people as well as human necessity. Several types of justification can be given to this view. In the following, I shall try to give justification on the basis of some of Ludwig Wittgenstein's insights. With the help of these insights, I shall try to demonstrate that it is possible to justify a non-descriptive and yet rational theory of value.

At times it has been said that there is no room in Wittgensteinian philosophy for ethics or moral standpoints. This view would appear to receive support from the fact that Wittgenstein did not have a specific theory of value, and for example his work "On Certainty" only deals with what I shall call the certainty basis of "empirical" propositions. As Henry Le Roy Finch observes, such a view seems to be in error.[65] As a matter of fact, ethics is immanently to be found in Wittgenstein's thought. I shall take up only one aspect of the problem; one that has the closest bearing to our subject.

The concept of action plays, as we have observed, a key role in the later philosophy of Wittgenstein. The language game is action, and the basis of the language game lies in action, in (primitive) acts that constitute forms of life. An ethical choice (an expression of a value judgement), in turn, is the same as playing with a language game. It is action, and at the same time its basis is to be found in certain acts.

In a way, hidden here is the core of Wittgenstein's ethics. Ethical choices are based on acts, and these acts in turn are ultimately unjustified. They are only bound to our form of life; we could say that the justification is there, in our life. Henry Le Roy Finch writes, "We have in Wittgenstein's philosophy (unnamed but presupposed) a primal freedom underlying language, forms of life, rites and ceremonies, religious belief and thinking, all of which have their source in this primal groundlessness".[66]

Thus, Wittgenstein does not give ethical choices anything external, no measure, no standard which would be given once and for all and which could be constructed so that every ethical choice can be weighed with that standard. All action is of value to the extent that it arises selflessly out of primal groundlessness.

Every value judgement can be justified within the framework of a game – it is this game that gives the measures of the evaluation – but the game itself cannot be justified. In this sense it is impossible to have rational justification between forms of life. Going from one form of life to another – and thus going from one value system to another – is a matter of persuasion.

Paul Taylor considers the same matter and observes that the basic norms of a certain value system are simply accepted. Certain norms become basic norms by "simply the fact that the person accepts them as supreme whenever he is asked to justify the standards and rules he has adopted".[67] What is interesting in this connection, at the same time, is that Taylor connects value systems specifically with forms of life. He writes, "A way of life may include a moral system, an aesthetic system, a political system, a system of etiquette and so on. Each system is made up of standards and rules arranged hierarchically, and all systems together are arranged hierarchically."[68] On the other hand, it does not appear to be quite clear to Taylor how the choice between different value systems takes place, and it is here that the difference lies, in my view, with what has been said in the foregoing. If I have understood him correctly, Taylor tends to think that the choice between value systems is in some way rational. Then, however, the connection with the form of life is cut off in the sense referred to above. As has been said, the form of life is ultimately action. It is not a matter for rational choice; it creates the *basis* for rational choice.

Thus, the relativity of evaluations is exactly as large as the array of language games and forms of life. This, however, does not lead us to chaos and arbitrariness. As has often been repeated, there is a relationship of family resemblance between forms of life. Thus, we can point out a number of criteria for value judgements so that these criteria "overlap" each other. And it is specifically this feature which makes the value relativism that I defend "moderately relativistic". If there is sufficient family resemblance among forms of life (language games), then it is possible to reach a *consensus* on the criteria of evaluation between those who belong to different forms of life. Not only do they understand each other, they are also capable of accepting the views of each other, even if this acceptance is *not* based on rational grounds. Very roughly speaking, we can speak of "compromises".

In the case, again, that there is not sufficient "family resemblance", consensus is not possible. It is here that the chasm between forms of life is the easiest to observe. In the present world, it is true, there is a relationship between most forms of life. Those in the different forms can thus understand each other. Even so, the forms of life may differ from each other in such a basic way that the acceptance of value-based positions becomes impossible. I shall try to illustrate my ideas with terminology which I have adopted from Charles Taylor.[69]

In order to clarify certain matters related to the understanding of social behaviour and the process of making social behaviour understandable, Taylor adopts the concept of "common meaning". An example of common meaning could be the concept of "the Finnish way of life". In a very general sense, this way of life keeps Finnish society together. A common meaning, however, is not the same thing as the mutual directions of the evaluations that different individuals have adopted. With this last comment I refer to the case where different people evaluate something in the same or in a similar way. A common meaning can be interpreted in different ways. Different groups may have different views of what the Finnish way of life contains. This feature also puts different social groups on a collision course. It can be said that if a common meaning is the force that holds Finnish society together (in a conceptual sense), the interpretation of the common meaning is a matter for the group supporting it. Let us denote the common meaning with Y. Interpretation Y_1 of the common meaning is based on the similarly directed evaluations of the members of a certain group on how matters should be in Finnish society. Another interpretation is based in a corresponding way on evaluations, but its contents differ from Y_1, as is the case with a third interpretation, and so on.

An "agreement" between two interpretations can be reached with sufficient family resemblance on how the common form of life should be understood. On this precondition, *A* and *B*, representing different interpretations of the common meaning, may accept a compromise. This is the most that human beings can achieve in the moral discretion. As Timothy Stroup says, "the point of ultimate moral disputes, when they really exist, is to get you to shift your pattern to something more like mine, and if this cannot be done, then it cannot be done by the objectivist or by the relativist". Referring to Edward Westermarck, Stroup continues "our moral judgements, instead of being complacent towards ourselves and critical of others, will through greater understanding become more critical of ourselves and more generous towards other persons and their circumstances".[70] This is in accord with the central idea of this contribution. The rational argumentation concerning evaluations will not prove to be useless although the ultimate differences in opinion are based on non-rational criteria.

On the other hand, the incommensurability of two interpretations does not mean that there are only two or, in every case, a very limited number of interpretations for the common meaning. On the contrary, there is a whole net of such interpretations valid at the same time. An individual may belong to more than one interpretation depending on the life situations. Hence, a person *A* may accept the interpretation Y_1 as far as the sexual morality is concerned but, at the same time, he belongs to the group that accepts the interpretation Y_2 concerning the basic assumptions of the economic order of society. From a slightly different point of view one can say that the concepts of form of life and of common meaning consist of an enormous net of fragments and that a certain individual may participate in some but not necessarily in every one of them. In saying this, however, we leave the concept of the form of life itself open.

2.6. *Knowledge, Certainty and Form of Life*

From 1949 to 1951 Wittgenstein dealt primarily with the problem of knowledge and certainty; it might be more to the point to say that he tried to demonstrate the difference between these concepts. One point of departure which is of importance in this connection is the conceptual distinction between knowledge and belief. The statement, "I believe", according to Wittgenstein, has subjective ("personal") truth. That statement is an expression: it does not need to be justified although it can be based on certain grounds. In a way such justification would not belong to the "logics" of the language game of belief.[71] If I have, for instance, a crossing of two paths before me, I can believe – on certain grounds – that path *A* is the proper one. Afterwards, my belief may be wrong. Then I must say that I did not know how the things were. However, also in this case I believed things to be in a certain way.

I can have believed it also without any grounds; I only believed. In this sense, justification does not belong as a necessary element to the "logic" of the believing-game. If, instead, I aver that I know something, I must be prepared to present justification for my position. This is the difference in respect of belief. In order for someone else to be able to formulate a view over how something can be known, we must know the language game that is played with the concept of knowledge. We must be able to play this game. When we are able to play it, we know the type of justification that should be presented in support of a proposition regarding knowledge. This is not to say that concrete arguments in an individual situation could not be called in question. On the contrary, calling the arguments in question is a natural part of the language game played with the notion of knowledge. This brings us to another problem, a problem that deals with the justification of arguments.

The warrants and arguments presented to back up an assertion form a kind of chain. This chain must be continued every time when the other party calls in question the warrants that have been put forward at a certain point in the chain. Let us briefly deal with the analogy between the arguments for interpretative standpoint and the strands of a rope: using these terms one also might say that the rope must be strengthened every time when the twine, in the light of an additional question, turns out to be too weak. However, this can not be continued *ad infinitum*. We can not doubt everything. "If you tried to doubt everything you would not get as far as doubting anything. The game of doubting itself presupposes certainty."[72] This being so, there must be some end point for putting forward grounds and justifications. There are times when we must be able to say: this rope does bear the strain, or, as Wittgenstein sees this, we must be able to trust something. However, bringing the doubt to an end is not "hasty". It is part of judging. For instance, if I supposed that all our calculations were uncertain, people would say that I am crazy and not that I am in error.[73]

However, the "ultimate foundations" of our judging, the columns supporting judgements, do not lie in our experience in the sense that we were able to find out the terminal point of the justification chain by learning from experience.[74] The ultimate links in the chain of arguments are propositions that "have a peculiar . . . role in the system of our empirical propositions".[75] The idea here is, I think, that these terminal points precede experience as well as the knowledge based on it. Bit by bit a system of what we believe is formed. In this system, "some things stand unshakeably fast and some are more or less liable to shift. What stands fast does so, not because it is intrinsically obvious or convincing; it is rather held fast by what lies around it".[76] In saying this Wittgenstein thinks that all argumentation every time takes place within some system (i.e., language game)[77] and that this system is fixed by certain foundations that will not be doubted any more. These foundations are not given to us in everyday experience. Neither do we realize them by means of intuition (i.e., "inward insight"). They are *given* to us. "Sure evidence is what we accept as sure".[78] Thus the assumption that the earth has existed long before my birth is neither an experiential statement nor an intuitive realization. It is "part of the whole picture which forms the starting-point of belief for me".[79]

This being so, every justification of an assertion presupposes that some part of the statements are beforehand fixed up in something. But "what I hold fast to is not *one* proposition but a nest of propositions", Wittgenstein says.[80] To use again the metaphor about the rope, the binding part is not one individual strand but a whole twine of strands between which a new strand, that is, the proposition at issue will be attached. Wittgenstein observes that the "nest" of statements is in a way fused into the foundations of our language games.[81] This nest forms the frame for all our considerations about truth and falsity, rightness and wrongness. At the same time, this is the foundation that makes linguistic communication possible. Without this foundation precising the bestowing of meaning, communication would dissolve.[82]

The foregoing already constrains Wittgenstein's implicit position on the relationship between knowledge and certainty. Knowledge presupposes the possibility of doubt as well as justification. What we take for certain, that we take for certain without any warrants, and we no more doubt it. And this is how certainty is a precondition of all knowledge.

When speaking of the "nest" of propositions that form the common ground of our knowledge Wittgenstein often uses the term "picture of the world" (*Weltbild*).[83] The world-picture should not be understood as a coherent and steadfast set of sentences. On the contrary, its boundaries are vacillating, and the set of sentences itself consists of a huge number of subsystems. Every such subsystem is as if a fragment of the world-picture, one of the interlocking parts of the whole. The fragments of the world-picture, in their turn, are the basis of language games. They fix the ultimate links of the language games. If we bear in mind the above considerations about the family resemblance of language games, we can easily grasp the idea of the subsystems of the world-picture being "interlocked". If we adopt the terminology of G. H. von Wright and call the set of sentences that forms the picture of the world preknowledge (*Vorwissen*), we may, following him, say that every language game has a foundation that forms a fragment of the game player's pre-knowledge.[84] This brings us to the core themes of the present discourse.

For Wittgenstein, the world-picture is not a matter of satisfying oneself of its correctness. "It is the inherited background against which I distinguish between true and false".[85] The sentences belonging to the picture of the world have a role not unlike that of the rules of a game. But the picture of the world is not fixed once and for all. It is not a petrification but something that is in the state of flux. The picture of the world is a dynamic foundation.[86] Paralleled by Wittgenstein with the bank of a river. The bank slowly changes its shape and yet every moment is somewhere; it determines the direction of the stream all the time. This world-picture dynamics is related with aspects that must be briefly discussed here before I pass on to a synthesis.

As its very bottom, the picture of the world is not a propositional matter. Rather we should say that the foundation of the picture lies in the non-propositional phenomenon called by Wittgenstein the form of life. Referring to this, he observes that the terminal point of the argumentation chain does not involve the realization (i.e., the "seeing") of some holding ground but the terminal point lies in our acting.[87] The form of life is a matter of action, of acts.[88] We shape our form of life with our action, and in our action ultimately are shown the things in which we trust. One also may say: the fact that I am able to act in a certain way in a certain situation shows that I belong to a certain form of life.

In this connection there is some reason to point out that it is possible to understand the form of life (and its propositional manifestation, the picture of the world) as an, as it were, "multilayered" phenomenon. Its founding layer consists of very elementary activities – the basic constituents of human culture. These in their turn make possible, say, a form of life in which there exist commands, prohibitions and permissions. At some stage legal norms interweave with the form of life, albeit this happens at a very high level of abstraction. This is how the network of the world-picture ("seamless net of subsystems", as von Wright puts it) little by little takes its form.

We are now in a position to understand what the idea about language being a manifestation of the form of life ultimately means. The form of life is the practical, non-propositional "phase" of the picture. On the other hand, the world-picture, or more correctly speaking, the fragment of the world-picture forms the foundation for a (certain) language game.

When Wittgenstein says that an expression receives its meaning in the use of language, he thinks that the meaning becomes apparent in the way that the language game is played. It is not a question of language in itself, as an autonomous phenomenon. On the contrary, an individual expression is a part of linguistic activity, i.e. of a language game. This, in turn, stands in connection with a form of life. Understanding action (the playing of a game) is not possible unless there are some common rules of action. To borrow the words of Karl-Otto Apel; language games are entities which combine the use of language, the form of life and the way of looking at the world.[89]

Lauri Mehtonen writes about the same matter in the following words: "Thus the study of a language game, the analysis of different semantic dimensions, is the study of one but not the only element in a totality (the form of life), and the carrying out of this study assumes that it be placed as one element in the totality where the focus is the form of life as a dynamic whole" (translated here)[90]. In other words, the analysis of language is always and in all circumstances the analysis of the form of life. Language, thought and form of life are combined in a way that always makes so-called language problems "material questions".

If we try to abstract the language game from its moorings, we cannot understand language. Language as action becomes understandable only when it is seen against its connections to the form of life. Words are "at home" within a form of life. Through this, belonging to a certain form of life is a requirement for participation in the language game. And *vice versa*: playing a language game is participation in a form of life. If a person is not a participant, he cannot understand the language, nor can he himself be understood.

Going from one form of life to another is not a matter for rational argumentation. Argumentation is only possible within the framework of a form of life. Wittgenstein observes that going from one form of life to another can only take place through some sort of persuasion.[91] If we argue over something with someone who belongs to another form of life, we cannot influence him through rational arguments. We must try to persuade him to join us and, thus, we must persuade him to change his form of life and his world picture.

Let us now return to the concept of rational acceptance. What connection does it have with the analysis of the form of life? I believe that the connection must be sought in three directions. First of all, the concept of the form of life has significance from the point of view of the concept of interpretation itself. In the foregoing, interpretation has been understood as a so-called linguistic matter. The focus of interpretation is language, and interpretation takes place through the use of language. This can easily give rise to wrong images of what interpretation is. It is often thought that interpretation is purely a semantic phenomenon. According to this view, interpretation deals with words and sentences without going outside of language, to reality itself. Interpretation is thus solely a linguistic matter (a *Sprachprobleme*). Those who have this view have misunderstood the concept of language. If language, as a semantic category, is seen together with the form of life, and the action element in language is picked out, the analysis of language can specifically be said to be the analysis of matters (of *Sachprobleme*). The analysis of language is the analysis of the form of life. Through it we can specifically understand our life, the acts of which our form of life is composed.

There is also a connection between the concepts of rational acceptability and the form of life in another sense. This connection has to do with values and evaluations. An example: A and B are members of the same form of life, F. They have the same shared meanings of matters. In other words, their common language makes it possible for them to understand one another. The common form of life F, however, can permit many different variations, different sections of the form of life. Let us assume two such sections, F_1 and F_2. Each section is matched by its so-called propositional side, i.e. its world picture. In this case there are two world pictures, WP_1 and WP_2. Within the framework of the world pictures, two different language games are played. Let us also assume that the difference between the world pictures is based (at least in part) on different acts. I shall call them "choices". A choice is a situation where it is possible to do I_1 and I_2, and I_1 is done. Within the framework of the world picture, it is possible to justify certain choices. This will be done by means of other acts. There are, however, basic acts that we cannot justify on a rational basis. They are merely (primitive) acts. Even so, they constitute in part the basis of the section of the form of life (F_1/F_2) and furthermore, the basis of the world picture. From this point of view, it would appear to be possible to say – as observed by Henry Le Roy Finch – that the choices are immanently in the concept of the form of life. When we are participants in the acts we are participants in a certain section of the world picture. This, in turn, means that perhaps we do not totally *accept* a world picture built on the basis of other basic acts and choices even though, through the common form of life foundation, we can understand these other choices. We understand them because we have a sufficient number of common terms to understand them. WP_1 and WP_2 have a sufficient family resemblance. Going from one world picture (WP_1) to another (WP_2), on the other hand, is always a nonrational matter. It is also a choice that cannot be justified.

Hence, belonging to a certain section of a form of life is not ultimately a matter of autonomous choice. We are participants in them since we are participants in an inherited background, to use a Wittgensteinian phrase. Complex social mechanisms tie a person to his form of life. To a large degree, these processes are not recognized and in this sense they stand outside of our choices. There is not just one explanation basis for why different individuals have a common fragment of a form of life, a common world picture. The explanation is not, for example, to be found in the fact that they would represent some common (for example, an economic) interest. One can always ask what common interest is possessed by those who, in defending life in all of its forms, oppose abortion and euthanasia.

It is not the purpose of this study to deliberate over the social process through which a common world picture is formed. What is most important is to observe that a common form of life justifies also the intersubjectivity of evaluations. It allows us to understand why values are not individual in an arbitrary fashion. Evaluations receive their intersubjectivity specifically from forms of life. A form of life is always in some way and to some extent a common matter. It specifically is a form of life. An individual cannot autonomously shape for himself a completely private form of life, a world picture and a language of his own. In doing this he would isolate himself from social interaction. It is the common aspect of the form of life that makes communication – and through this, interaction – possible. It is the factor that brings about contact among people.

Thus, on one hand, the form of life is the link that ties language and reality together, and on the other hand it is the factor that creates interaction between individuals. For this reason it is utterly misleading and superficial to say that hermeneutic points of departure accept interpretation theory merely as a matter standing on the level of language. It would be as wrong to connect a view that emphasizes the relativity of values with pure arbitrariness. Social life and society in themselves create to a large extent contacts between people, and through this, values and evaluations are also social matters belonging to groups of individuals. Values are just as intersubjective as society in itself is.

What is said above is also an answer to the often presented counter argument that value relativism (noncognitivism) waters down the entire preconditions of rationality. If it is possible to justify an interpretative position on a rational basis in a satisfactory manner by using any value system whatsoever, every decision would then be justified. After all, it is rational, and it is based on *some* value code. Thus we can "rationally" present arguments for interpretation I_i on the basis of the value system we have adopted. It is "just as good" a position as is another interpretation, I_j, which is built on the basis of a different value code.

Such criticism, which emphasizes the cognitive features of value theory, does not do justice to the relativism that has been outlined above. The purpose is not to argue that any value system whatsoever is as relevant socially as from the point of view of the ideology of legal certainty. On the contrary, those values which can generally be accepted in society are significant from this point of view. As it is here that there lies an important watershed between moderate value relativism and various types of cognitive value theories, there is reason to examine that matter from yet another point of view.[92]

In the foregoing, the point of departure has been that an interpretation is directed at a certain recipient, either an individual or a group. In speaking of acceptability, we assumed that the recipient is a group called "the legal community". In the theory of argumentation, the recipient group has generally been called the audience or the auditory. In a way, this is the "human" side of the form of life. The audience is composed of those individuals who share a common form of life. And it is precisely in this sense that the concept of the audience is in a key position from the point of view of moderate value relativism.

2.7. *The Audience and the Form of Life*

2.7.1. *Perelman's theory of the audience.* In the theory of knowledge, a traditional distinction has been made between generalization on the basis of experience (induction) and logical reasoning (deduction). One of Chaim Perelman's leading ideas has been the supplementing of this dual view with other forms of rational reasoning.[93] The approach that he represents has been called new rhetorics. It can just as well be called, following Robert Alexy, the "practical use of reason" ("der praktische Gebrauch der Vernunft").[94]

Perelman calls logical reasoning "demonstration". The goal of new rhetorics is to enrich the demonstration or, in Perelman's own words, "The new rhetoric does not aim at displacing or replacing formal logic, but at adding to it a field of reasoning that, up to now, has escaped all efforts at rationalization, namely, practical reasoning."[95]

The key concept in Perelman's argumentation theory is the audience (*auditoire*). Justification is always presented to someone, imagined or real. The recipient can be a concrete group, for example the listeners at a lecture, the members of a court or of a committee of Parliament. When the justification is presented to a concrete group, it is often a question of persuasion.[96] Depending on the situation, the justification is either effective or ineffective. The persuasion either succeeds or it does not do it. Rational argumentation, in turn, is according to Perelman directed to a so-called universal audience. This is the audience where the members accept the position on the basis of rational arguments after they have become convinced of the justification of the position. In this context Perelman speaks of convincing as the opposite of persuasion.[97] The justification used in convincing is sound ("valuable") as opposed to the arguments used in persuasion, which merely involve efficacy. The acceptance by the universal audience is thus a criterion of rational and objective argumentation.[98]

The universal audience is composed of enlightened persons who are capable of using justification if they make use of this capability. Briefly stated, all "rational" persons belong to the universal audience. It is thus an ideal audience: no one has the possibility of assuming that he is directing his arguments at the universal audience so that every possible member of the audience would *de facto* take a position on the matter.

What is important in the concept of the universal audience used by Perelman is that also value judgements receive an objective nature. Perelman's point of departure is that a value judgement is reasonably justified only when everyone (every reasonable person) can accept it.[99] Thus, those evaluations which pass through the sieve of acceptance of the universal audience at the same time become rationally justified and receive propositions relating to reality.[100]

2.7.2. *Some clarifications.* Perelman's theory of the audience offers a good basis for the continuation of the discussion. The audience can primarily be defined as a group which accepts the general conditions of rationality and where the value system that is the basis of the interpretative position has been accepted. Perelman's position on the concept of the audience, however, has some ambiguous details. For example, he claims that the universal audience, although it is ideal, is bound both socially and culturally. Thus, in part, it depends on contingent matters. Can the audience, however, at the same time be both universal and something that is tied to contingent facts? Answering this question requires a further development of the concept of the audience.

First of all, we must distinguish between two levels of notions, on one hand, the separation between a concrete and an ideal audience, and on the other hand, between a universal and a particular audience. There is a need to analyze these combinations of concepts in somewhat greater detail.

2.7.2.1. *The concrete audience.* A concrete audience can be composed of one or more persons. The number of persons, however, is always limited. Such an audience is real; it exists. Its members are physically existing individuals. There can be two types of a concrete audience:

(a) A universal concrete audience is composed of all the human individuals living on the world at moment t_i, regardless of their other properties. When defined in this way, the number of persons in the concrete audience is constantly changing. Even so, at every moment, it is real.

With an eye on argumentation, there are many problems related to a concrete audience that is regarded as universal. It is true that the interpreter can be imagined to direct his arguments at all the members of this audience, but it would be unrealistic to think that the arguments would even come to the attention of each and every member. Thus, we could also not think that the arguments would receive the acceptance of the audience in question. One cannot accept something which one is not aware of. For the same reason, it is impossible to even speak of acceptability. In the theory of argumentation, therefore, this type of audience does not have any real significance.

(b) A particular and at the same time concrete audience is composed of those really existing persons who fulfill the characteristics set for the audience. In the foregoing, the listeners at a lecture and the members of a committee of Parliament to whom a standpoint on a certain problem in the interpretation of law has been presented were given as examples.

We can also regard as a concrete audience one in which the members can be identified on the basis of certain characteristics even though the interpretative position and/or its justification has not come to the attention of every member. In this respect a particular audience differs from the universal one referred to above. If we consider the element of being aware of something, it would perhaps be proper to speak of an individualized audience or an audience which can be individualized. In the former, each member even in reality is aware of the position that is being discussed. This is the case in regard to the listeners at a lecture – at least with certain reservations. In the latter, this condition has not been met, but in principle the position can be brought to the attention of every member. An example of the latter type of audience is the group formed by those who have graduated in law in Finland.

If a particular audience is defined in the foregoing manner, an interpretative position is either acceptable or not acceptable in a certain audience. For example, it is possible that some of the listeners at a lecture accept the view of the lecturer, while others do not. This has significance from the point of view of rational acceptability.

A justification directed at a particular audience may be rational. The interpreter may follow the conditions of rationality. It is also possible, however, that the sole intention of the lecturer is to influence the audience through persuasion. In this case, the justification is nonrational, or it at least has nonrational elements. But no matter how rational the justification itself is, the definition of the audience accepted above does not give any guarantees of rational acceptability. Nothing entitles us to expect that for example a concrete audience, A_i, will behave rationally when considering the content of an interpretative position. The possible acceptance may be based purely on random factors, for example the authority of the interpreter. The factor that the position, for example, is largely accepted by lawyers is not necessarily a consequence of rational consideration. In principle also the so-called prevailing opinion may be built completely on nonrational points of view. Therefore, a particular and concrete audience does not offer a basis for the further development of the idea of rational acceptance. The ultimate content of the expectation of legal certainty is not to be found in the fact that a certain concrete group, no matter how large, accepts an interpretation, nor is it to be found in the fact that it can be accepted in such a group. The element of rationality is in a key position.

What has been said above is true also of a particular audience where the members are tied to the evidence of the same reality and to the same values. Such a group could, for example, be the group of judges who think in the same way in respect to society. There is no guarantee that when these criteria prevail the interpretative position would be accepted on the basis of rational consideration. It is just as possible that it will strike a responding chord due to social psychological factors without each member of the group considering the basis of the position. It is also possible that the acceptance is found through physical or mental coercion, as could be the case in a dictatorship. As has already been observed, such a position has nothing to do with the so-called expectations of legal certainty.

For these reasons neither a universal nor a particular concrete audience can form the basis for the idea of rational acceptability. Another concept of the audience must be taken as assistance – the ideal audience.

2.7.2.2. *The ideal audience.* Once again there is reason to distinguish between two types of audience. Not only do they help in understanding Perelman's theory of the audience outlined above, but they also help in clarifying the concept of the audience adopted in this study.

(a) An ideal audience can be universal. Such an audience, for example, is to be found in the audience formed of "all rational persons" referred to by Perelman. It includes all those who are enlightened in the sense that they are capable of rational discourse. As Robert Alexy has observed, Perelman's concept of the universal audience corresponds to the concept adopted by Jürgen Habermas, the "Ideale Sprechsituation". In such a situation all the participants are in the same position. The possibility of any persuasion and manipulation has been eliminated.

If we accept the view that it is also possible to justify evaluations through rational discourse in a way that can lead to agreement being reached in the audience, we have come to some kind of cognitive value theory. As has been observed earlier, Perelman's presentation would appear to refer to such a possibility. This means that in a universal audience, the positions of two members who originally had different views can be brought together by the introduction of evidence. The moral philosophical choice that lies at the basis of this study does not accept this thesis of convergence. For this reason the concept of the universal audience, in the sense used here, cannot offer a basis for rational acceptability. There remains a fourth possibility, i.e. the one that the present study relies upon.

(b) The particular ideal audience is defined through the use of two criteria. First of all, its members bind themselves to the rules of rational discourse. In this respect, this type of audience resembles the type just dealt with above. The difference lies in the fact that the members of the particular audience have adopted common values. The audience is tied to a certain form of life, to use a Wittgensteinian phrase.

This audience differs from the concrete audience in an important respect. It is assumed that its members fulfill the condition of rationality. As this demand is not normally adequate in respect of societal reality, it is thus specifically a question of an ideal audience. However, it is not universal in the sense used by Perelman, since there is no assumption of universal (objective) values lying behind it. On the contrary, it meets another condition set by Perelman. An ideal particular audience is culturally and socially determined.

2.7.3. *Rational acceptability as a regulative principle for legal dogmatics.* To summarize what has been said above, two persons, *A* and *B*, can meet the condition of rationality, but even so, their system of values may differ in respect of the basic values. For example, they may have adopted different positions on sexual morals, positions which cannot be brought together on rational grounds. *A* and *B* then belong to different audiences. On the other hand, this does not mean that *A* and *B* cannot understand each other. They can and usually do have a common form of life, more basic than the above; this gives them a common language. A different attitude towards a certain moral principle, in addition, does not mean that *A* and *B* cannot have the possibility of agreeing in some other respect, shall we say in respect of the economic basis of society. In this last respect, they are members of the same audience. In other words, a person may be a participant in a number of audiences according to the matter that is being dealt with in the interpretation. In this way of thinking, society is an enormous, interlocking and hierarchical network of opinions (world pictures). Thus, an audience theory based on relativism does not permit an either/or situation with black and white alternatives.[101]

Just as little is such an audience theory a consequence – let this be repeated once more – of a superindividualistic opinion of evaluations and, further, of legal interpretations. The members of a certain society are participants in relatively uniform forms of life, where there are dividing lines separating individuals into camps only in respect of certain basic values. Social life in itself shows that people are capable of far-reaching communication, even of far-reaching communication on what is essential in society. It is on this basis that the management of our everyday social affairs takes place. Participation in a common form of life (or in a fragment of it) creates the requirements for joint activity which in turn makes the birth of consensus possible.

As a matter of fact we have thus come to one of the central contentions of this study. An ideal and particular audience is a group in which a rational consensus can be achieved. This has great significance from the point of view of the societal relevance of interpretations in legal dogmatics. In many connections in the foregoing we have emphasized the nature of justification of interpretative standpoints as a dialogue. Justification succeeds if and only if we have convinced an addressee accepting the principles of *D*-rationality that it is right to accept the offered interpretation. This specifically means that the parties of the dialogue have, on a rational basis, achieved consensus on the matter. According to this, an interpretative standpoint which is supported by the greatest rational consensus has the greatest societal relevance. This idea calls for some clarification.

Let us assume that community *C* only consists of members who bind themselves to the principles of *D*-rationality, and that there are more than two members. Let us also assume that the members fulfill the additional criteria on the basis of which we can call the community a legal community. On the basis of the preceding discussion, we can denote the community as an ideal audience. The majority of the members accept value system *V*. It is these members who form a particular part of the ideal audience.

Let us further assume two scholars, *A* and *B*, who both belong to community *C*, i.e. both of them bind themselves to the principles of *D*-rationality. They are "sensibly reasoning" persons. Scholar *A* presents a norm standpoint P_1 to the effect that norm *N* is valid in community *C*. The other scholar, in his turn, supports standpoint P_2 that contains norm *M* (which is not identical with *N*). P_1 is according to value system *V*, and P_2 to value system *U*.

If, on legal grounds (*G*, *D*) and on the basis of value system *V*, the majority of the members of *C* could accept P_1, it is rationally acceptable in *C*. It is acceptable for the majority of those members of the community who accept the principles of *D*-rationality and, at the same time, who bind themselves to the value system *V*. In this regard, we can say that the norm standpoint of the scholar *A* has greater weight in *C* than does that of scholar *B*. The majority of the rationally reasoning members of *C* who bind themselves to value system *V* would come to the same conclusion as *A*. The views of scholar *B*, on the other hand, are shared only by the minority of *C*.

On the basis of these conditions we can derive the following regulative principle:

R: Legal dogmatics ought to attempt to reach such legal interpretations that could secure the support of the majority in a rationally reasoning legal community.

Rational acceptability as a regulative principle for legal dogmatics has the same *role* as truth has in empirical sciences. In the same way as empirical investigations are trying to approximate truth the goal of legal dogmatics is to maximalize the rational acceptability. On the other hand, rational acceptability makes it meaningful to evaluate (weigh) norm standpoints from the point of view of legal certainty.

This does not mean an acceptance of some kind of "voting theory of truth". The idea is not to say that people must have an opportunity to vote about a norm standpoint and, if the majority votes for that standpoint, it also is true in that society. There are several mistakes in this way of thinking.

First, the theory of rational acceptability does not deal with the dichotomy true/false at all. On the contrary, norm standpoints do not belong in the realm of truth. There can be more than one "true" norm standpoint in society quite dependent on the starting point. The core of the criticism concerning the theories of one right answer lies just in this conception. The refusal of one right answer is a direct consequence of the value -relativism thesis.

On the other hand, the majority referred to here is an ideal phenomenon. It is composed of rational persons who share certain evaluations relevant to the legal problem at issue. The more rational members of that ideal audience who accept the standpoint the more societal relevance this standpoint has. If the standpoint *would be* accepted by the majority of such members it would be the most relevant of all rival standpoints concerning that legal problem. No better means to "measure" the legitimacy of the norm referred to in the standpoint can be found in that society. Majority principle is, understood in this way, connected with the legitimacy problem and not with the truth problem.

From the point of view of the meaningful management of our common matters it is necessary but also sufficient that we achieve a representative consensus on the value system which is the basis of the legal order. It is the core of the Western view of democracy. Democracy certainly does not mean that we try to achieve true results. The goal is the creation of an acceptable basis of action from the point of view of the community. Through this, moderate value relativism is nothing other than part of the demand for democracy. It expresses an ideal of the management of social affairs: the goal of the management is to produce results supported by those reasonable persons who represent the values adopted and accepted in general in society. It is thus not a question of any consensus whatsoever, or a consensus that would have come about through chance. On the contrary, in this way the acceptance of legal norms is closely tied to social mechanisms. Law, its interpretation and the value consensus that is shaped through different channels in society form a whole, where one part cannot be removed without breaking the whole.

The rational acceptability has societal relevance in a very important respect. If the majority of members of the legal community, following *D*-rationality, would come to the conclusion that it is rational and reasonable to accept the standpoint presented, then this standpoint has greater societal relevance in C than any other corresponding standpoint has. The relevance is not based on persuasive arguments, wielding power or otherwise on mere formal authority, but on the *rational strength of the justification*. Such an interpretation also maximally satisfies the expectation of legal certainty in society. And furthermore, the standpoint has the maximal legitimacy in that society.

This has important consequences as regards the research strategy that is to be followed in legal dogmatics. If the strategy is based e.g. on the

Kelsenian model concerning the formal validity of legal norms one is close to the idea that legal dogmatics has merely the task of describing the proper alternative interpretations. The model of legal realism, on the other hand, emphasizes the predictive aspect of legal science. In the present study, the third alternative has been emphasized. The concept of legal validity is connected to legal certainty, and, furthermore, to the concept of the rational acceptability. As to the research strategy, this means that the justification of interpretations has the key role. Justification, furthermore, is necessary for the sound functioning of society. The official can make a decision in a hard case situation if he has certain basic information about the legal order in question. The result as such, however, is of no importance at all. It may be right or wrong, good or bad, depending upon the criteria of evaluation. If we try to criticize the decision as far as its legitimacy is concerned the problem turns out to be of quite another character. In that case we need a yardstick for our criticism. The expectation of legal certainty is perfectly fulfilled only if (a) the decision (or interpretation) falls within the legal framework, (b) the discourse proceeds in a rational way, and (c) the decision complies to the prevailing value code. This means that rational acceptability is not merely an abstract ideal but a valid and effective principle functioning in the everyday praxis. It is a guide for the decision-maker and legal scholar permitting him to find the most appropriate interpretation. In practice, the degree to which this yardstick is applied will vary because interpreters do not always follow the standards of rational discourse nor do they use the sources of law in an optimal way. Sometimes an interpretation is rejected because it departs from the prevailing value code. However, rational acceptability maintains its role as a yardstick also in those cases. It is the regulative principle for the legal community as a whole. Therefore, an interpretation can be criticized by means of rational acceptability. This "measure" guides not only an individual interpreter but also his critics. Hence rational acceptability fulfills our strictest requirements concerning the most appropriate legal reasoning in modern democratic society.

EPILOGUE

The main attention in this study has been directed at legal dogmatics. In certain respects, it differs from the application of the law. A researcher has no obligation to reach a decision. Perhaps the most important difference is the fact that legal dogmatics does not deal with concrete cases. These differences, however, are not significant from the point of view of the theory of interpretation. What is essential is that epistemically also the legal scholar is bound to the same type of factors as is the person applying the law. The decision must be produced in the same type of "circumstances". For this reason the drawing of parallels to the theory of the interpretation of law is in order.

As is the case with every corresponding theory, interpretation theory has three dimensions: an ontological, an epistemological and a methodological one. Each of these is significant from the point of view of the theory of justification. Questions dealing with knowledge and methods cannot be satisfactorily dealt with without taking a standpoint on what should be assumed to exist (in respect of interpretation of the law). Epistemology and the research methods, in turn, have some important internal dependence. For this reason this study has been systemized on the basis of this tripartite classification.

The point of departure of the study is the fact that both the focus of interpretation and the arguments that are presented as justification for the interpretation results are expressed in everyday language. Loosely stated, interpretation is a linguistic matter. On the basis of this statement, interpretation in legal dogmatics has been understood as the totality formed by so-called language games. In order for this totality to be grasped, a certain language game has been constructed, a game where arguments have been used optimally and where the use of arguments takes place as reasonably as possible.

The choice of the language game is based on the guiding view in the study, the view that the expectation of legal certainty prevailing in society demands that matters be decided in a just and rational manner. For this reason the theory of interpretation is based on two central focal points. These are the demand for rationality and the demand for the acceptability of the contents. The expectation of justice is specifically connected with the latter.

In order to understand this, one must keep in mind what Ludwig Wittgenstein thought about the nature of philosophy. For him, the life of individuals and thus also the manifestations of the human culture are "deeply entrenched in the basic structures of a social nature" as Georg Henrik von Wright has written.[1] That basic structure mentioned above is the so-called form of life (*Lebensform*). It is not given once for all, but it is partially produced by human beings, and therefore the form of life is also changing with history. However, the form of life is something that is "before us", i.e. independently of an individual. Language games are rooted in this basic structure. One can also say that language games are manifestations of the form of life, and here lies the deepest nature of philosophy. Quoting von Wright again: "The problems of philosophy have their roots in a distortion or malfunctioning of the language games which in its turn signalizes that something is wrong with the ways in which men live".[2]

In this study, no attempts are made to draw conclusions concerning the impact that Wittgenstein has had on contemporary thinking. Even so, certain basic features characteristic of Wittgenstein's view give a fruitful impetus to recall the theory of rational discourse. As was noted above, the background philosophy of this theory is presented by Jürgen Habermas. Like Wittgenstein, Habermas is also interested in what is wrong with the ways in which men live. For Wittgenstein the malfunctioning of language is a symptom of a cancer in the way of life itself (*Lebensweise*). In his own way, Habermas has made an interesting approach just in that direction. I do not claim that Habermas gives an interpretation to the "malfunctioning of language games". But as von Wright says, "had Wittgenstein lived to see the sixties and seventies of our century he would, no doubt, have found plenty to reinforce his view of the dangers of self-destruction inherent in the nature of modern industrial society." Habermas has lived during this period and tried in different contexts to make these phenomena understandable. Here lies the kernel of my interest to compare these two – in many senses very different – philosophers.

I introduce the reader to follow me for a while in order to get a rough picture of certain ideas presented by Habermas in his previous massive work.[3] The most important of these ideas is the distinction between the system (*System*) and the world of life (*Lebenswelt*). The last mentioned term is a clumsy translation of a German word that refers to a meaning content that is difficult to describe in a short way. The other expressions for the same purpose may be "the reality of everyday life" or "the everyday world". However, the first mentioned expression has been chosen for our purposes.

According to Habermas, there are in society two intertwined but theoretically different aspects, the system and the world of life:

(a) The system is objective and systematic reality that manifests in external relations between the members of the society. The co-ordination of the activities is based on non-linguistic means, i.e. on money and power. In the system the economic activity is organised by means of the concept "money". On the other hand, the administrative and legal activities, the bureaucratic structure of society, are co-ordinated by the concept "power" and law.

(b) Yet, in society we meet also another reality, world of life (*Lebenswelt*). It is based on a mutual communication between the members of society. In *Lebenswelt* the goal of all activities is the understanding of each other. In this sense, the world of life is a necessary precondition for all communicative interaction. As an intersubjective whole, *Lebenswelt* forms a given interpretation of the world. Nobody can choose it, and the world of life cannot be questioned, either. It really is "given" as far as an individual member of society is concerned. As a comparison, one can easily recall here the Wittgensteinian concept "form of life". In this very regard, it has the same role in Wittgenstein's conception as the notion "Lebenswelt" has in the Habermasian one.

The system and the world of life manifest also two different types of rationality, and – at the same time – two kinds of social activity. The system is dominated by instrumental-technical rationality. It is characteristic of, for instance, the bureaucracy where all activities are subordinated to certain given goals. Hence, we can also speak about goal rationality. A typical example can be found in the technological development. In the system, nearly everything is ordained in accordance with the technological goals. They define what is welfare in modern societies.

In *Lebenswelt* the rationality is of quite another type. Habermas himself calls it communicative rationality. It is not instrumental as to its nature. On the contrary, the communicative rationality serves as a tool by means of which people can reach mutual understanding. This kind of rationality deals with argumentation and convincing and, according to Habermas, people can in an ideal situation reach a perfect understanding with each other if they follow the rules of rational discourse. Hence, Habermas' idea of communicative rationality is based on the logic of argumentation. The subject matter of it can be fact statements (propositions), norms as well as values. As regards the fact statements the idea is to give reasons for the veracity (*Wahrheit*). Norms are associated with legitimacy (*Richtigkeit*) whereas values are attached to the authenticity (*Wahrhaftigkeit*).

Social activity that is directed by the communicative rationality does not try to further its own interests but seems to reach mutual understanding. In this regard, the concept of communicative rationality is, to some extent, an explication of the notion "symbolic interaction" presented by Georg Herbert Mead.

As far as the relation between the system and the world of life is concerned, Habermas makes two further steps. First, analysing the development of modern societies we can identify several subsystems that have disengaged from the system. These subsystems are not regulated any more by the idea of mutual understanding. On the contrary, communication has been replaced by non-linguistic means, i.e. by money and power. The social integration based on the communicative activity has been changed to an integration governed by instrumental rationality. The relations between human beings are no more communicative but external relations defined by the money and power. An individual member of society is not a participant in a communicative procedure. He is subservant who is overruled by the "emperors" of the system.

However, the system and the world of life have not originally been separated from each other. It is a symptom of modern societies that the system (and subsystems as constituents of the system) are disengaging from the world of life all the time. The system has began to live its own life. At the same time another phenomenon is going on in society. The world of life is also differentiating, i.e. the internal parts of this "level" are disengaging from each other. From a theoretical point of view, one can identify the following three subelements: the culture, social community and personality. Also the procedures by means of which those elements will be renewed are differentiating: renewing the culture, social integration and socializing (adopting an individual to society).

The kernel of Habermas's thinking is not, however, this procedure of differentiation but an opposite phenomenon.[4] According to Habermas, the system and the instrumental rationality manifested in the system begin to pervade the world of life. Habermas calls this colonization. The structure of symbols and the systems of understanding typical for the world of life do not withstand this development. *Lebenswelt* is, so to speak, getting narrower, i.e. the genuine forms of the world of life will disappear. The media that are typical for the system, in other words, money and power begin to cover the original spheres of *Lebenswelt*. The everyday life of an individual member of society is becoming more and more bureaucratic, more and more economically coloured, and more and more technologically structured.

For Habermas, the crucial point is the place of incision where the system and *Lebenswelt* meet each other. Here the system, for instance, colonizes the world of life. However, the critics have often pointed out that Habermas does not describe when the system pervades the world of life in that sense. According to the criticism, Habermas has not presented a historical description of the pervading procedure. This is true but not very important from our point of view. I would claim that one must try to understand Habermas in relation to his own basic ideas. The theory of communicative rationality is not an empirical description of what is happening in the world but a tool by means of which one can analyse modern societies and identify the pathologies of them. This theory is simply an attempt to clarify what it means to say that something is wrong with the ways in which men live.

In this regard, Habermas's analysis seems to be fruitful for our purposes, too.[5] Let us deal with legal order as a part of the system. Legal order consists of legal norms. As a special subsystem it has disengaged from the world of life. Indeed, legal order is (a part of) a system. As such, legal order also follows the instrumental rationality. Generally speaking, legal norms are means for reaching certain goals, i.e. goals that are given in advance and defined, for instance, by the technological rationality.

Using legal norms as tools the power center in society directs the social development. On the other hand, in the procedure of disengagement the legitimacy of legal norms is more and more based on the formal validity. A norm *N* is legitimate if and only if it is given according to a proper procedure. This typically Kelsenian validity is enough in the situation where the system "lives its own life" independent of the *Lebenswelt*.

This is the case when a judge or a civil servant applies the law. In doing so, he does not ask if the law (the statute) is formally valid or not.

He simply *applies* the law, i.e. follows the rule. This kind of attitude has in the foregoing been called legal positivism. According to it, the statute alone is enough as the basis of legitimacy for a decision.

In modern societies formal validity is not, however, the only basis of legitimacy. On the contrary, one can speak about the crisis of legitimacy in the situations where more than one well-founded interpretation can be given for a certain statute. In several countries the problem has become manifest in the activities of the so-called green movements. The value system they represent may radically differ from the official one that is referred to by the courts or administrative organizations. The mere statute is then not enough to fulfill the demands of "green values". Without taking any stand against or for these movements, the phenomenon itself is interesting. It makes sense to the Habermasian analysis: the legitimacy of legal norms is based in modern societies not only on the formal validity but also on the values accepted or acceptable (rationally) in society. The basis of legitimacy is thus "behind" the norms. It is rooted in the world of life (*Lebenswelt*).

"The red thread" of this contribution can easily be understood, I suppose, on this background. The idea has not been to build up any visions of the future society. The work is therefore anything but prophetic – following the expression of von Wright. The purpose has only been to identify and to analyse the pathologies in the legal culture, i.e. situations where the malfunctioning of the system can be observed.

From this point of view, the crisis of legitimacy is often a crisis of value systems. Therefore it is impossible to conceptualize the problem only by means of the system (of the legal order as a formally valid system of norms). On the other hand, it would be rather naive to defend the primacy of *Lebenswelt* as the genuine basis of legitimacy. Legal order is a power order and applying law is using this power. This is the reason why the law is – at the same time – "a citizen of two different worlds". It is a formal tool to organize social life in a predictable way, but the legitimacy of the law (or legal interpretations/decisions) is dependent on linguistic communication and mutual understanding that results in that communication. If for instance the court decisions only follow (blindly) the letter of the law and represent a different value system than the majority of society, people do not trust in decision-making any more. This controversy is not a phenomenon that could in a manifest way be identified at a certain moment in a certain society. But the lack of the trust on courts may, by and by, lead to a deep crisis in that society if the courts do not begin to take into account the demands growing up in the *Lebenswelt.*

In this sense, the final source of the legitimacy is in society (in *Lebenswelt*) itself. Only such an interpretation that is directing toward the expectations of the majority of society, can receive, in the long run, acceptability by that majority. What is important in this regard is the expectation of legal certainty. It is a measure, how and when the rational acceptability can be reached. As we have seen, legal certainty is tightly connected to the value system of society why acceptable interpretations must not only be rational but also reasonable.

Therefore, the rational acceptability is the "meeting point" where the system and Lebenswelt find each other. A good judge or a good civil servant tries all the time to orientate along the main lines of the everyday life practice. Then the decisions they give receive a maximal acceptability and the use of legal power is not just the use of mere power. It is a peaceful construction of society according to the expectations of ordinary people. Then we are, I hope, more mature than otherwise to overcome "the dangers of self-destruction inherent in the nature of modern industrial society" (von Wright).

NOTES

CHAPTER I

[1] Makkonen, Kaarle, *Zur Problematik der jurisdischen Entscheidung* pp. 175 ff. In this connection, H. L. A. Hart uses the term "the plain case." Cf. *The Concept of Law*, p. 123. See also Benditt, Theodore M., *Law as Rule and Principle*, p. 36.
[2] See *Benditt*, *op. cit.*, p. 36. See also Saarenpää, Ahti E., *Rutiinijuttu*. Reports from the Project for the Study of Legal Research, pp. 2 and 5.
[3] This is connected to the distinction between legal problem and fact description. See Aarnio, Aulis, *On Legal Reasoning*, pp. 63 ff.
[4] See Aarnio, Aulis, *Perillisen oikeusasemasta*, pp. 313 ff.
[5] The nature of decisions of discretion comes up exceptionally well in the decision of the Court of Appeals of Eastern Finland (R 1974/99/496) where it is observed,

> . . . Sence . . . the provision regarding the right of a party with a traffic service licence to engage in commercial traffic is so open *to interpretation* that *X* cannot be seen to have been guilty of the offence . . .

The Court of Appeals acquitted the defendant on, among others, the grounds that the defendant could not be assumed to have been familiar with the details of a provision that provided a very large scope for discretion.

In this connection, cf. the concept of the "hard case". Cf. Hart, *op. cit.*, pp. 123–125, Benditt, *op. cit.*, pp. 36 and 38, and MacCormick, Neil, *Legal Reasoning and Legal Theory* pp. 195 ff.
[6] Regarding this, cf. Makkonen, *op. cit.*, pp. 25 ff., and Strömholm, Stig, *Rätt, rättskällor och rättstillämpning*, p. 135. See also Brusiin, Otto, *Tuomarin harkinta normin puuttuessa*, pp. 127 ff.
[7] For example Kauko Wikström remarks on this power. *Oikeuskäytännön tulkinnasta*, pp. 98 ff.
[8] Cf. Brusiin, *op. cit.*, pp. 92 ff.
[9] Brusiin, *op. cit.* p. 95–98.
[10] See about this e.g. Aarnio, *Denkweisen der Rechtswissenschaft* pp. 121 ff.
[11] An excellent analysis of the matter can be found in Kaarle Makkonen's article 'Ajatuksia juridisen kielen loogisesta anlyysistä', *LM*, 1959, pp. 49 ff.
[12] Cf. Aarnio, Aulis, Robert Alexy and Aleksander Peczenik, The Foundation of Legal Reasoning, *Rechtstheorie* **2** (1981) (Introduction), pp. 134–135.
[13] Cf. about the Finnish situation during the 1960's Blom, Raimo, 'Tuomioistuimen toiminnan puoluettomuus rikosasioissa, Tampereen yliopiston tutkimuslaitos, *D tiedotteita* **40**, 1970.
[14] Regarding the concept of typical examples, cf. Koch, Hans-Joachim and Rüssman, Helmut, *Juristische Begründslehre*, p. 209. See also Pöyhönen, Juha, *Juridisista teorioista* pp. 41 ff.

[15] Brusiin, *op. cit.*, pp. 8–11 and Peczenik, *Wartosc Naukowa Dogmatyki Prawa, 1966* (according to the author, this study attempts to analyze specifically the matter dealt with in the text). See also Klami, Hannu Tapani, *Anti-Legalism* pp. 37 ff.
[16] Cf. Holopainen, Toivo, 'Normien mukaista vai tavoitteiden suuntaista', *LM*, 1977, pp. 627 ff. and Klami, Hannu Tapani, *Finalistinen oikeusteoria*, pp. 128 ff.
[17] As Klami observes, already Chapter 24, Section 3 of the Finnish Code of Judicial Procedure requires that decisions be based on norms. Klami, *op. cit.*, p. 126.
[18] See about the internal connection between fact- and norm-questions Aarnio, On Legal Reasoning, pp. 63 ff. and Wróblewski, Jerzy, 'Facts in Law'. In: *Meaning and Truth in Judicial Decision*, pp. 104 ff.
The position of the legal dogmatician is described in, for example, Strömholm, *Allmän rättslära*. Section 7.2.2. *See also Peczenik, Juridikens metodproblem* p. 54.
[19] Regarding this in general, see Hart, *op. cit.*, p. 86 and Aarnio, *On Legal Reasoning*, pp. 3 ff. There is reason to emphasize that in both studies the distinction between the internal and the external perspective is connected with the *acceptance* of norms, in other words with a binding of oneself to them. Thus Hart notes that the internal perspective is represented in a person when he acts "as a member of the group which accepts and used them (i.e. rules) as guides to conduct". This can be termed an *organizationally* internal (resp. external) perspective.
[20] Winch, Peter, *The Idea of a Social Science and Its Relation to Philosophy*. Sixth Impression, pp. 83 ff.
[21] The matter is dealt with in an interesting manner by Kauko Wikström, *op. cit.*, pp. 86 ff.
[22] Wittgenstein, Ludwig, *Philosophical Investigations* § 30. Cf. also § 31–32.
[23] Strömholm, *Rätt, rättskällor och rättstillämpning*, p. 68.
[24] Cf. von Wright, G. H., *Humanismi elämänasenteena* pp. 96 ff.
[25] Aarnio, Aulis, 'The Significance of the Theoretical Element in Legal Research'. In: *Philosophical Perspectives in Jurisprudence*, pp. 119 ff. The task of practical legal dogmatics is to interpret certain texts (or to solve certain problems formulated in an abstract manner). It is pragmatically oriented. On the other hand, the theoretical legal dogmatics is interested mainly in systematic frameworks of the legal order. In the research practice, however, there are continuous internal connections between these two orientation models.
[26] Patoluoto, Ilkka, Post scriptum in: *Runciman, Social Science and Political Theory* (Finnish transl.).
[27] Cf. Kuhn, Thomas S., *The Structure of Scientific Revolutions*, 1st ed., 1962, as compared to 2nd ed., pp. 66 ff. Cf. also Brante, Thomas, *Vetenskapens struktur och förändring*, pp. 14 ff.
[28] Regarding this Aarnio, Aulis, Jääskinen, Niilo Pöyhönen, Juha and Uusitalo, Jyrki *Paradigms, Change and Progress in Legal Dogmatics*, Chapter 3 (in press).
[29] Cf. Aarnio, 'On the Paradigm Articulation in Legal Research', *Rechtstheorie*, Beiheft 3, pp. 51 ff. See also Zuleta Puceiro, Enrique, *Paradigma Dogmatico y Ciencia del Derecho*, pp. 11 ff. and pp. 139 ff. and Zuleta Puceiro, 'Scientific Paradigms and Legal Change', pp. 331 ff. Cf. Wróblewski, Jerzy, 'Paradigms of Justifying Legal Decisions', pp. 253 ff. where Wróblewski deals with the problem of adjudication.
[30] Regarding the concept of legal positivism cf. Aarnio, 'The Form and Content of Law': Aspects of Legal Positivism', *Archivum Juridicum Cracoviense* **XII** (1980), pp. 17 ff. See also Hart, H. L. A., 'Positivism and the Separation of Law and Morals'. In: *Philosophy of Law*, pp. 49 ff.

[31] Hintikka, Jaakko, 'Arvokäsitteistä sosiaalitieteiden metodiopissa', *Ajatus* **XX** (1957), pp. 27 ff., esp. p. 39. Regarding values in legal science, cf. Makkonen, *op. cit.*, p. 220.
[32] The term "legal theory" can also refer to *juridical theory*, for example the theory about ownership or – as is more common – to a *theoretical approach*, such as conceptual dogmatics (*Begriffsjurisprudenz*). Regarding the ways of using this latter sense cf. Wimmer, Franz, 'By What Criteria Can Progress in Legal Theory Be Determined?', *Rechtstheorie*, Beiheft **3** (1981), pp. 35 ff.
[33] Aarnio, *On Legal Reasoning*, pp. 47 ff. See also Klami, 'Legal Heuristics: A Theoretical Skeleton', *Oikeustiede* 1982, pp. 7 ff.
Regarding justification in general cf. MacCormick, *op. cit.*, pp. 13 ff. An excellent analysis of the concept of justification in itself can be found in Wróblewski, Jerzy, 'Verification and Justification in the Legal Sciences', *Rechtstheorie*, Beiheft **1** (1979), pp. 195 ff.
[34] Regarding the concept of a facade of justification cf. Benditt, *op. cit.*, pp. 4 ff., and Ross, Alf, *Law and Justice* pp. 167 ff. Ross speaks about *a facade of legitimation*, which more or less differs from the formulation of a true decision. See also Aarnio, Aulis and Alexander Peczenik, *Mas alla del realismo*, pp. 131 ff.
[35] This intuition-based approach has been represented by, for example, Jerome Frank. Cf. *Law and the Modern Mind* p. 125. Frank uses the term "hunch" in this connection. Cf. Hutcheson, Joseph C. Jr., *The Judgement Intuitive*, p. 279.
Hannu Tapani Klami's "heuristic" point of view is problematic precisely in the sense that it is not clear what the theory tests. Cf. *Legal Heuristics*, p. 36 ff, which emphasizes the rational features of heuristics. In this, however, the theory loses its heuristic content to the same extent as the theory approaches rational reconstruction.
[36] Regarding this cf. Aarnio, *On Legal Reasoning*, pp. 134 ff. and Wikström, *op. cit.*, p. 124 ff.
[37] Cf. Alexy, Robert, *Theorie der juristischen Argumentation*, pp. 225 ff. Cf. Klami's observation of the normativeness of the approach mentioned in the text. Review of Aarnio, *Denkweisen der Rechtswissenschaft*, *LM*, 1980, pp. 180 ff. See also Klami, *Finalistinen oikeusteoria*, pp. 17 ff. and pp. 52 ff.
[38] In this context it is interesting what G. H. von Wright writes on the Wittgensteinian view concerning the adequacy of certain ways of understanding history: "One cannot speak of true and false as attributes of a way of viewing things, a *Betrachtungsweise*. But it gets its significance, of course, from the phenomena it illuminates, and its justification from how much it contributes to our understanding history". von Wright, Wittgenstein in relation to his Times, pp. 117 ff.
[39] The importance of the justification lies in the fact that without any justificatory background it is impossible to solve if the result is "correct" or not. The result itself may be good or bad, but only by means of justification the *quality* or the result can be evaluated.
[40] It is important to observe that the ontology, the epistemology and the methodology have internal connections with each other. Thus, for example, the ontology is connected with the epistemology. Cf. Niiniluoto, Ilkka, *Johdatus tieteen filosofiaan*, p. 139.
[41] The problem of the present study is how to build such a justificatory theory for legal dogmatics that is adequate from the *societal* point of view.

CHAPTER II

[1] Armstrong, D. M., *Nominalism & Realism*: Universals & Scientific Realism. Volume I, p. 12. Cf. also Niiniluoto, *op. cit.*, pp. 123 ff.
[2] Cf. for example Tolonen, Juha, *Der Allgemeine Erklährungshintergrund der wirtschaftlichen Ordnung und seine Anwendung auf das Aktiengesellschaftsrecht*, pp. 17 ff.
[3] Finch, Henry Le Roy, *Wittgenstein – the Later Philosophy*, pp. 243–244.
[4] *Ibid.*, p. 243.
[5] In the theory of law, this type of ontology has been defended by Osvi Lahtinen. Cf. his article 'Kuolinpesä-konstruktiosta', *LM* 1955, pp. 112 ff. and a comment on this article, Aarnio 'On Finnish Legal Theory in the 20th Century', in *Legal Point of View*, pp. 25 ff.
[6] Niiniluoto, *op. cit.*, p. 129.
[7] Klami, *Finalistinen oikeusteoria*, pp. 3 ff. See also Klami, 'Dualism of Law', In: *Objektivierung des Rechtsdenkens*, pp. 475 ff.
[8] Popper, Karl R., *Objective Knowledge: An Evolutionary Approach*, pp. 74 and 154 ff.
[9] Niiniluoto, *op. cit.*, p. 129. Cf. also Popper, *op. cit.*, pp. 156–160, which deals with the objectivity of World 3 and its nature as a Man-made product. Regarding the contingence and necessary existence of norms, see von Wright, G. H., *Norm and Action*, pp. 107 ff. In this connection it should be noted that if the ontology accepts so-called *institutional facts* in addition to entities and properties, many traditional problems regarding existence will find a solution. It is not, however, self-evident where (in the ontological sense) facts receive their institutional nature. For example Searle connects them with so-called constitutive rules, in which case we have come around once again to the problem of the existence of rules. Regarding constitutive rules and the concept of the institutional fact, see Searle, J. R., *Speech Acts: An Essay in the Philosophy of Language*, and also Searle, *What is a Speech Act?*, pp. 39 ff.
[10] See Makkonen, *op. cit.*, pp. 119 ff. Hans Kelsen often specifically equated existence with validity. He writes, "Mit dem Worte 'geltung' bezeichnen wir die spezifische Existenz einer Norm", *Reine Rechtslehre*, 2nd Ed. p. 9. As will be observed in the following (Sections 3.2 and 3.4) sentence (1) has not been turned into sentence (2) in the sense intended by Kelsen.

Regarding the existence of a norm, see also von Wright, G. H., *Norm and Action*, pp. 107 ff. and Sintonen, Matti, Problems of Interpretation and Truth in Legal Dogmatics, *Rechtstheorie*, Beiheft **2**, p. 83. From a legal point of view, see also Peczenik, Aleksander, *Legal Data: An Essay About the Ontology of Law*, pp. 99 ff.
[11] Wróblewski, Jerzy, 'Verification and Justification in the Legal Sciences'. *Rechtstheorie*, Beiheft **1** (1979), pp. 207 ff. See also Wróblewski, 'Dilemmas of the Normativistic Concept of Legal System', *Rechtstheorie*, Beiheft **5** (1984), pp. 320 ff. where Wróblewski presents a more detailed analysis of the problem. Cf. Ross, Alf, Validity and the Conflict Between Legal Positivism and Natural Law, pp. 76 ff.

See also Aarnio, Aulis, 'On the Validity, Efficacy, and Acceptability of Legal Norms'. In: *Philosophical Perspectives in Jurisprudence*, pp. 152 ff. Cf. Guastini, Riccardo, 'A Tentative Analysis of Two Juristic Sentences', pp. 573 ff.
[12] Kelsen, Hans, *Reine Rechtslehre*, pp. 209 ff. Seppo Laakso gives an exceptionally lucid analysis of the matter. In: *Oikeuden systeemiyhteys*, pp. 51 ff. Regarding Kelsen's theory, see e.g. Raz, Joseph, *The Concept of a Legal System*, pp. 93 ff. See also Laakso, 'Puhtaan oikeusopin problematiikkaa', *Oikeustiede* 1980, pp. 150 ff.

[13] See e.g. Kelsen, *Reine Rechtslehre*, pp. 206–208. According to Kelsen, the fundamental norm is a logical necessity ("logisch unerlässich"). Such a conception, however, was rather late in being developed in Kelsen's theory. In this connection see Laakso, 'Puhtaan oikeusopin problematiikkaa', pp. 152–153.
[14] Kelsen, *op. cit.*, pp. 208 ff.
[15] Peczenik, *Grundlagen der juristischen Argumentation*, pp. 42 ff.
[16] See here especially the criticism presented by Hermann Klenner about the "emptiness" of the Kelsenian system. Klenner, *Vom Recht der Natur zur Natur des Rechts*, pp. 139 ff., and Klenner, *Rechtsleere*, *passim*. See also Peschka, Vilmos, *Die Theorie der Rechtsnormen*, pp. 224 ff.
[17] Alchourrón, Carlos – Bulygin, Eugenio, *Normative Systems*, pp. 94 ff. For a more detailed analysis, see Peczenik, 'On the Nature and Function of the Grundnorm', pp. 282 ff. See also Raz, *op. cit.*, pp. 95 ff. and Vernengo, Roberto J., 'La Funcion Sistematica de la Norma Fundamenta', pp. 3 ff., especially pp. 17 ff.
[18] Kelsen, *op. cit.*, p. 219. The giving of a norm and its efficacy are *conditions* of the validity of the norm (*Bedingung der Geltung*) but the foundation (*Grund*) of a norm is always another, superior norm, and ultimately the fundamental norms. Regarding efficacy, see also Raz, *op. cit.*, pp. 203 ff. See also Petev, Valentin, 'Rechtsquellenlehre und Reine Rechtslehre', *Rechtstheorie*, Beiheft **5**, pp. 274–277.
[19] Kelsen, Die philosophischen Grundlagen der Naturrechtslehre und Rechtspositivismus, pp. 8–9 and 18. See also *Reine Rechtslehre*, pp. 1–3.
[20] Wróblewski, 'Verification and Justification in the Legal Sciences', *Rechtstheorie*, Beiheft **1** p. 212 ff. See also Weinberger, Ota, 'Logik, Wirklichkeit und Positivität in der Reinen Rechtslehre', *Rechtstheorie*, Beiheft **5** (1984), pp. 425 ff., especially pp. 436 ff. where Weinberger analyses the existence of law from the Kelsenian point of view.
[21] Peczenik 'On the Nature and Function of the Grundnorm', *Rechtstheorie*, Beiheft **2**, pp. 279 ff. and Peczenik, The Basis of Legal Justification, pp. 2 ff. and Peczenik, *Grundlagen der juristischen Argumentation*, pp. 5 ff. Regarding the concept of transformation, see Aarnio, Alexy, and Peczenik, *Rechtstheorie* **2** (1981), pp. 136 ff.
[22] Regarding the concept of "underpinning reasons", see MacCormick, *Legal Theory and Legal Reasonings*, pp. 64 ff. and pp. 138–140.
[23] Cf. about "minimum demands" e.g. Hart, *op. cit.*, pp. 189 ff.
[24] Alf Ross refers to the ambiguity of the term "validity" in his contribution 'Validity and the Conflict Between Legal Positivism and Natural Law', pp. 77–78. Ross seems to be inclined to reserve the term "validity" only for systemic validity, not for the efficacy. Cf. however, Aarnio and Peczenik, Mas alla del realismo, pp. 132 ff. *passim*. where the authors make an attempt to point out the ambiguity of Ross' own terminology.
Regarding this matter see e.g. Illum, Knud, 'Some Reflection on the Method of Legal Science and on Legal Reasoning'. *SSL* 1968 pp. 49 ff. and Illum, *Lov og ret*, pp. 53 ff.
[25] See about organic reactions, see Kelsen, *Reine Rechtslehre*, pp. 182 ff. and Ross, *op. cit.* pp. 66 ff.
[26] Holmes, Oliver Wendell, 'The Path of the Law', in *Collective Legal Papers*, 1921, p. 173.
See also Summers, Robert S., *Instrumentalism and American Legal Theory*, especially p. 239 ff. and Summers, 'Pragmatic Instrumentalism in Twentieth Century American Legal Thought – A Synthesis and Critique of Our Dominant General Theory about Law and Its Use', *Cornell Law Review* **66** (1981), pp. 861 ff. and esp. pp. 904 ff. Summers

remarks give a clear picture of the goals and contents of the tendency known as American realism.

See also Krawietz, Werner, *Juristische Entscheidung und wissenschaftliche Erkenntnis*, pp. 97 ff.

[27] Cf. Benditt, *op. cit.*, pp. 12 ff.

[28] von Wright, G. H., 'Normien eksistenssi'. Lecture (mimeograph), *passim*.

[29] Regarding this distinction see Hart, *op. cit.*, pp. 77 ff. Ross (*op. cit.*, p. 46) observes that a *primary* norm is always a directive for the judge.

[30] Frank, Jerome, *Law and the Modern Mind*, p. 134 ff. See also Benditt, *op. cit.*, pp. 10–11 and Summers, 'Pragmatic Instrumentalism in Twentieth Century American Legal Thought', p. 896 ff.

[31] Ross, *Om ret og retfaerdighed*, p. 55. This is a literal translation, with minor stylistic adjustments. Thus, "conditions" has been put instead of "conditioning facts". Cf. Ross, *On Law and Justice*, pp. 42 ff., where the translator of that book omitted the words "justify" and "justification", and inserted the words "form the basis" and "reasoning" instead of them.

Cf. also what Ross himself says in the article 'Validity and the Conflict Between Legal Positivism and the Natural Law', pp. 74 ff.

[32] Ross, *Om ret og retfaerdighed*, p. 41. A literal translation with very minor stylistic adjustments. In *On Law and Justice* Ross writes as follows:

> The working hypothesis implies that the legal norms, like the norms of chess, serve as a scheme of interpretation for the corresponding set of social acts, the law in action, in such a way that it becomes possible to comprehend those actions as a coherent whole of meaning and motivation and to predict them within certain limits.

Ross thus left out references to "supraindividual" and "common ideology". He repeated these omissions systematically throughout the book. Cf. Ross, *On Law and Justice*, e.g. pp. 35, 36 and 71. The reader of the last mentioned book cannot fully understand the Rossian theory only on the basis of Law and Justice.

See also Aarnio and Peczenik, Mas alla del realismo, Section 2.

[33] Ross, *op. cit.*, pp. 48 ff. See also Bjarup, Jes, *Skandinavischer Realismus*, pp. 68 ff., Strömholm, *op. cit.*, p. 100 and Lauridsen, Preben Stuer, *Studier i retspolitisk argumentation*, pp. 125 ff. and p. 234 ff. See also in general Bulygin, Eugenio, 'El Concepto de Vigencia en Alf Ross, pp. 3 ff.

[34] Ross, *op. cit.*, pp. 38 ff.

[35] Aarnio and Peczenik, *Mas alla del realismo*, Section 7.

[36] Jørgensen, Stig, *Law and Society*, pp. 86 ff. and Jørgensen, *Argumentation and Decision*, pp. 381 ff.

[37] Benditt, *op. cit.*, pp. 13 ff.

[38] Makkonen, *Zur Problematik der juridischen Entscheidung*, p. 59. See also Hart, *op. cit.*, p. 143.

[39] Hart, *op. cit.*, pp. 132 ff and especially pp. 141–142.

Hart criticizes Ross' view also in another respect, i.e. referring to the fact that Ross does not deal with the formal validity. Hart, *op. cit.*, pp. 28 ff. and pp. 100 ff.

Ross has answered to the criticism pointing out that the main reason for the confusion is the ambiguous meaning of the word "validity". When Ross speaks about (factual) validity, Hart discusses about the *existence* of a norm. To my mind, Ross is right in this respect. Hart himself writes, e.g. that when we assert that a legal system exists "we in fact refer in compressed, portemantean form to a number of heterogeneous social facts". The truth of this assertion can be confirmed by "reference to actual practice; to the way in which courts identify what is to count as law", Hart, *op. cit.* pp. 245–246.

On the other hand, the Hartian criticism is correct as far as Ross' own terminology in his books (*Om ret of retfaerdighed* and *On Law and Justice*) is concerned. See Notes 31 and 32 in this section.

40 In this regard there are good reasons to refer to a conception according to which a legal norm is valid if it is in correspondence with the *general* view of law and justice prevalent in society. See e.g. Illum, Knud, *Lov og* Ret, passim. This conception is liable to such criticism that has been presented e.g. by Alf Ross. He pointed out that "the general view of law and justice" leads to "an individual psychological basis of valid law".

Here it is also *very* important to note how the Fascist concept of valid law was based on "general view of law and justice". What is in accordance with the consciousness of people was the real expression of (Fascist) German law. See e.g. Dietze, H. H., *Naturrecht in der Gegenwart*, p. 184 and in general Kaufman, Arthur, Rechtsphilosophie und Nationalsozialismus, pp. 19ff.

This kind of conception is really very alien to the view defended in this contribution although the *basic idea* of the connection between the valid law and societal value base is a parallel one. Cf. what is observed later regarding the views of Otto Brusiin (Note 44). See also Aarnio, 'Eternal and Changing Law'. In: *Philosophical Perspectives in Jurisprudence*, pp. 94 ff.

41 Niiniluoto, Ilkka, 'On the Truth of Norm Propositions'. *Rechtstheorie*, Beiheft **3** (1981), pp. 171 ff. See also Niiniluoto, 'On Truth and Argumentation in Legal Dogmatics', *Rechtstheorie*, Beiheft **2** (1981), pp. 53 ff.

42 Niiniluoto, Beiheft **3**. p. 176.

43 In this connection reference should be made to the concept of validity represented by Otto Brusiin. The basis of his point of departure is that legal norms are part of the set of norms in society. These "societal norms", in turn, are the result of historical development. They reflect the *value consciousness* of the citizens. This is something more than the general opinion. Value consciousness is the result of development over a number of centuries; as it were, it grows up from societal reality. Brusiin observes that value consciousness (legal Convictions) need not be general; it is enough that it is built on a factual power relation.

This view clearly demonstrates the core of value-based validity (axiological validity), the connecting of validity to social historical facts and, at the same time, to the value consciousness of citizens. On the other hand, not even Brusiin is fully able to defend himself against the criticism which is directed in the text against the randomness of acceptance. Value consciousness which is based on factual power relations may lay the foundation for a totally manipulative order. If Brusiin's observation about the historical nature of value consciousness is taken to mean that value consciousness which truly and justifiably comes to the level of awareness can be the basis for the legal order, we are near the conception presented in the text. Value consciousness is a matter that is reached only when it is unaffected by random factors.

CHAPTER III

[1] Aarnio, *Denkweisen der Rechtswissenschaft*, pp. 49 ff. Aleksander Peczenik has pointed out to me that the distinction between text-oriented and problem-oriented viewpoints only concerns the so-called *context of discovery*. With the reservations made in the text, this holds true. Worth mentioning is, however, that the research *strategy* may be slightly different depending on from which "end" one takes his starting point.

[2] Regarding the concept of norm propositions see Niiniluoto, Beiheft **3**, p. 172, Wróblewski, 'Verification and Justification in the Legal Sciences', pp. 196 ff. and esp. pp. 201 ff., and Sintonen, Matti, Problems of Interpretation and Truth in Legal Science, *Rechtstheorie*, Beiheft 2, pp. 77 ff. See also Klami, *Finalistinen oikeusteoria*, pp. 19 ff. See also Aarnio, Alexy, and Peczenik, *Rechtstheorie* 1982, pp. 427 ff.

[3] Niiniluoto, 'Truth and Legal Norms', In: *Conditions of Validity and Cognition in Modern Legal Thought, ARSP*, Beiheft **25** (1985), pp. 168 ff. and especially pp. 182 ff.

[4] See von Wright, G. H., 'Is and Ought', In: Man, Law and Modern Forms of Life, 1985, pp. 263 ff. especially p. 272.

[5] In connection with the conceptual relation between the norm standpoint and the norm recommendation, R. M. Hare's distinction between the frastic and neustic parts of a sentence is interesting. According to Hare, the neustic component shows whether it is a question of an indicative or imperative use of language. In a corresponding manner the persuasive component has a role to play in norm recommendations. See Hare, *Language of Morals*, pp. 15 ff. and esp. p. 18.

[6] Regarding definitions in general, see Niiniluoto, *Johdatus tieteenfilosofiaan*, p. 160. See also Koch, Hans-Joachim and Rüssman Helmut, *Juristische Begründslehre*, pp. 147 ff. and pp. 280 ff. and Klug, Ulrich, *Juristische Logik*, 3rd ed., pp. 87 ff. Especially in regard to the analytical nature of interpretative statements, see Niiniluoto, 'Language, Norms and Truth', p. 177 ff.

[7] Aarnio, *On Legal Reasoning*, p. 59 ss.

[8] Cr. also Klami, *Finalistinen oikeusteoria*, p. 62. and Peschka, Vilmos, *Die Theorie der Rechtsnormen*, pp. 44 ff.

[9] Hart, *op. cit.*, pp. 77 ff., MacCormick, Neil, *op. cit.*, p. 229 and Ross, *Directives and Norms*, p. 91.

[10] Ross, *op. cit.*, pp. 84 ff: "a set of secondary rules is required to specify what sanctions may be exacted of those who violate the substantive law. . . Such rules are directed to the judge. . ."

[11] In this connection Kelsen uses the term, "Zurechnung". See *Reine Rechtslehre*, p. 22. About the relation between "Is" and "Ought": von Wright, G. H., Is and Ought. *Man, Law and Modern Forms of Life*. pp. 263 ff. and Weinberger, Ota, ' "Is" and "Ought" Reconsidered', *ARSP* 1984, p. 454 ff.

[12] Alchourron, Carlos and E. Bulygin, *Normative Systems*, p. 41 ff.

[13] Cf. Dworkin, Ronald, 'The Model of Rules', In: *Taking Rights Seriously*, sections 1-4.

[14] Searle, J. R., *op. cit.*, pp. 56 ff. and Ross, *Directives and Norms*, p. 53. – A good analysis is presented by Riccardo Guastini in: 'Six Concepts of "Constitutive Rule" ', p. 488 ff. and also *Tuori, K.*, Oikeusnormien asettamismenettelyt ja oikeuden, Kriisitendenssit, *Politiikka* **3** (1985), pp. 189 ff.

[15] Regarding competence norms, see Ross, *op. cit.*, pp. 130 ff. and Zitting, Simo, 'Omistajan oikeuksista ja velvollisuuksista I', *LM* 1952, pp. 394 ff.

[16] Regarding this, see Aarnio, *Perillisen oikeusasemasta*, p. 71 ff.
[17]Makkonen, *Zur Problematik der jurisdischen Entscheidung*, pp. 27 ff.
[18] For general comments on this, see Weinberger, Christiane and Ota, *Logik, Semantik und Hermeneutik*, pp. 64 ff. and pp. 96 ff. See also Esser, Josef, *Vorverständnis und Methodenwahl in der Rechtsfindung, passim*, and Jonsson, Inge, 'Riktningar inom 1800-talets hermeneutik', pp. 65 ff. Aarnio, *Denkweisen der Rechtswissenschaft*, pp. 150 ff. and Aarnio, 'Outline of a Hermeneutic Approach in Legal Theory', In: *Philosophical Perspectives*, pp. 47 ff. Cf. Villa, Vittorio, 'Legal Science and Hermeneutic Point of View', pp. 509 ff., and in general Villa, *Teorie della Scienza Giuridica e Teorie delle Scienze Naturali, passim*. Stig Strömholm emphasizes the general differences between linguistic interpretation and the legal interpretation of texts. He particularly points to four aspects: (a) legal interpretation has a broader and more relevant connection to the social context than do other forms of interpretation, (b) there is an hierarchial division of roles among the interpreters, (c) legal interpretation must fulfill certain axiological goals such as justice, and (d) the focus of interpretation, legal norms, form a system. Cf. Strömholm, 'Juridisk tolkningsmetodik före 1800-talets "moderna genombrott"', pp. 47 ff.
[19] This is especially the case in classical text hermeneutics, Cf. Aarnio, 'Philosophical Perspectives in Jurisprudence', pp. 56 ff. Hans-Georg Hinderling gives a good analysis of the problem in *Rechtsnorm und Verstehen, passim*. See also Larenz, Karl, *Methodenlehre der Rechtswissenschaft*, p. 85 ff.
[20] Cf. Aarnio, Denkweisen der Rechtswissenschaft, pp. 154–155. The philosophical problematics of "conventions" is dealt with in a very interesting manner in Lars Hertzberg's paper, 'Science and Certainty', pp. 60 ff. especially pp. 72 ff.
[21] See about these types of sentences p. ff.
[22] Aarnio, *Denkweisen der Rechtswissenschaft*, pp. 75 ff.
[23] Cf. Aarnio, *op. cit.*, p. 90.
[24] Cf. Aarnio, *op. cit.*, p. 122.
[25] See also what is said in Note 32 of Part IV below concerning Robert Alexy's contribution to the problem.
[26] In this context it is interesting what Wittgenstein thought of the nature of philosophy. Anthony Kenny points out that Wittgenstein saw the philosophy as a tool against the philosopher in us. Every one of us is trapped in philosophical errors. Therefore, philosophical analysis has a therapeutic role for us. It strengthens us to resist certain temptations the origin of which is in our own language. So: "Know Thyself". – See about this Kenny, Wittgenstein on the Nature of Philosophy', pp. 13 ff.
[27] Regarding sources of law, see Peczenik, *Juridikens metodproblem*, pp. 109 ff. and Strömholm, *op. cit.*, pp. 287 ff. and Ross, *On Law and Justice*, pp. 82 ff. See also Makkonen, Kaarle (ed.), *Oikeudellinen lähdemateriaali*, 1979, pp. 16 ff.
[28] See e.g. Björne, Lars, *Deutsche Rechtssysteme im 18. und 19. Jahrhundert*, especially p. 131 ff. where one can find a really remarkable analysis about the historical development of the so-called systematic thinking in legal science.
[29] Alanen, Aatos, *Yleinen oikeustiede ja kansainvälinen yksityisoikeus*, 1965, p. 56 and Peczenik, *Juridikens metodproblem*, pp. 136–137. About the customary law in general: Klami, Hannu Tapani, *Gewohnheitsrecht als Rechtsquelle*, pp. 4 ff. and pp. 44 ff.
[30] Brusiin, *op. cit.*, pp. 7 ff. and Alanen, *op. cit.*, p. 57. See also Strömholm, *op. cit.*, pp. 187 ff.

[31] Alanen, *op. cit.*, pp. 58 ff.
[32] Makkonen, *Zur Problematik der juridischen Entscheidung*, p. 65.
[33] Alanen, *op. cit.*, p. 60.
[34] Aarnio, *Denkweisen der Rechtswissenschaft*, pp. 135 ff. Regarding precedent in general, see Brusiin, *op. cit.*, pp. 167 ff. Peczenik, *op. cit.*, pp. 104 ff., Strömholm, *op. cit.*, pp. 333 ff. Regarding the position of precedents in American law, see Radin, Max, 'Case Law and Stare Decisis', pp. 3 ff. An excellent analysis can be found in: Saarenpää, Ahti E., 'Court Decisions as the Focus of Study', *SSL* 1984, pp. 123 ff.
[35] On the distinction *Aarnio, A., Oikeussäännösten tulleinnasta*, pp. 89 ff.
[36] See, however, the Supreme Court decision KKO 2649/19.10.1966 and *Miettinen, M* in *Minutes of the XXI Annual Meeting of the Lawyer's Union in Finland*, 1970, pp. 80 ff.
[37] The Royal Letter to the Court of Appeal in Gōta 1682 and *Nehrman, D.*, Inledning til then swenska jurisprudentiam civilem, 1729, p. 72.
[38] Brusiin, *op. cit.*, pp. 157 ff. and Makkonen, *Zur Problematik der juridischen Entscheidung*, pp. 153 ff. See also Jørgensen, Stig, *Law and Society*, pp. 110 ff. For comments on the relationship between general principles of law and juridical induction, see Aarnio, *Denkweisen der Rechtswissenschaft*, pp. 201 ff.
[39] Perelman, Chaim, *Juristische Logik als Argumentationslehre*, p. 109.
[40] Aarnio, 'Eternal and Changing Law', In: *Philosophical Perspectives in Jurisprudence*, p. 100 ff. In this connection, the criticisms that Dworkin directs at Hart's views of *legal* principles is interesting. What is important is what turns principles into legal principles. Cf. Dworkin, *Taking Rights Seriously*, pp. 36 ff.
[41] Regarding this criticism, see Aarnio, 'The Development of Legal Theory and Philosophy of Law in Finland', pp. 9 ff. See also Aarnio, '150 anni di filosofia del diretto in Finlandia', pp. 809 ff.
[42] Aarnio, *The Development of Legal Theory and Philosophy of Law in Finland*, pp. 20 ff.
[43] As far as the goal reasoning according to the pragmatic instrumentalism is concerned one can find an excellent analysis in: Summers, Robert S., *Instrumentalism and American Legal Theory*, pp. 60 ff. Regarding the consideration of consequences in general, see MacCormick, *op. cit.*, pp. 100 ff. See also Aarnio, *Denkweisen der Rechtswissenschaft*, pp. 84 ff, which deals with interpretation presented in the form of so-called technical norms, Klami, *Finalistinen oikeusteoria*, pp. 42 ff. and Peczenik, *Juridikens metodproblem*, p. 150 ff. Peczenik presents the so-called teleological interpretation method in general.
[44] Perelman, *op. cit.*, p. 79 and p. 109.
[45] Perelman, *op. cit.*, p. 43 and Germann, O. A., *Methodische Grundfragen*, pp. 4 ff. See also Rahlf, Joachim, 'Die Rolle der historischen Auslegungsmethode in der Rechtsprechung des BGH', pp. 27 ff. In Scandinavian realism, criticism of the will of the legislator has been presented especially by Karl Olivecrona, Cf. e.g. *Law as Fact*, pp. 65 ff.
[46] See Note 21 of Part III.
[47] Aarnio, *Rechtstheorie*, Beiheft **3**, pp. 51–53.
[48] Also on the basis of this doctrine four sources of law rise over all others: written law, *travaux préparatoires*, court decisions and customary law. See also Aarnio, *Denkweisen der Rechtswissenschaft*, pp. 133 ff.
[49] Peczenik, *op. cit.*, pp. 48 ff., Peczenik, 'The Structure of a Legal System', *Rechtstheorie* **6** (1975), p. 7 ff. and Peczenik, *Rechtstheorie* **2** (1980), pp. 150 ff. Cf. H. L. A. Hart's concepts "permissive" and "mandatory", *The Concept of Law*, p. 246 ff.

[50] In this regard, we can speak of an obligation to justify the decision. This is not only an epistemic but also a legal obligation. First, the matter can be referred back to the lower court if there is no sufficient justification in the decision (See Finnish Supreme Court 1980 II 79). Secondly, the judge will be sentenced if he has given a decision without any justification (Brusiin, *Tuomarin harkinta normin puuttuessa*, pp. 59 pp.). According to a reform proposal (Commitee Report 1966: B27) Chapter 24, Section 5 of the Code of Judicial Procedure should be rewritten in such a way that the judge would have a legal obligation to refer to the law and, in the case of ambiguity, to the reasons of the interpretation. Until now, this proposal is not valid law in Finland.
[51] For a more detailed analysis of this, see Summers, Robert S., 'The Types of Substantive Reasons: The Core of a Theory of Common Law Justification', pp. 724 ff. (Also available in *ARSP*, Beiheft **11**). See also Summers, Robert S. and Leigh B. Kelley, '"Economist Reasons" for Common Law Decisions – A Preliminary Inquiry', pp. 213 ff. Cf Golding, Martin P., *Legal Reasoning*, pp. 39 ff.
[52] Summers, *op. cit.*, pp. 726 ff.
[53] Summers, *op. cit.*, pp. 728 ff.
[54] See Dworkin, *Taking Rights Seriously*, pp. 25 and 44. Regarding these comments, see Alexy, Robert, 'Zum Begriff des Rechtsprincips', Rechtstheorie, Beiheft **1**, 1979, pp. 59 ff., esp. pp. 63 ff. See also Eckhoff and Sundby, *Rettssystemer: Systemteoretisk innføring i rettsfilosofin*, 1976, pp. 128 ff. Regarding this, see Jareborg, Nils, 'Regler och riktlinjer', *TfR* 1979, pp. 385 ff. With the reservations made, the text corresponds to Jareborg's view of the matter. Cf., however, Eckhoff, *TfR* 1980, p. 145. Regarding the term "guiding standard", see Eckhoff, 'Guiding Standards in Legal Reasoning', p. 205 ff.
[55] Regarding Wittgenstein's concept of rules, see *Philosophical Investigations*, § 218–219. In this, Wittgenstein emphasizes that following a rule is similar to "following blind". There is no choice in the matter. Rules are like the tracks of a railroad: "and infinitely long rails correspond to the unlimited application of a rule (§ 218). Henry Le Roy Finch observes, on the other hand, that we have no *obligation* to follow a rule (*op. cit.*, p. 197). A rule compels us only if we begin to follow it. In this sense, it is a question of an "either-or" situation. See also Brand, Gerd, The Central Texts of Wittgenstein, pp. 125 ff. An excellent analysis about the Wittgensteinian concept of rule, Kripke, Saul A.: *Wittgenstein on Rules and Private Language*, esp. pp. 7 ff.
[56] *Peczenik, Juridikens metodproblem*, p. 86 and concerning the standards of preference pp. 118–120.
[57]Regarding analogy in general, see Frändberg, Ake, *Om analog användning av rättsnormer*, pp. 16 ff., Koch and Rüssman, *op. cit.*, pp. 259 ff. and especially Peczenik, *op. cit.*, pp. 74 ff. See also Aarnio, *On Legal Reasoning*, pp. 70 ff. and Alexy, *Theorie der juristischen Argumentation*, pp. 343 ff. About case-analogy Golding, Martin P., *Legal Reasoning*, pp. 44 ff. and pp. 97 ff.
[58] *Peczenik, op.cit.*, p. 76.
[59] *Ibid.*, p. 74.
[60] Koch and Rüssman, *op. cit.*, pp. 257 ff. and Klug, *op. cit.*, pp. 132 ff.
[61] Aarnio, *Denkweisen der Rechtswissenschaft*, p. 130.
[62] Aarnio, *On Legal Reasoning*, p. 72.
[63] Alanen, *op. cit.*, p. 159.
[64] See e.g. Larenz, Karl, *Methodenlehre der Rechtswissenschaft*, pp. 255 ff., Engisch, K.

Einführung in das juristische Denken, p. 256 and Zippelius, Reinhold, *Rechtsphilosophie*, pp. 221 ff.

[65] Cf. Aarnio, *On Legal Reasoning*, p. 76. According to the model presented by Robert Alexy, the formula for analogy reasoning can be written as follows:

(1) $(x)\,(Fx \vee Fsim\,x \rightarrow OGx)$

(2) $(x)\,(Hx \rightarrow \text{Fsim x})$

(3) $(x)\,(Hx \rightarrow OGx)$

or, in a simplified form (1) if every *x* is either *F* or similar to *F*, *x* ought to be *G*; (2) if *x* is *H*, it is similar to *F*; (3) every *x* that is *H* ought to be *G*. Cf. Alexy, *Theorie der juridischen Argumentation*, p. 343. See also Klug, *op. cit.*, p. 120.

[66] Regarding isomorphic situations, see Stenius, Erik, 'Wittgensteinin "puhtaan kielen kritiikki" ', p. 45 ff.

[67] In general, see Alexy, *op.cit.*, p. 342, Klug, *op. cit.*, p. 128 and Koch and Rüssman, *op. cit.*, p. 258. Cf. Golding, M. P., 'Principled Decision-Making and the Supreme Court', pp. 208 ff.

[68] Alanen, *op. cit.*, p. 159.

[69] Allowing extending analogy in criminal law will lead to a conflict with the principle of *nulla poena sine lege*. On the other hand, a complete prohibition on analogy will lead to an unevenness of application, as similar cases cannot be dealt with in a similar fashion. For this reason, in the Finnish literature, it has been usual to warn only against analogy *in malam partem*. Cf. Honkasalo, Brynolf, 'Suomen rikosoikeus', *Yleiset opit* **I**, p. 50. See also Peczenik, *op. cit.*, pp. 89–90.

[70] Peczenik, *op. cit.*, p. 85.

[71] Alanen, *op. cit.*, p. 161.

[72] *Ibid.*

[73] Peczenik, *op. cit.* p. 76. See about the methods of legal interpretation in general Bydlinski, F., *Juristische Methodenlehre und Rechtsbegriff*, pp. 437 ff., Larenz, Karl, *Methodenlehre der Rechtswissenschaft*, pp. 188 ff. See also Vernengo, Roberto J., *Curso de Teoria General del Derecho*, pp. 411 ff.

[74] Alanen, *op. cit.*, p. 159.

[75] Alexy, *op. cit.*, p. 319.

[76] See MacCormick, *op. cit.*, p. 15. Hannu Tapani Klami has described the general function of the reasoning in judicial decisions by distinguishing between the following functions:

- the *informative* function: the how and the why of the final result is given;
- the *controlling* function: the reasoning makes it possible to check on the validity and solidity of the conclusion, a feature which Klami regards as especially important from the point of view of appeal;
- the persuasive function: the decision-maker tries to justify his decision so that it can be approved by an audience; and
- the *pedagogic* function: the decision is justified in a way that would make it easy to understand.

On the above functions, the controlling function is the most significant from the point of view of this study. When we speak of the reasoning of a decision from the point of view of justification, it is actually a question of the problem of *the possibility of controlling the decision* and guaranteeing control in order to fulfill the requirements of legal security. See Klami, *Finalistinen oikeusteoria*, Chapter 3, 2.

[77] Regarding these concepts see Victor, Dag, *Rättssystem och vetenskap*, 1977, pp. 21 ff.
[78] *Ibid.*, pp. 25 ff.
[79] *Ibid.*, pp. 27–28.
[80] Regarding the so-called "intertwinement thesis", see Aarnio, The Significance of the Theoretical Element in Legal Research, In: *Philosophical Perspectives in Jurisprudence*, pp. 120 ff.
[81] It is a question of subsumption. See e.g. Koch and Rüssmann, pp. 64 ff. Cf. Larenz, *op. cit.*, p. 256 and Alexy, *op. cit.*, pp. 274 ff.
[82] See, in general, Ahmavaara, Yrjö, *Informaatio*, p. 112. The expression used as an example, "someone", is an unspecified singular term. See Jareborg, Nils, *Begrepp och brottsbeskrivning*, p. 94. To supplement the text, see Chapter 4 of Jareborg's book, p. 93 ff. See also Hart, *op. cit.*, p. 4, pp. 15 ff. and pp. 122 ff., Vernengo, Roberto, J., *Curso de Teoria General del Derecho*, pp. 406 ff. and Wróblewski, Jerzy, 'Fuzziness of Legal System', pp. 311 ff.
[83] In this connection there is reason to recall *Wittgenstein's* characterization of the concept of "family resemblance". It is precisely in connection with open terms that we can say that individual meaning contents are "related" to each other only in the sense that the strands of a rope form the rope. See *Philosophical Investigations*, § 66–75. The problem of open terms has been dealt with in a noteworthy manner by *Furberg Mats*, in *Saying and Meaning*, pp. 72 ff. See also Hart, *op. cit.*, pp. 121 ff, which touches upon the problem of the so-called "open texture".
[84] Regarding this concept, see e.g. Regnell, Hans, *Semantik*, p. 69 and Ross, *op. cit.*, pp. 135 ff. See also Ekelöf, Per Olof, Semantik och juridik. *Svensk Juristtidning* 1966, pp. 497 ff. and *Jareborg, op. cit.*, pp. 98 ff.
[85] Aarnio, 'Formal Incorrectness and the Invalidity of Legal Acts', *SSL*, pp. 19 ff.
[86] Ahmavaara, *op. cit.*, p. 112 and Jareborg, *op. cit.*, p. 108. See also Regnell, *op. cit.*, pp. 75 ff.
[87] Jareborg, *op. cit.*, pp. 121 ff.
[88] *Ibid.*, p. 108. When the same term refers to several different matters, the concept of "polysemia" has often been used.
[89] See von Wright, G. H., 'Normit ja logiikka', *Ajatus* 1963, pp. 255 ff.
[90] Regarding the concept of the legislator, see Peczenik, *Juridikens metodproblem*, pp. 112–113.
[91] See Brusiin, *op. cit.*, pp. 24 ff., Coing, Helmut, *Grundzüge der Rechtsphilosophie*, pp. 328 ff., *Makkonen, Zur Problematik der juridischen Entscheidung*, pp. 122 ff. and Peczenik, *op. cit.*, pp. 76 ff.

A rather complete definition of the concept of the gap is given by Alchourrón and Bulygin. See *Normative Systems*, pp. 145 ff. and the comments on this in Aarnio, *On Legal Reasoning*, pp. 60 ff.
[92] See also Wróblewski, Jerzy, 'System of Norms and Legal System', *Rivista Internationale di Filosofia del Diritto* **2** (1972).
[93] Alchourrón and Bulygin, *op. cit.*, p. 146.
[94] *Ibid.*, p. 147.
[95] Kelsen, Hans, *Reine Rechtslehre*, p. 348 ff.
[96] Alchourrón and Bulygin, *op. cit.*, p. 51 ff.
[97] *Ibid.*, p. 146; cf. pp. 31 ff. and pp. 106 ff.
[98] *Peczenik, op. cit.*, p. 77.

[99] From the general point of view it is a question of a more precise outlining of the meaning content of the expression in question. Regarding this concept, see Naess, Arne, *Empirisk semantik*, pp. 6–13 and pp. 26 ff. and Naess, Arne, *Interpretation and Preciseness*, p. 350 ff.

[100] See Aarnio, *Denkweisen der Rechtswissenschaft*, pp. 120–121. The basis of the diagram is Naess' presentation of pro- and counter-argumentation. See *Empirisk semantik*, pp. 67 ff. Ilmar Tammelo has called this type of reasoning "a zetetic process". See Tammelo, Zetetischer Verfahren für juristisches Aufweisen; *Rechtstheorie* 1978, pp. 421 ff. For comments on this see Wimmer, Franz, 'Überlegungen zu Tammelos Unterscheidung von Euduktion, Produktion und Seduktion,' *Rechtstheorie* 1979, pp. 338 ff.

[101] *Peczenik, The Basis of Legal Justification*, pp. 33 ff. Peczenik makes, on good grounds, a distinction between the contextually sufficient and the deep justification. See also *op. cit.*, pp. 1 ff., 28 ff, and 110 ff.

[102] See Alexy, *op. cit.*, pp. 272 ff and Wróblewski, 'Legal Syllogism and Rationality of Judicial Decision', '*Rechtstheorie* **5** (1974), pp. 39 ff., Wróblewski, 'Legal Decision and Its Justification', *Proceedings of the World Congress for Legal and Social Philosophy*. 1971, pp. 412 ff. and Wróblewski, 'Justification of Legal Decisions', *Revue Internationale de Philosophie. La Nouvelle Rhétorique. Essais en hommage à Chaim Perelman 127–128* (1979), pp. 277 ff.
According to Alexy, a simple syllogistic form is as follows:

(a) $(Tx - ORx)$
Ta
ORa

where x is an individual variable, O an ought operator, a an individual name, T and R random predicates. The syllogism may be presented in the following example:

A witness ought to tell the truth in court
a is a witness
a ought to tell the truth in court

A more extensive analysis of syllogistic deduction is to be found in Tammelo, Ilmar and Helmut Schreiner, Grundzüge und Grundverfahren der Rechtslogik. I., pp. 110 ff. See also Aarnio, *On Legal Reasoning*, pp. 59–60, Koch- Rüssmann, *op. cit.*, pp. 14 ff. and pp. 59 ff. and Makkonen, *op. cit.*, pp. 47 ff. Regarding deductive reasoning, very clear criticism is to be found in MacCormick, *op. cit.*, pp. 19 ff.

[103] See MacCormick, *op. cit.*, pp. 19–52 and esp. pp. 100 ff., which separates "second-order justification" from the deductive reasoning in a decision. This latter justification corresponds to the term, "external justification".
The description of Ex-justification is, in this section, based on the discussions and common work that the author has had with Aleksander Peczenik in 1984–85. See also Peczenik, *Creativity and Transformations in Legal Reasoning*, pp. 280 ff.

[104] Aarnio, *Perillisen oikeusasemasta*, pp. 362 ff.

[105] Aarnio, *Denkweisen der Rechtswissenschaft*, pp. 133 ff.

[106] Alexy, *op. cit.*, pp. 221 ff.

[107] Larenz, *op. cit.*, pp. 198 ff.
[108] Regarding these principles, see Ross, *op. cit.*, pp. 164 ff. and Peczenik, *op. cit.*, pp. 110 ff and Strömholm, *op. cit.*, pp. 428 ff.
[109] See *Kommentar zum Allgemeinen Gesetzbuch* (hrsg. von Heinrich Klang und Franz Gschnitzer), p. 103 and p. 107. Regarding the significance of *travaux préparatoires* in general. See Strömholm, *Legislative Material and Constitution of Statutes. SSL* 1966, pp. 175 ff. and Rahlf, *op. cit.*, pp. 28 ff.
[110] Aarnio, *Denkweisen der Rechtswissenschaft*, pp. 134 ff. and Aarnio, *On Legal Reasoning*, pp. 109 ff.
[111] Aarnio, *On Legal Reasoning*, pp. 216 ff.
[112] Cf. Peczenik, *op. cit.*, p. 113, where he states that lawyers know whose intention is to be taken into consideration. Peczenik's view would seem to oversimplify the situation, as research praxis has shown countless examples where different decisions on the same matter have made use of the disparate views of various instances.
[113] Larenz, Karl, *Methodenlehre der Rechtswissenschaft*, p. 322. Larenz uses a concept of an "objective-teleological" argument. This concept refers to the objective goal involved in legal order.
[114] See e.g. *Strömholm*, Rätt, rättskällor och rättstillämpning, p. 405
[115] Perelman, *op. cit.*, p. 79.
[116] Peczenik expresses the matter in an apt manner when he writes that we can speak of the "true meaning of the law" in two senses:

(a) the meaning in a linguistic sense, in other words the literal, lexical or contextual meaning
(b) the interpretation of the law in accordance with the accepted ("gällande") intepretative and methodical principles ("lagbudets verkliga mening i juridisk bemärkelse").

Peczenick, *op. cit.*, p. 191. It is this that is referred to in the text as the "objective" meaning (interpretation).
[117] Klang and Gschnitzer, *op. cit.*, p. 104. See also Zippelius, Reinhold, *Rechtsphilosophie* 1982, pp. 199 ff.
[118] Regarding this, see Alexy, *op. cit.*, pp. 322 ff., who distinguishes between systemic interpretation in a strict and in a broad sense. The former ("systematische überprüfung im engeren Sinne") is connected with the logical consistency between the statement being interpreted and the statements used to support it. The latter ("systematische überprüfung im weiteren Sinne") can be characterized by speaking of the practical consistency between statements. Alexy calls the former "logical control of consistency" and the latter "practical control of consistency" ("Konsistenz-kontrolle"). Regarding systemic points of view in interpretation in general, see Peczenik, *op. cit.*, pp. 99 ff. and Strömholm, *op. cit.* pp. 401 ff. In Finnish legal science, Saarenpää has been the most consistent in emphasizing systemic points of view. See *Tasajaon periaate*, pp. 18 ff, and Aarnio, *Denkweisen der Rechtswissenschaft*, pp. 121 ff.
[119] Regarding this problem, see Aarnio, *Denkweisen der Rechtswissenschaft*, p. 137.
[120] Cf. Alexy, who presents an interesting analysis of the significance of legal dogmatical statements in justification. He summarizes his analysis in the form of a *rationality*

principle: "If a dogmatic argument is possible, it must be used". See Alexy, *op. cit.*, pp. 320 ff., and esp. p. 334. In other words a rational interpreter refers to a legal dogmatical opinion, too. At the same time, Alexy regards legal dogmatics as having several functions, such as the stabilization function, the technical task of furthering the learning and teaching of legal material and the heuristic function, in other words the task of presenting decision models with practical applications. See Alexy, *op. cit.*, pp. 326–332.

[121] Aarnio, *On Legal Reasoning*, pp. 183 ff.

[122] Regarding the so-called finalistic interpretation in general, see MacCormick *op. cit.*, pp. 129 ff. See also Alexy, *op. cit.*, pp. 295 ff., who deals with the problematics of so-called teleological interpretation, Larenz, *op. cit.*, p. 322 and Peczenik, *op. cit.*, pp. 150 ff.

In Finnish legal science the matter has been dealt with especially by Aarnio, *Denkweisen der Rechtwissenschaft*, pp. 84 ff. and Klami, *Finalistinen oikeusteoria*, esp. pp. 61 ff. and Klami, *Legal Heuristics*, pp. 20 ff.

Regarding the teachings of pragmatic instrumentalism (American realism), see Summers, 'Pragmatic Instrumentalism', pp. 882 ff., esp. pp. 908 ff.

[123] Klami, *Legal Heuristics*, esp. pp. 21–36.

[124] Cf. Klami, *Finalistinen oikeusteoria*, p. 62, cf. pp. 128–129 and p. 133.

[125] The situation may also be described by saying that the other arguments show what interpretations can *not* come into the question in accordance with the law, and finalistic interpretation locks in one of the remaining ones as the preferable alternative.

[126] See Peczenik, *Juridikens metodproblem*, p. 191. Cf. Walter, Robert, 'Das Auslegungsproblem im Leichte der Reinen Rechtslehre', p. 194 ff.

[127] Alchourrón and Bulygin, *Normative Systems*, pp. 21 ff.

[128] Brusiin, *op. cit.*, p. 195. See also Alchourrón and Bulygin, *op. cit.*, p. 53 and Krawietz, *op. cit.*, p. 88 and p. 153.

Brusiin's position on the matter is not quite clear, as on the other hand he believes that all legal interpretation "arises" from the reality of societal norms. Even so, for Brusiin "order" is a volitive concept, "system" a cognitive concept. An interesting analysis about the concept of legal system is presented in: Kerimov, D. A., *Philosophische Probleme des Rechts*, pp. 199 ff. especially p. 202 ff.

[129] Alchourrón and Bulygin, *op. cit.*, pp. 50 ff.

Alchourrón, Carlos, 'Systematization and Change in the Science of Law', *Proceedings of the XI World Congress on Philosophy of Law and Social Philosophy, 1983* (in print), Bulygin, Eugenio, 'Legal Dogmatics and the Systematization of Law', in: *op. cit.* and Aarnio, Aulis, 'On the Change of Legal System', in: *op. cit.*

[130] Alchourrón and Bulygin, *op. cit.*, pp. 9 ff.

[131] *Ibid.*, pp. 54–55.

[132] *Ibid.*, pp. 72 ff.

[133] *Ibid.*, pp. 78 ff.

[134] Kuhn, *op. cit.*, Chapt. 3 and e.g. Chapt. 9.

[135] See Ross, *On Law and Justice*, pp. 211 ff. and Zitting, Simo, An Attempt to Analyse the Owner's Legal Position. *SSL*, 1959, pp. 234 ff.

[136] I am indebted for the clarification in the text to Niilo Jääskinen who has demonstrated in our discussions the imprecision of the set of concepts in my earlier writings. Cf. Aarnio, *On Legal Reasoning*, pp. 272 ff. and Aarnio, *Denkweisen der Rechtswissenschaft*, pp. 50 ff.

[137] Tolonen, Juha, *op. cit.*, pp. 36 ff., cf. pp. 174 ff.

[138] Saarenpää, *Tasajaon periaate*, p. 22.

[139] Peczenik, 'Norms and Reality', in *Essays in Legal Theory*. 1969, pp. 9 ff. and Peczenik, 'Empirical Foundations of Legal Dogmatics', in *ibid.*, pp. 60 ff.
[140] Aarnio, Aulis, Jääskinen Niilo, Pöyhönen Juha and Uusitalo Jyrki, *Paradigms, Change and Progress in Legal Dogmatics* (in print); Section 2. See also Ralf Dreier's excellent analysis in: 'Zur Theoriebildung in der Jurisprudenz' in *Recht-Moral-Ideologie*, 1981, pp. 70 ff. See also Dalberg-Larsen, Jørgen, *Five Essays on Legal Science*, pp. 68 ff., especially pp. 80 ff.
[141] A detailed analysis is to be found in Aarnio, *Perillisen oikeusasemasta*, pp. 49 ff. (German summary), and for some comments on this, Saarenpää, 'Court Decisions as the Focus of Study, pp. 128 ff. See also Aarnio, 'En analys av arvinges rättsliga ställning'. Tidskrift utgiven av Juridiska Föreningen i Finland **6** (1980), pp. 363 ff.
[142] See Ross, *On Law and Justice*, pp. 199 ff. Cf. Borum, O. A., *Arvefaldet*, pp. 22 ff. and Malmström, Åke, *Successionsrättsliga studier*, pp. 38 ff. and pp. 198 ff.
[143] Zitting, Simo, 'An Attempt to Analyse the Owner's Legal Position, *SSL*, 1959, pp. 234 ff.
[144] See Zitting, *op. cit.* p. 229.
[145] See Aarnio, *Perillisen oikeusasemasta*, pp. 89 ff. for an analysis of these doctrines.
[146] Legal dogmatics which attempts to construct a systematic framework can be called theoretical legal dogmatics. See Aarnio, *Denkweisen der Rechtswissenschaft*, pp. 69 ff. and pp. 231 ff. as well as Aarnio, 'The Significance of the Theoretical Element in Legal Research', in: *Philosophical Perspectives in Jurisprudence*, pp. 123 ff. Cf. also Peczenik, Aleksander, 'Legal Research, Growth of Science and Moral Theory', pp. 137 ff., especially pp. 146 ff.

CHAPTER IV

[1] Wróblewski, 'Legal Syllogism and Rationality of Judicial Decision', *Rechtstheorie* 1974, pp. 33 ff.
[2] Perelman, *Juristische Logik als Argumentationslehre*, p. 40.
[3] Cf. Niiniluoto, Ilkka, 'Fallibilismista', *Sosiologia* **5–6** (1974), pp. 275 ff., where he deals with the question of whether it is possible to obtain incontestable knowledge outside of logical reasoning. In this connection, see Hertzberg, Science and Certainty, p. 63 ff.
[4] See Aarnio, *On Legal Reasoning*, pp. 55 ff.
[5] Dworkin, *Taking Rights Seriously*, pp. 85 ff.
[6] *Ibid.*, e.g., pp. 88–89.
[7] Regarding this concept, see MacCormick, *op. cit.*, pp. 195 ff. See also Benditt, *op. cit.*, pp. 36 ff.
[8] MacCormick, 'Dworkin as Pre-Benthamite', Philosophical Review LXXXVII/4, pp. 585 ff., esp. p. 591.
[9] *Ibid.* p. 592.
[10] *Ibid.* p. 593.
[11] Oker-Blom, Max, En enda riktiga lösning trots allt? Dworkin mot finländsk bakgrund, *JFT* 1968, pp. 251 ff., esp. p. 310 ff.
[12] See about predictions in general Aarnio, *On Legal Reasoning*, pp. 237 ff. Predictions from the socialist point of view, Kerimov, D. A., *Philosophische Probleme des Rechts*, pp. 278 ff.

[13] Aarnio, *On Legal Reasoning*, pp. 243 ff.
[14] See Aarnio and Peczenik, Beyond the Behavioural Idealism, Section 3. Cf. Bulygin, Eugenio, 'El Concepto de Vigensia en Alf Ross', pp. 6 ff.
[15] Albert, Hans, 'Theorie und Prognose in den Sozialwissenschaften', pp. 60 ff. See also what Bulygin says about the dispositive Character of predictions. Bulygin *op. cit.*, pp. 11–14.
[16] See Niiniluoto, 'On the Truth of Norm Propositions', *Rechtstheorie*, Beiheft **3** (1981), pp. 171 ff. and Niiniluoto, On the Truth and Argumentation in Legal Dogmatics, *Rechtstheorie*, Beiheft **2**, (1981) pp. 53 ff. Cf. also Wikström, Kauko, 'How to Prove Propositions in Legal Dogmatics', pp. 297 ff., especially p. 306.
[17] Niiniluoto, *Rechtstheorie*, Beiheft **3** (1981), p. 176. For Niiniluoto, many rules in society are conventions although they are not based on "an agreement". A convention Niiniluoto defines – following D. Lewis – as a regularity *R* in the behaviour of the members of a community *C* such that it is true, and it is common knowledge in *C*, that in almost every instance of a social co-ordination situation *S*

(i) almost everyone in *C* conforms to *R*
(ii) almost everyone in *C* expects almost everyone else in *C* to conform to *R*
(iii) almost everyone in *C* prefers to conform to *R* on the condition that most of the others do.

Furthermore, it is *common knowledge* in community *C* that *p* if and only if
(a) (almost) everyone in *C* has reason to believe that *p*
(b) (almost) everyone in *C* has reason to believe that (almost) everyone in C has reason to believe that *p*.

See Niiniluoto, Truth and Legal Norms. *Proceedings of XI World Congress on Philosophy of Law and Social Philosophy*, p. 180.
[18] Regarding the above, see Niiniluoto, 'Language, Norms and Truth', pp. 186 ff. In particular in regard to the question of language as a social and contingent phenomenon see Lars Hertzberg's and Matti Sintonen's article 'On Language as an Object of Empirical Investigation', *Ajatus* **38**, pp. 149 ff. The writers observe, for example, "For to know what categories are relevant to a given language is already to know something about that language." (p. 150). To add on to what is presented in the text, it can be noted that language is connected to the form of life (cf. Section IV 2.5.). It is an inherited background; it is not open to agreement.
[19] Ilkka Niiniluoto admits also that there is a difference between linguistic and legal norms as far as the "official status" of these norms is concerned. This difference is, however, not significant, to Niiniluoto's mind.
See 'Language, Norms and Truth', pp. 181 ff.
[20] Cf. Helin, Markku, 'On the Semantics of the Interpretative Sentences in Legal Dogmatics', pp. 63 ff. especially pp. 83 ff. Helin presents a thorough-going and important criticism against the theory of rational acceptability. The criticism is based on a linguistic analysis of a Searlean type. One kernel in Helin's criticism is that the idea of rational acceptability makes legal scholars "Besserwissers", "whose task is to tell the misguided legal community what their true law is" (p. 86). In this regard, the criticism is not tenable. If one takes the demands of rationality seriously, he cannot adopt this kind of "Besser-

wisser" – attitude. Rational acceptability is, for him, only an ideal, a regulative principle of research, not a genuine measure to express the true interpretation.
See also Gizbert-Studnicki, Tomasz, 'How Many Theories of Truth Are needed in Jurisprudence', pp. 157 ff.

[21] With this in mind we can say that, with the criteria presented, an interpretation can be demonstrated to accord with law but not necessarily with the legal order. See also Perelman, Juristische Logik als Argumentationslehre, p. 118. and Aarnio, *Rechtstheorie*, Beiheft **2** (1980), p. 44 ff.

[22] See also what Ilkka Niiniluoto writes in his article 'Truth, and Legal Norms', *ARSP*, Beiheft **25**, pp. 181 ff.

[23] See about this kind of syllogism Aarnio, *On Legal Reasoning*, pp. 147 ff.

[24] *Ibid.* pp. 304 ff.

[25] *Ibid.* pp. 307 ff.

[26] *Ibid.* pp. 309 ff.

[27] *Ibid.* pp. 310 ff.

[28] See e.g. Eriksson, Lars, D., 'Om olika argumentationsmodeller', *JFT* 1979, pp. 25 ff. and Eriksson, *Marxistisk teori och rättsvetenskap*, pp. 106 ff. See also Pöyhönen, Juha, Knowledge in Law and the Possibility of an Alternative Legal Dogmatics, *passim* and Simmonds, N. E., 'Law as a Rational Science', *ARSP* 1980, pp. 535 ff. especially, pp. 538 ff.

[29] Cf. Aarnio, *Denkweisen der Rechtwissenschaft*, pp. 144 ff.

[30] Here lies the kernel of the whole legal interpretation. Only if the interpretation is according to these rules and principles, it is legal as to its nature.

[31] See especially Aarnio, 'Argumentation Theory and Beyond', *Rechtstheorie* **4** (1983) p. 387 where the distinction between a semantically and legally possible alternatives has been argued.

[32] Perelman, *Juristische Logik als Argumentationslehre*, p. 144 and Perelman, '*The Rational and the Reasonable*', pp. 117 ff.

[33] Lucas, J. R., *On Justice*, p. 37.

[34] Schelsky, Helmut, *Die juristische Rationalität*, pp. 5 ff. and pp. 16 ff. *et passim*. Schelsky points out that "rationale Einheit oder Identität der Wissenschaft des Rechts mit der jurisdisch-institutionellen Praxis des Rechts als Gesetzgebung oder Justiz ist eine 'Illusion". Even so, the juridica-institutional rationality is an ideal for lawyers. See also Krawietz, Werner, 'Begründung des Rechts – anthropologisch betrachtet: zur Institutionentheorie von Weinberger und Schelsky', pp. 546 ff.

[35] Krawietz, Werner, 'Rechtssystem und Rationalität in der juristischen Dogmatik', *Rechtstheorie*, Beiheft **2** (1981), pp. 299 ff. See also Krawietz, *Recht als Regelsystem*, e.g. pp. 110 ff.

[36] Habermas, Jürgen, *Theorie des kommunikativen Handelns II*, pp. 51 ff. See also Habermas, Moralbewusstsein und kommunikatives Handeln, pp. 31 ff.

[37] Alexy, Robert, *op. cit.*, pp. 219 ff.

[38] See Aarnio, Argumentation Theory — and Beyond. *Rechtstheorie* **4**/1983 p. 393 ff.

[39] Perelman, Chaim, '*The Rational and the Reasonable*', p. 118.

[40] Peczenik, Aleksander, *Grundlagen der juristischen Argumentation*, p. 1 ff., cf. p. 28.

[41] *Ibid.*, p. 28 ff.

[42] Cf. Alexy, Robert, *op. cit.*, p. 225. See also *Aarnio*, 'Argumentation Theory – and Beyond', *Rechtstheorie* **4** (1983), pp. 394–395.

In principle, we can imagine several types of justification for rules of rationality. *Alexy* lists four justification possibilities: (a) a technical justification, which assumes that rationality is a means towards reaching a goal, (b) an empirical justification, which refers to actual praxis, (c) a definition-oriented (*definitorisch*) justification, which attempts to set rules for the language game of justification, and (d) a transcendental justification, which takes as its point of departure the necessities of linguistic communication; in other words its attempts to construct the general and necessary conditions for the process of understanding. See Alexy, *op.cit.*, p. 225. See also Perelman, *Juristische Logik als Argumentationslehre*, p. 155. Perelman writes: "Deshalb ist die Idee des gesunden Menschenverstandes mit seiner Idee der Rationalität aufs engste verbunden". What is said in the text is connected primarily with this last aspect, Alexy's "universal pragmatic" justification. There is, however, a difference in weight in the ways of justifying something. My own point of departure is the concept of rationality as a component of language; it is a central element in human communication. In this respect my ideas are the same as those of G. H. von Wright, who has analyzed the concepts of act and action. See von Wright, *Explanation and Understanding*, pp. 86 ff. and von Wright, *An Essay in Deontic Logic and the General Theory of Action*, pp. 41 ff. For comments on this, see Aarnio, *On Legal Reasoning*, pp. 142 ff. Regarding Alexy's catalogue of rules, see also MacCormick, 'Legal Reasoning and Practical Reason', *Passim*.

[43] Peczenik, Aleksander, *Grundlagen der juristischen Argumentation*, pp. 167 ff and pp. 189 ff.

[44] See Alexy, *op. cit.*, pp. 234 ff., who presents four basic rules (*Grundregeln*) regarding consistency. They are: (a) None of the discussants may be inconsistent, (b) Everyone has the right to state only what they believe, (c) the treatment of analogous cases must be consistent, and (d) everyone must use expressions to mean the same thing.

[45] von Wright, *Logiikka, filosofia ja kieli*, 1958, pp. 100 ff.

[46] Alexy, *op. cit.*, pp. 234 ff.

[47] Alexy, *op. cit.*, pp. 250 ff. See also Hare. R. M., Moral Thinking, 1981, pp. 107 ff. Here one may object that in certain cases the principle of subjective openness cannot be followed. If a participant in the discussion aims at establishing a cruel dictatorship, we may ask ourselves whether it is a "rational obligation" to accept such a person as a participant in the discussion. (This question has been raised by Antti Koura and Matti Wiberg).

This criticism does not touch at all our concept of rationality because the latter concerns the *procedure* of discourse, not the material result. Thus also people advocating alien values or unacceptable beliefs should be admitted as participants in the dialogue. The standards of rational discourse are neutral as far as the substance of the discussion is concerned.

The same applies to the principle of honesty (discussed in the text). In certain cases it would be "profitable" to the person concerned not to reveal all his arguments. Such a behaviour could even be well-founded from the moral point of view. However, he does not act in a rational way in doing so. Again, we should distinguish between the standards of rational discourse and the acceptability of the conclusion.

[48] Alexy, *op. cit.*, p. 240.

[49] Alexy, *op. cit.*, p. 240. Regarding the significance of impartiality see Niiniluoto, *Tiede 2000* **1** (1980), p. 4.

[50] Alexy, *op. cit.*, p. 240. In this regard a critic may also claim that the principle of objectivity cannot always be observed in practice. Let us take an example (formulated by Antti Koura and Matti Wiberg): (1) *A* knows that *p*, (2) he cannot reveal all evidence proving *p*, (3) *p* has happened. In other words, *A* knows "more" than he (or she) can tell.

In such a case it may be better for *A* not to tell all his information about *p*. The reason for his behaviour may be that he wants to protect his friend *B* who is accused of a crime. Here the situation is the same as the one discussed in Note 47. The standards of rational discourse presuppose objectivity irrespective of the material consequences. Naturally, *A* may refrain from using certain arguments for the sake of his friend's security, but in doing so he does not behave in a rational way though his behaviour may be approved from a material point of view.

51 *Ibid.*, p. 214. See also Perelman, 'Fünf Vorlesungen', pp. 85 ff., esp. p. 157.

52 *Ibid.*, p. 239. Alexy gives this rule in a general formulation as what amounts to the basic rule of the rationality of discussion: "Jeder Sprecher muss das, was er behauptet, auf Verlangen begründen . . . ".

53 Alexy, *op.cit.*, p. 242.

54 Peczenik, *The Basis of Justification*, p. 86. Cf. Baum Levenbook, Barbara, 'The Role of Coherence in Legal Reasoning', pp. 362 ff.

55 Aarnio, *Denkweisen der Rechtswissenschaft*.

56 Taylor, Charles, 'Interpretation and the Sciences of Man', pp. 8 ff.

57 Perelman, 'Fünf Vorlesungen', p. 92.

58 Alexy, *op. cit.* p. 216.

59 *Ibid.*, p. 244.

60 *Ibid.*

61 See Rescher, Nicholas, *Introduction to Value Theory*, p. 9. See also Toulmin, Stephen, *Reason in Ethics*, pp. 43 ff. Jareborg, in turn, observes, "Value is not a fact. But that *V* is a value is a fact if it is true that *V* is a value" Jareborg, Värderingar, p. 187 (translated here). Regarding this matter, see also Hare, What is a Value Judgement?, pp. 383 ff.

Cf. Brandt, Richard B., *Ethical Theory*, pp. 271 ff. I have dealt with these thematics previously in *Denkweisen der Rechtswissenschaft*, pp. 155 ff. See also Hermerén, Göran, *Värdering och objektivitet*, pp. 82 ff. and Raphael, D. D., *Moral Philosophy*, pp. 11 ff.

62 Stroup, Timothy, 'Edward Westermarck: A Reappraisal', *Man* (*N. S.*) **19**, p. 578.

63 Westermarck, Edward, *Ethical Relativity*, 1932, pp. 195–196.

64 Hare, *Moral Thinking*, p. 228. See also MacCormick, *Legal Reasoning and Legal Theory*, p. 274: "Whatever one's own beliefs, one lives among human beings in a community or various communities. One's fellows have, and one knows they have, moral attitudes towards and moral expectations of oneself, which reflect their moral principles and, perhaps, rules – their moral code".

65 Finch, *op. cit.*, p. 217.

66 *Ibid.*, p. 218.

67 Taylor, Paul W., *Normative Discourse*, p. 168.

68 *Ibid.* p. 171.

69 Taylor, Charles, 'Interpretation and the Sciences of Man', p. 11.

70 Stroup, *op. cit.* pp. 580–581.

71 This section is based on Wittgenstein's 'On Certainty' (published in Finnish as *Varmuudesta* in 1975). I have written a previous article on it: 'Linguistic Philosophy and Legal Theory', *Rechtstheorie*, Beiheft **1** (1979), pp. 17 ff. In general, see Ayer, A. J., Wittgenstein on Certainty, p. 226.

72 *On Certainty*, § 115, cf. § 163.2.

73 *Ibid.*, § 217.

74 *Ibid.*, § 131.

[75] *Ibid.*, § 136.
[76] *Ibid.*, § 144.
[77] *Ibid.*, § 105.
[78] *Ibid.*, § 196.
[79] *Ibid.*, § 209.
[80] *Ibid.*, § 225.
[81] *Ibid.*, § 558.
[82] von Wright, G. H., 'Wittgenstein on Certainty', Section 4.
[83] Cf. Taylor, Charles, *op. cit.*, pp. 6 ff.
[84] von Wright, *op. cit.*, Sections 4 to 6.
[85] Wittgenstein, *On Certainty*, § 94.
[86] Here one can find, however, an interesting link to the idea language grows organically. See about this and its connection to Wittgenstein's conservative attitude J. C. Nyiri, 'Wittgenstein's Later Work in relation to Conservatism', in: *Wittgenstein and his Times* (ed. by Brian McGuinness), pp. 48 ff.
[87] Wittgenstein, *On Certainty*, § 204, cf. § 402.
[88] *Ibid.*, 402.
[89] Aarnio, *On Legal Reasoning*, pp. 126 ff. In general, see Apel, Karl-Otto, 'Analytic Philosophy of Language and the Geisteswissenschaften', *Foundation of Language*, pp. 37 ff. See also Tolonen, Thomas, 'Über die Hermeneutik von Karl-Otto Apel', *Ajatus* XXXIII, pp. 280 ff., esp. p. 282.
[90] Mehtonen, Lauri, 'Näköaloja Ludwig Wittgensteinin myöhäisfilosofiaan', 1973 (mimeograph), p. 16.
[91] Wittgenstein, *On Certainty*, § 262, cf. § 608–612.
[92] Cf. Perelman, 'The New Rhetoric, in Pragmatics of Natural Language' (Y. Bar-Hillel, ed.). 1971, p. 148.
[93] Perelman, 'Eine Studie über Gerichtigkeit', p. 36 ff.
[94] See Alexy, *op. cit.*, pp. 213 ff.
[95] Perelman, 'Fünf Vorlesungen', p. 146 ff. See also p. 153. For a criticism of the universal audience, see Weinberger, Ota, 'Topik und Plausibilitätsargumentation', *ARSP* **1** (1973), pp. 17 ff.
[96] Perelman, op. cit., pp. 153–155. See also *Perelman*, 'Rhetoric and Philosophy', In: *Philosophy and Rhetoric I*, p. 21 and Perelman, *Juristische Logik als Argumentationslehre*, p. 141, which contains the following observation about the universal audience: "In einem solchen Fall appelliert man an die Ratio und branch Argumente, die jedes rationale Wesen akzeptieren müsste".
[97] Perelman, Ch and L. Olbrechts-Tyteca, 'Act and Person in Argument', In: *The Annual Ethics* **61**, 1950/51, p. 252, reprinted in Perelman, *The Idea of Justice and the Problem of Argumentation*, pp. 168 ff. See esp. pp. 188–190.
[98] See e.g. Perelman, 'Fünf Vorlesungen', p. 159.
[99] Habermas, Jürgen, 'Wahrheitstheorien', pp. 255 ff.
[100] Matti Sintonen argues that unanimity is not possible even within an audience. See *Rechtstheorie*, Beiheft **2**, p. 81.
[101] It is important to note another connection with rational acceptability. It is also connected with the question of national sovereignty. See Tolonen, Juha, 'Oikeustieteen edistymisestä', In: (the mimeograph) *Tieteen puolesta*, pp. 42 ff. Tolonen examines the problem of legitimacy in his article. He notes that in the theory of rational acceptability it

is in fact a question of a formulation of a dilemma that was central to the French Revolution: what is a nation and how can it be sovereign.

This can also be used to answer the criticism that accuses the theory represented in this study of arbitrariness. See Klenner, Hermann, a review of Chaim Perelman, *Juristische Logik als Argumentationslehre*, in *Deutsche Literaturzeitung* **1** (1980), pp. 74 ff. Klenner observes *inter alia*, "Droht micht der als neue Rhetorik angepreisenen Juristenlogik . . . also Technik der Rabulistik ge-oder missgebrauch werden?" See also *Backman, Eero*, The Concept of Legal Order and the Problem of Its Determination in the Hermeneutical Theory of Law, p. 33 ff.

EPILOGUE

[1] von Wright, G. H., *Wittgenstein*, p. 207.

[2] von Wright, *op.cit.*, pp. 207–208.

[3] Habermas, Jürgen, *Theorie des kommunikativen Handelns I-II*. See also Habermas, *Moralbewusstsein und kommunikatives Handeln*, especially pp. 53 ff. and pp. 127 ff. Here I only refer to these works in general. See also Panou, Stavros, *Handlungstheorie und Sozialphilosophie*, p. 16 ff.

[4] For Habermas, an evolution is also typical for *Lebenswelt*. The rationality of Lebenswelt is changing – and developing – all the time. This means that the forms of communicative rationality differentiate. Hence, different "parts" of Lebenswelt, i.e. certain types of human relations form their own unities. The disengagement of the system from Lebenswelt presupposes this kind of rational evolution in *Lebenswelt*. The last mentioned must be "mature" for the disengagement.

[5] In this approach the Habermasian theory has not been accepted as such. For instance, the theory of truth (*Wahrheitstheorie*) that is based on the idea of consensus is not the background theory of this work. "Ideale Sprechsituation" (ideal speech situation) – the universal audience in the Perelmanian terminology – guarantees the truth of empirical statements – and for Perelman, the validity of moral statements. Rationality as an ideal for legal discourse does not give such a guarantee. Legal interpretation is neither true nor false. At its best, an interpretation is acceptable by the majority of the rational legal community. However, acceptability is not the same as the truth of a statement. Rationality only guides the optimal procedure of discourse. The contents, i.e. the final result of this procedure depends also e.g. on the values and evaluations. Therefore, legal interpretations cannot be universally "right". Values are relative although people evaluate things in a quite intersubjective way.

The consensus theory of truth is thus not the proper basis for the theory of legal intepretation. On the other hand, in legal reasoning the correspondence theory of truth is too strong. An adequate epistemic model is "between" these two theories. Yet, the theory of communicative actions and the distinction between the system and the world of life is a fruitful framework as far as the deep justification of legal reasoning is concerned. This is so independent of the possible weaknesses in the details of the Habermasian theory.

Summing up: legal reasoning, especially legal decision-making is connected both to the use of societal power and to the human communication. Every theory of legal reasoning must take into account both of these elements. And therefore, Habermas has given valuable clues for us how to solve this dilemma.

See also what Andrés Ollero says about the role of legal philosophy in the above respect. Ollero, *Rechtswissenschaft und Philosophie*, pp. 22–23.

ABBREVIATIONS

ARSP	=	*Archiv für Rechts- und Sozialphilosophie*
JFT	=	*Tidskrift utgiven av Juridiska Föreningen i Finland*
LM	=	*Lakimies* (Journal Published by the Association of Lawyers in Finland)
SSL	=	*Scandinavian Studies in Law*

BIBLIOGRAPHY

Aarnio, Aulis: 1981, '150 anni di filosofia del diritto in Finlandia', in: *Rivista Trimestrale Di Diritto e Procedura Civile* **3**, 809 ff.

Aarnio, Aulis: 1983, 'Argumentation Theory- and Beyond: Some Remarks on the Rationality of Legal Justification', *Rechtstheorie* **4**, 385 ff.

Aarnio, Aulis: 1986, 'On Changes in the Systematics of Law', in: *Vernunft und Erfahrung im Rechtsdenken der Gegenwart* (Hrsg. Torstein-Eckhoff, Lawrence M. Friedman, Jyrki Uusitalo. *Rechtstheorie*, Beiheft **10**, Berlin, 161 ff.)

Aarnio, Aulis: 1979, *Denkweisen der Rechtswissenschaft* (Wien).

Aarnio, Aulis: 1980, 'En analys av arvinges rättsliga ställning', *JFT* **6**, 363 ff.

Aarnio, Aulis: 1983, 'Eternal and Changing Law', in: *Philosophical Perspectives in Jurisprudence*, pp. 94 ff.

Aarnio, Aulis: 1978, 'Kan ett påstående on en rättsregels innehåll vara riktigt?" in: *Uppsalaskolan – och efteråt* (ed. S. Strömholm) (Uppsala), pp. 143 ff.

Aarnio, Aulis: 1969, *Kysymyksiä testamenttioikeuden alalta* (Vammala).

Aarnio, Aulis: 1979, 'Linguistic Philosophy and Legal Theory', *Rechtstheorie, Beiheft* **1**, 17 ff.

Aarnio, Aulis: 1982, Oikeussäännösten tulkinnasta (Helsinki).

Aarnio, Aulis: 1978, 'On Legal Policy Research', *Rechtstheorie* **3**, pp. 301 ff.

Aarnio, Aulis: 1977, *On Legal Reasoning* (Loimaa).

Aarnio, Aulis: 1985, 'On the Justification of Legal Integration', *Revue de Synthèse* **118–119**, pp. 269 ff.

Aarnio, Aulis: 1981, 'On the Paradigm Articukation in Legal Research', *Rechtstheorie, Beiheft* **3**, pp. 45 ff.

Aarnio, Aulis: 1981, 'On the Truth and Acceptability of Interpretative Propositions in Legal Dogmatics', *Rechtstheorie, Beiheft* **2**, 33 ff.

Aarnio, Aulis: 1985, 'Outline of a Hermeneutic Approach in Legal Theory', in: *Philosophical Perspectives in Jurisprudence*, pp. 47 ff.

Aarnio, Aulis: 1983, 'Philosophical Perspectives in Jurisprudence', *Acta Philosophica Fennica* **36**.

Aarnio, Aulis: 1967, *Perillisen oikeusasemasta* (Vammala).

Aarnio, Aulis: 'The Development of Legal Theory and Philosophy of Law in Finland', in: *Philosophical Perspectives in Jurisprudence*, pp. 9 ff.

Aarnio, Aulis: 1980, 'The Form and Content of Law: Aspects of Legal Positivism', *Archivum Juridicum Cracoviense* **XIII**, pp. 17 ff.

Aarnio, Aulis: 1979, 'The Grounding Structures of Law: Reflections on Helmut Coing's Conception of Natural Law', *Rechtstheorie* **9**, 281 ff.

Aarnio, Aulis: 'The Significance of the Theoretical Element in Legal Research', in: *Philosophical Perspectives in Jurisprudence*, pp. 119 ff.

Aarnio, Aulis: 1984, 'Värdena och domarreglerna: Tankar om förhållandet mellan rätt och moral', in: *Festskrift till Jan Hellner* (Stockholm), pp. 7 ff.

Aarnio, Aulis, Robert Alexy, Aleksander Peczenik: 1981, 'The Foundation of Legal

Reasoning, *Rechtstheorie* 1981, pp. 133 ff., pp. 257 ff. and pp. 423 ff. (for a German translation of the article, see Krawietz, Werner and Robert Alexy, 'Methatheorie juristischer Argumentation'.

Aarnio, Aulis and Aleksander Peczenik: 1985, 'Mas alla del realismo: Una critica de la reconstruccion de la dogmatica juridica por Alf Ross', in: *Revista de Ciencias Sociales* **5**, 127 ff. (The same in English: Beyond the Reality, A Criticism of Alf Ross' Reconstruction of Legal Dogmatics. In: *Meaning Interpretation and the Law* (ed. by Alexander Peczenik). Helsinki, 1986, pp. 10 ff.)

Ahlander, Björn: 1952, *Om rätt och rättstillämpning*.

Ahrens, H.: 1870–71, *Naturrecht oder Philosophie des Rechts und des Staates*, Vols. I–II (Berlin) (orig. 1837).

Ahmavaara, Yrjö: 1969, *Informaatio* (Helsinki).

Alanen, Aatos: 1965, *Yleinen oikeustiede ja kansainvälinen yksityis-oikeus* (Vammala).

Albert, Hans: 1957, 'Theorie und Prognose in den Sozialwissenschaften', *Schweitzerische Zeitschrift für Volkswirtschaft und Statistik* **93**, 60 ff.

Alchourrón, Carlos E.: 1983, 'Systematization and Change in the Science of Law, in: *Vernunft und Erfahrung im Rechtsdenken der Gegenwart* (Hrsg. Torstein Eckhoff, Lawrence M. Friedman, Jyrki Uusitalo. *Rechtstheorie*), *Beiheft* **10**, 171.

Alchourrón, Carlos E. and Eugenio Bulygin: 1971, *Normative Systems* (Wien).

Alexy, Robert: 1978, *Theorie der juristischen Argumentation* (Frankfurt am Main).

Alexy, Robert: 1979, 'Zum Begriff des Rechtsprinzips', *Rechtstheorie, Beiheft* **1**, 59ff.

Apel, Karl-Otto: 1967, 'Analytic Philosophy of Language and the Geisteswissenschaften', *Foundation of Language*, Supplementary Series, Vol. 4. (Dordrecht).

Armstrong, D. M.: 1980, 'Nominalism and Realism', *Universals & Scientific Realism*, Volume I (Cambridge).

Ayer, A. J.: 1974, 'Wittgenstein on Certainty', in: *Understanding Wittgenstein*, pp. 266 ff.

Backman, Eero': 1979, 'The Concept of Legal Order and the Problem of Its Determination in the Hermeneutical Theory of Law', in: *Reasoning on Legal Reasoning*, ed. by A. Peczenik and J. Uusitalo (Helsinki), p. 33 ff.

Ballweg, Ottmar and Thomas-Michael Seibert (Hrsg.): 1984, *Rhetorische Rechtstheorie.*

Baum Levenbook, Barbara: 1984, 'The Role of Coherence in Legal Reasoning', in: *Law and Philosophy* **43**, 355 ff.

Benditt, Theodore M.: 1978, *Law as Rule and Principle* (Stanford).

Bjarup, Jes: 1978, *Skandinavischer Realismus* (Freiburg/München).

Björne, Lars: 1984, *Deutsche Rechtssysteme im 18. und 19. Jahrhundert* (Ebelsbach am Main).

Blom, Raimo: 1970, 'Tuomioistuimien toiminnan puolueettomuus rikosasioissa', *Tampereen yliopiston tutkimuslaitos*', D-tiedotteita, No. 40 (Tampere).

Borum, O. A.: 1949, 'Arvefaldet', *Bidrag til arverettens anden del* (København).

Brand, Gerd: 1980: *The Central Texts of Wittgenstein* (Bristol).

Brandt, Richard B.: 1959, *Ethical Theory* (Englewood Cliffs, N.J.).

Brante, Thomas: 1980, *Vetenskapens struktur och förändring* (Lund).

Brusiin, Otto: 1938, *Tuomarin harkinta normin puuttuessa* (Vammala).

Brusiin, Otto: 1959, *Zum Ehescheidungsproblem* (Hyvinkää).

Brusiin, Otto: 1951, *Über das juristische Denken* (Helsinki).

Brusiin, Otto: 1949, *Über die Objektivität der Rechtssprechung* (Helsinki).

Bulygin, Eugenio: 1963, 'El Concepto de Vigencia en Alf Ross', in: *Revista del Colegio de Abogados de la Plata*, pp. 1 ff.
Bulygin, Eugenio: 1986, 'Legal Dogmatics and the Systemazation of Law', in: *Vernunft und Erfahrung im Rechtsdenken der gegenwart*, Hrsg. Torstein Eckhoff, Lawrence M. Friedman, Jyrki Uusitalo. *Rechtstheorie. Beiheft* **10**, 193 ff.
Bydlinski, F.: 1982, Juristische Methodenlehre und Rechtsbegriff (Wien).
Coing, Helmut: 1976, *Grundzüge der Rechtsphilosophie*, 3. Aufl. (Berlin).
Cossio, Carlos: 1969, *La "Causa" Y La Comprension En El Derccho* (Buenos Aires).
Dalberg-Larsen, Jørgen: 1984, *Five Essays on Legal Science* (Kopenhagen).
Dalberg-Larsen, Jørgen: 1977, *Retsvidenskab som samfundsvidenskab* (København).
Dietze, H. H.: 1936, *Naturrecht in der Gegenwart* (Berlin).
Dreier, Ralf: 1981, 'Zur Theoriebildung in der Jurisprudenz', in: *Dreier, Recht – Moral – Ideologie* (Berlin), pp. 70 ff.
Dworkin, Ronald: 1977, 'No Right Aswer?', in: *Law, Morality, and Society: Essays in Honour of H. L. A. Hart*, ed. by P. M. S. Hacken and J. Raz (Oxford), pp. 58 ff.
Dworkin, Ronald: 1978, *Taking Rights Seriously*, 2nd ed. (London).
Eckhoff, Torstein: 1976, 'Guiding Standards in Legal Reasoning', *Current Legal Problems* **29**, 205 ff.
Eckhoff, Torstein and Nils-Kristian Sundby: 1976, *Rettssystemer: Systemteoretisk innforing i rettsfilosofien* (Oslo).
Ekelöf, Per Olof: 1966, 'Semantik och juridik', *SvJT*, pp. 497 ff.
Ekelöf, Per Olof: 1958, 'Teleological Construction of Statutes', *SSL* **2**, 75 ff.
Ekelöf, Per Olof: 1951, *Är den juridiska Doktrinen en teknik eller en vetenstap*? (Stockholm).
Engish, K.: 1971, *Einführung in das juristische Denken*, 5. Aufl. (Stuttgart, Berlin, Köln, Mainz).
Eriksson, Lars D.: 1980, *Marxistisk teori och rättsvetenskap* (Helsinki).
Eriksson, Lars D.: 1979, 'Om olika argumentationsmodeller', *JFT*, 25 ff.
Esser, Josef: 1972, *Vorverständnis und Methodenwahl in der Rechtsfindung*, 2. Aufl. (Frankfurt am Main).
Finch, Henry LeRoy: 1977, *Wittgenstein – The Later Philosophy* (Atlantic Highlands, N.J.).
Frank, Jerome: 1963, *Law and the Modern Mind* (Garden City, N.J.).
Frändberg, Åke: 1973, *Om analog användning av rättsnormer* (Uppsala).
Furberg, Mats: 1971, *Saying and Meaning, A Main Theme in J. L. Austin's Philsophy* (Oxford).
Gizbert-Studnicki, Tomasz: 1985, 'How Many Theories of Truth are Needed in Jurisprudence?', in: *Conditions of Validity and Cognition in Modern Legal Thought* (ed. by Neil MacCormick, Stavros Panou and Luigi Lombardi Vallauri), *ARSP. Beiheft* **25** (Stuttgart), pp. 153 ff.
Germann, O. A.: 1946, *Methodische Grundfragen* (Bern).
Golding, Martin P.: 1984, *Legal Reasoning* (New York).
Golding, Martin P.: 1970, 'Principled Decision-Making and the Supreme Court', in: *Essays in Legal Philosophy* (ed. by Robert S. Summers) (Oxford), pp. 208 ff.
Guastini, Riccardo: 1982/1983, 'Six Concepts of "Constitutive Rule"', in: *Annali della Facolta di Giurisprudenza di Genova* **1–2**, 487 ff.

Guastini, Riccardo: 1984, 'A Tentative Analysis of Two Juristic Sentences', in: *Theory of Legal Science* (A Peczenik *et al.* eds.) (Dordrecht), pp. 571 ff.

Habermas, Jürgen: 1983, *Moralbewusstsein und kommunikatives Handeln* (Frankfurt am Main).

Habermas, Jürgen: 1972, *Theorie und Praxis*, 4. Aufl. (Frankfurt am Main).

Habermas, Jürgen: 1981, *Theorie des kommunikativen Handelns: Zur Kritik der funktionalistischen Vernunft* I–II (Frankfurt am Main).

Habermas, Jürgen: 1973, 'Wahrheitstheorien', in: *Wirklichkeit und Reflexion. Festschrift für W. Schulz* (Hrsg. H.Fahrenbach) (Pfullingen).

Hare, R. M.: 1952, *Language of Morals* (London).

Hare, R. M.: 1981, *Moral Thinking* (London).

Hare, R. M.: 1954/1955, 'Universalisability', in: *Proceedings of the Aristotelian Society* **55**, 295 ff.

Hart, H. L. A.: 1961, *The Concept of Law* (Oxford).

Helin, Markku: 1983, 'On the Semantics of the Interpretative Sentences in Legal Dogmatics', in: *Essays in Legal Theory in Honor of Kaarle Makkonen*(Vammala), pp. 63 ff.

Hermerén, Göran: 1972, *Värdering och objektivitet* (Lund).

Hertzberg, Lars and Matti Sintonen: 'On Language as an Object of Empirical Investigation', *Ajatus* **38**, pp. 148 ff.

Hertzberg, Lars: 1981, 'Science an Certainty', in: *Essays in Philosophical Analysis* (ed. Ingemar Pörn) (Helsinki), pp. 60 ff.

Hinderling, Hans-Georg: 1971, *Rechtsnorm und Verstehen* (Bern).

Hintikka, Jaakko: 1957, 'Arvokäsitteistä sosiaalitieteiden metodiopissa', *Ajatus* **XX**, 27 ff.

Holmes, Oliver Wendell:1921, 'The Path of the Law', in: *Collective Legal Papers* (New York), pp. 173 ff.

Holopainen, Toivo: 1977, 'Normin mukaista vai tavoitteiden suuntaista?', *LM*, pp. 627 ff.

Honkasalo, Brynolf: 1965, *Suomen rikosoikeus. Yleiset opit.* Ensimmainen osa. 2 ed. (Hämeenlinna).

Hutcheson, Joseph C., Jr.: 1928, 'The Judgement Intuitive: The Function of the 'Hunch' in Judicial Decision', *Cornell Law Quarterly* **14**, 279 ff.

Illum, Knud: 1945, *Lov og Ret* (København).

Illum, Knud: 1968, 'Some Reflections on the Method of Legal Science and on Legal Reasoning', *SSL*, pp. 49 ff.

Jareborg, Nils.: 1974, *Begrepp och brottsbeskrivning* (Stockholm).

Jareborg, Nils: 1979, 'Regler och ritlinjer', *TfR*, pp. 385 ff.

Jareborg, Nil: 1975, *Värderingar* (Lund).

Jonsson, Inge: 1982, 'Riktningar inom 1800-talets hermeneutik', in: *Symposium Proceedings, "Tolkning och tolkningsteorier"* (Stockholm), pp. 65 ff.

Jørgensen, Stig: 1969, 'Argumentation and Decision', *Festskrift til professor, dr. jur. & phil. Alf Ross* (København), p. 381.

Jørgensen, Stig: 1983, *Law and Society* (Aarhus).

Jørgensen, Stig: 1970, *Ret og samfund* (København).

Karsten, Rafael: 1941, *Filosofinen etiikka* (Loviisa).

Kaufmann, Arthur: 1982, *Analogie und der Natur der Sache*, 2 Aufl.

Kaufmann, Arthur: 1983, 'Rechtsphilosophie und Nationalsozialismus', *ARSP Beiheft* **18**, 14 ff.

Kaufmann, Arthur and Winfried Hassemer: 1977, *Einführung in Rechtsphilosophie und Rechtstheorie der Gegenwart* (Heidelberg-Karlsruhe).
Kelsen, Hans: 1928, *Die philosophischen Grundlagen der Naturrechtslehre und Rechtspositivismus* (Charlottenburg).
Kelsen, Hans: 1960, *Reine Rechtslehre*, 2 Aufl. (Wien).
Kenny, Anthony: 1982, 'Wittgenstein on the Nature of Philosophy', in: *Wittgenstein and his Times* (ed. Brian McGuinness) (Oxford), pp. 13 ff.
Kerimov, D. A. A.: 1977, *Philosophische Probleme des Rechts* (Berlin).
Kerimov, D. A. A.: 1981, *Verfassung der USSR und politisch-rechtliche Theorie* (Berlin).
Kivivuori, Antti: 1969, *Suomen vahingonkorvauslainsäädännön kehitys* (Joensuu). I.
Klami, Hannu Tapani: 1980, 'Anti-Legalism', *Five Essays in the Finalistic Theory of Law* (Turku).
Klami, Hannu Tapani: Dualism of Law. In: *Objektivierung des Rechtsdenkens: Gedächtnisschrift für Ilmar Tammelo* (Berlin), pp. 471 ff.
Klami, Hannu Tapani: 1979, *Finalistinen oikeusteoria* (Turku).
Klami, Hannu Tapani: 1984, *Gewohnheitsrecht als Rechtsquelle* (Turku).
Klami, Hannu Tapani: 1982, 'Legal Heuristics: A Theoretical Skeleton', in: *Oikeustiede* (Vammala), s. 7ss.
Klemner, Hermann: 1972, *Rechtsleere* (Berlin).
Klemner, Hermann: 1980, Review about: 'Chain Perelman, Juristische Logik als Argumentationslehre', in: *Deutsche Literaturzeitung* **1**, 74 ff.
Klemner, Hermann: 1984, *Vom Recht der Natur des Rechts* (Berlin).
Klug, Ulrich: 1966, *Juristische Logik*, 3 Aufl. (Berlin, Heidelberg, New York).
Koch, Hans-Joachim and Helmut Rüssman: 1982, *Juristische Begründungslehre* (München).
Kommentar zum Allgemeinen Gesetzbuch: 1964 (hrsg. von Heinrich Klang und Franz Gschnitzer). Erster Band, erster Halbband (Wien).
Krawietz, Werner and Robert Alexy (Hrsg.): 1983, *Metatheorie juristischer Argumentation* (Berlin).
Krawietz, Werner: 1984, 'Begründung des Rechts – antropologisch betrachtet: zur Institutionentheorie von Weinberger und Schelsky', in: *Theorie der Normen. Festgabe für Ota Weinberger zum 65. Geburtstag* (Hrsg. Werner Krawietz, Helmut Schelsky, Günther Winkler, Alfred Schramm) (Berlin), pp. 541 ff.
Krawietz, Werner: 1978, *Juristische Entscheidung und wissenschaftliche Erkenntnis* (Wien, New York).
Krawietz, Werner: 1981, 'Rechtssystem und Rationalität in der juristischen Dogmatik', *Rechtstheorie, Beiheft* **2**, 299ff.
Krawietz, Werner: 1984, 'Recht und Rationalität in der modernen Systemtheorie', in: *Objektivierung des Rechtsdenkens: Gedächtnisschrift für Ilmar Tammelo*(Hrsg. Werner Krawietz, Theo Mayer-Maly, Ota weinberger) (Berlin), pp. 724 ff.
Kripke, Saul, A.: 1982, *Wittgenstein on Rules and Private Language* (Oxford).
Kuhn, Thomas S.: 1970, *The Structure of Scientific Revolutions*, 2 ed. (1 ed. 1962) (Chicago).
Laakso, Seppo: 1980, *Oikeuden systeemiyhteys puhtaassa oikeusopissa* (Tampere).
Laakso, Seppo: 1980, *Puhtaan oikeusopin problematiikkaa. Oikeustiede*, s. 91ss.
Laakso, Seppo: 1980, *Über die Dreidimensionalität des Rechts und des juristischen Denkens* (Tampere).

Lahtinen, Osvi: 1966, 'Von konstruierten Denkschemas und von der Sprache', in: *Ius humanum. Studia in honorem Otto Brusiin* (Turku), pp. 87 ff.
Lahtinen, Osvi: 1951, *Zum Aufbau der rechtlichen Grundlagen* (Helsinki).
Larenz, Karl: 1975, *Methodenlehre der Rechtswissenschaft*, 3 Aufl.
Lauridsen, Preben Stuer: 1974, *Studier i retspolitisk argumentation* (København).
Lucas, J. R.: 1980, *On Justice* (Oxford).
MacCormick, Neil: 'Dworkin as Pre-Benthamite', *Philosophical Review* **LXXXVII** (4), pp. 585 ff.
MacCormick, Neil: 1978, *Legal Reasoning and Legal Theory* (Oxford).
MacCormick, Neil: 1982, 'Legal Reasoning and Practical Reason', *Mid-West Studies in Philosophy*.
MacCormick, Neil: 1974, 'Principles of Law', in: *Juridical Review* **19**, pp. 217 ff.
Makkonen, Kaarle: 1959, 'Ajatuksia juridisen kielen loogisesta analyysista', *LM*, p. 49 ff.
Makkonen, Kaarle: 1966, 'Der Ausdruck "subjektives Recht" in der juristischen Sprache', in: *Ius humanum: Studia in honorem Otto Brusiin* (Turku), pp. 112 ff.
Makkonen, Kaarle: 1965, *Zur Problematik der juridischen Entscheidung* (Turku).
Malmström, Åke: 1938, *Succionsrättsliga studier* (Stockholm).
Mehtonen, Lauri: 1973, 'Näköaloja Ludwig Wittgensteinin myöhäisfilosofiaan', *Dialectica ry, Dilemma ry: julkaisusarja nro* **2** (Tampere) (moniste).
Naess, Arne: 1961, *Empirisk semantik* (Oslo).
Naess, Arne: 1953, *Interpretation and Preciseness: A Contribution to the Theory of Communication* (Oslo).
Niiniluoto, Ilkka: 1983, 'Analogy and Legal Reasoning', in: *Essays in Legal Theory in Honor of Kaarle Makkonen* (Vammala), pp. 177 ff.
Niiniluoto, Ilkka: 1974, 'Fallibilismista', *Sosiologia* **5** (6), 275 ff.
Niiniluoto, Ilkka: 1980, *Johdatus tieteenfilosofiaan* (Keuruu).
Niiniluoto, Ilkka: 1981, 'Language, Norms and Truth', Essays in Philosophical Analysis (ed. Ingemar Pörn), *Acta Philosophica Fennica* **32**, 168 ff.
Niiniluoto, Ilkka: 1981, 'On Truth and Argumentation in Legal Domatics', *Rechtstheorie, Beiheft* **2**, pp. 53 ff.
Niiniluoto, Ilkka: 1981, 'On the Truth of Norm Propositions', *Rechtstheorie, Beiheft* **3**, 171 ff.
Niiniluoto, Ilkka: 1980, 'Tieteen tuntomerkit', *Tiede 2000* **1**, 5 ff.
Niiniluoto, Ilkka: 1985, 'Truth and Legal Norms. Condition of Validity and Cognition in Modern Legal Thought' (ed. by Neil MacCormick, Stavros Panou and Luigi Lombardi Vallauri), *ARSP Beiheft* **25**, 168 ff.
Oker-Blom, Max: 1968, 'En enda riktig lösning trots allt? Dworkin mot finländsk bakgrund', *JFT*, pp. 251 ff.
Ollero, Andrés: 1978, *Rechtswissenschaft und Philosophie*, Grundlagendiskussion in Deutschland (Edelsbach).
Olivecrona, Karl: 1971, *Law as Fact*, 2nd ed. (London).
Olivecrona, Karl: 1966, *Rättsordningen*, 2 uppl. (Lund).
Panou, Stavros: 1984, *Handlungstheorie und Sozialphilosophie* (München).
Patoluoto, Ilkka: 1975, *Yhteiskuntatieteen ja politiikan suhteet. Jälkipuhe N. G. Runcimanin teoksen Yhteiskuntatiede ja poliittinen teoria suomennoksen toiseen painokseen* (Helsinki), pp. 194 ff.
Peczenik, Aleksander: 1984, 'Creativity and Transformation in Legal Research', in: *Theo-*

rie der Normen. Festgabe für Ota Weinberger zum 65. Geburtstag (Hrsg. Werner Krawietz, Helmut Schelsky, Günther Winkler, Alfred Schramm) (Berlin), pp. 277 ff.

Peczenik, Aleksander: 1969, 'Empirical Foundations of Legal Dogmatics', in: *Essays in Legal Theory* (Copenhagen), pp. 9 ff.

Peczenik, Aleksander: 1983, *The Basis of Legal Justification* (Lund).

Peczenik, Aleksander: 1969, *Essays in Legal Theory* (Copenhagen).

Peczenik, Aleksander: 1983, 'Is there Always a Right Answer to a Legal Question?', in: *Essays in Legal Theory in Honor of Kaarle Makkonen* (Vammala), pp. 239 ff.

Peczenik, Aleksander: 1983, *Grundlagen der juristischen Argumentation* (Wien, New York).

Peczenik, Aleksander: 1974, *Juridikens metodproblem* (Stockholm).

Peczenik, Aleksander: 1984, 'Legal Data. An Essay about the Ontology of Law', in: *Theory of Legal Science* (eds. A. Peczenik *et al.*) (Dordrecht), pp. 97 ff.

Peczenik, Aleksander: 1984, 'Legal Research. Growth of Science and Moral Theory', in: *Objektivierung des Rechtsdenkens. Gedächtnisschrift für Ilmar Tammelo* (Berlin), pp. 137 ff.

Peczenik, Aleksander: 1979, 'Non-equivalent Transformations and the Law', in: *Reasoning on Legal Reasoning* (eds. A. Peczenik and J. Uusitalo) (Helsinki), pp. 96 ff.

Peczenik, Aleksander: 1969, 'Norms and Reality', in: *Essays in Legal Theory*, pp. 9 ff.

Peczenik, Aleksander: 1981, 'On the Nature and Function of the Grundnorm', *Rechtstheorie, Beiheft* **2** (Berlin), pp. 279 ff.

Peczenik, Aleksander: 1975, 'The Structure of a Legal System', *Rechtstheorie* **1** (2), pp. 1 ff.

Perelman, Chaim: 1967, 'Eine Studie über die Gerechtigkeit', in: *Über die Gerechtigkeit* (München), pp. 9 ff.

Perelman, Chaim: 1967, 'Fünf Vorlesungen über die Gerechtigkeit', in: *Über die Gerechtigkeit* (München), pp. 85 ff.

Perelman, Chaim: 1979, *Juristische Logik als Argumentationslehre*.

Perelman, Chaim: 1963, *The Idea of Justice and the Problem of Argument* (London).

Perelman, Chaim: 1971, 'The New Rhetoric', in: *Pragmatics of Natural Language* (ed. Y. Bar-Hillel) (Dordrecht), pp. 148 ff.

Perelman, Chaim: 1979, 'The Rational and the Reasonable', in: *The New Rhetoric and the Humanistics: Essays on Rhetoric and its Applications* (Dordrecht), pp. 117 ff.

Perelman, Chaim: 1968, 'Rhetoric and Philosophy', in: *Philosophy and Rhetoric I*, pp. 15 ff.

Perelman, Chaim and L. Olbrechts-Tyteca: 1950/1951, 'Act and Person in Argument', *Ethics* **61**, 252 ff.

Peschka, Vilmos: 1982, *Die Theorie der Rechtsnormen* (Budapest).

Petev, Valentin: 1984, 'Rechtsquellenlehre und Reine Rechtslehre', *Rechtstheorie, Beiheft* **5**, 273 ff.

Popper, Karl R.: 1972, *Objective Knowledge: An Evolutionary Approach* (Oxford).

Pöyhönen, Juha: 1985, 'Knowledge in Law and the Possibility of an Alternative Legal Domestics', in: *On the Utility of Legal Theory* (eds. A. Aarnio and M. Van Hoecke (Kangasala).

Pöyhönen, Juha: 1981, *Juridisista teorioista*.

Radin, Max: 1963, 'Case Law and Stare Decisis', in: *Essays on Jurisprudence from the Columbia Law Review*, pp. 3 ff.

Rahlf, Joachim: 1976, 'Die Rolle der historischen Auslegungsmethode in der Rechtsprechung des BHG', in: *Juristische Dogmatik und Wissenschaftstheorie* (Hrsg. E. van Savigny, V. Neumann and J. Rahlf) (München), pp. 27 ff.

Raphael, D. D.: 1981, *Moral Philosophy* (Oxford).

Raz, Joseph: 1979, *The Authority of Law* (Oxford).

Raz, Joseph: 1970, *The Concept of a Legal System* (Oxford).

Regnell, Hans: 1982, *Att beskriva och förklara. Vad det kan innebära inom olika forskningsområden* (Stockholm).

Regnell, Hans: 1965, *Semantik* (Stockholm).

Rescher, Nicholas: 1973, *Coherence Theory of Truth* (Oxford).

Rescher, Nicholas: 1969, *Introduction to Value Theory* (Englewood Cliffs, N.J.).

Ross, Alf: 1968, *Directives and Norms* (London).

Ross, Alf: 1953, *Om ret og retfaerdighed* (København).

Ross, Alf: 1958, *On Law and Justice* (London).

Ross, Alf: 1961, 'Validity and the Conflict Between Legal Positivism and Natural Law', *Revista Jurídica de Buenos Aires* **IV**, 71 ff.

Saarenpää, Ahti E.: 1984, 'Court Decisions as the Focus of Study', in: *SSL*, pp. 123 ff.

Saarenpää, Ahti E.: 1980, *Rutiinijuttu*, Reports from the Project for the Study of Legal Research. No. 2 (Helsinki).

Saarenpää, Ahti E.: 1980, *Tasajaon Periaate* (Vammala).

Searle, J. R.: 1969, *Speech Acts: An Essay in the Philosophy of Language* (London).

Searle, J. R.: 1972, 'What is a Speech Act?', in: *The Philosophy of Language* (ed. J. R. Searle), pp. 39 ff.

Simmonds, N. E.: 1980, 'Law as a Rational Science', *ARSP*, pp. 535 ff.

Sintonen, Matti: 1981, 'Problems of Interpration and Truth in Legal Dogmatics, *Rechtstheorie, Beiheft* **2** (Berlin), pp. 77 ff.

Stenius, Erik: 1970, 'Wittgensteinin "puhtaan kielen kritiikki"', in: *Filosofian tila ja tulevaisuus* (eds. J. Hintikka ja L. Routila) (Helsinki), pp. 45 ff.

Stroup, Timothy: *Edward Westermarck: A Reappraisal*, Man (N.S.) 19, pp. 575 ff.

Strömholm, Stig: 1976, *Allgemeine Rechtslehre* (Göttingen).

Strömhlm, Stig: 1982, 'Juridisk tolkningsmetodik före 1800-talets "moderna genombrott"', in: *Symposium Proceedings 'Tolkning och tolkningsteorie'* (Stockholm), pp. 47 ff.

Strömholm, Stig: 1966, 'Legislative Material and Constitution of Statutes', *SSL*, pp. 173 ff.

Strömholm, Stig: 1981, *Rätt, rättskällor och rättstillämpning* (Stockholm).

Summers, Robert S. (ed.): 1970, *Essays in Legal Philosophy* (Reprint Oxford).

Summers, Robert S. (ed.): 1982, *Instrumentalism and American Legal Theory* (Ithaca).

Summers, Robert S. (ed.): 1971, *More Essays in Legal Philosophy* (Oxford).

Summers, Robert S. (ed.): 1981, 'Pragmatic Instrumentalism in Twentieth Century American Legal Thought – A Synthesis and Critique of Our Dominant General Theory about Law and Its Use', *Cornell Law Review* **66**, 861 ff.

Summers, Robert S. (ed.): 1978, 'The Types of Substantive Reasons: The Core of a Theory of Common Law Justification', *Cornell Law Review* **63**, 724 ff. (Published also in *ARSP, Beiheft* **11**).

Summers, Robert S. and Leigh B. Kelley: 1981, '"Economist Reasons" for Common Law Decisions – A Preliminary Inquiry', *Oxford Journal of Legal Studies* **1** (2), 213 ff.

Tammelo, Ilmar: 1977, *Theorie der Gerechtigkeit* (Freiburg-München).
Tammelo, Ilmar: 1978, 'Zetetische Verfahren für juristischen Aufweisen', *Rechtstheorie* **4**, 421 ff.
Tammelo, Ilmar and Helmut Schreiner: 1974, *Grundzüge und Grundverfahren der Rechtslogik. 1* (Pullach bei München).
Taylor, Charles: 1971, 'Interpretation and the Sciences of Man', *Review of Metaphysics*, pp. 1 ff.
Taylor, Paul W.: 1961, *Normative Discourse* (Englewood Cliffs, N.J.).
Tolonen, Juha: 1974, *Der allgemeine Erklärungshintergrund der wirtschaftlichen Ordnung und seine Anwendung auf das Aktiengesellschaftsrecht* (Helsinki).
Tolonen, Juha: 1982, 'Oikeustieteen edistymisestä', in: *Tieteen puolesta* (Turku), pp. 49 ff.
Tolonen, Tuomas: 'Über die Hermeneutik von Karl-Otto Apel', *Ajatus* **XXXIII**, pp. 280 ff.
Toulmin, Stephen: 1976, *Knowing & Acting. An Invitation to Philosophy* (New York).
Toulmin, Stephen: 1968, *Reason in Ethics* (Cambridge).
Toulmin, Stephen: 1958, *The Uses of Argument* (Cambridge).
Toulmin, Stephen, Richard Rielke, and Allan Janik: 1979, *An Introduction to Reasoning* (New York).
Tuori, Kaarlo: 1985, 'Oikeusnormien asettamismenettelyt ja oikeuden krüsitendenssit', *Politiikka* **3**, 189 ff.
Uusitalo, Jyrki: 1980, *Tieteen dynamiikka tutkimusilmiönä.* Reports from the Project for the Study of Legal Research: No. 1 (Helsinki).
Vernengo, Roberto J.: 1976, *Curso De Teoria General Del Derecho* (Buenos Aires).
Vernengo, Roberto J.: 1960, 'La Funcion sistematica de la Norma Fundamental', in: *Revista Juridica de Buenos Aires* **I–II**, 3 ff.
Victor, Dag: 1977, *Rättsystem och vetenske* (Stockholm).
Villa, Vittorio: 1984, Legal Science and Hermeneutic Point of View', in: *Theory of Legal Science* (eds. A. Peczenik *et al.*) (Dordrecht), pp. 509 ff.
Villa, Vittorio: 1984, *Teorie della Scienza Giuridica e Teorie Delle Scienze Naturali.* Modelli Ed Analogie.
Walter, Robert: 1983, 'Das Auslegungsproblem im Lichte der Reinen Rechtslehre', in: *Festschrift für Ulrich Klug zum 70. Geburtstag* (Mainz), pp. 187 ff.
Weinberger, Ota: 1981, 'Analytisch-Dialektische Gerechtigkeitstheorie', *Rechtstheorie, Beiheft* **3** 307 ff.
Weinberger, Ota: 1984, '"Is and "Ought" Reconsidered', *ARSP*, pp. 474 ff.
Weinberger, Ota: 1984, 'Logik und Objektivierung der juristischen Argumentation', in: *Objektivierung des Rechtsdenkens. Gedächtnisschrift für Ilmar Tammelo* (Hrsg. Werner Krawietz, Theo Mayer-Maly, and Ota Weinberger) (Berlin).
Weinberger, Ota: 1984, 'Logik, Wirklichkeit und Positivität in der Reinen Rechtslehre', *Rechtstheorie, Beiheft* **5**, 425 ff.
Weinberger, Ota: 1973, 'Topik und Plausibilitätsargumentation', *ARSP* **1**, 17 ff.
Weinberger, Christiane & Ota: 1979, *Logik, Semantik und Hermeneutik.* Westermark, Edward: 1908, *The Origin and Development of the Moral Ideas*, Vol. II (Vol. I 1906).
Wikström, Kauko: 1983, 'How to Prove Propositions in Legal Dogmatics', in: *Essays in Legal Theory in Honor of Kaarle Makkonen* (Vammala), pp. 297 ff.
Wikström, Kauko: 1979, *Oikeuskäytännön tulkinnasta.* Erittely oikeusnormien sovelta-

mistoiminnasta esitettävien väitteiden teoreettisista perusteista ja oikeuskäytännön rakenteesta (Vammala).

Wimmer, Franz: 1981, 'By What Criteria Can Progress in Legal Theory be Determined?', *Rechtstheorie, Beiheft* **3**, 35 ff.

Wimmer, Franz: 1979, 'Überlegungen zu Tammelos Unterscheidung von Euduktion, Perduktion und Seduktion', *Rechtstheorie* **3**, 338 ff.

Winch, Peter: 1970, *The Idea of a Social Science and Its Relation to Philosophy*, Sixth Impression (London).

Wittgenstein, Ludwig: 1969, *On Certainty*, eds. G. E. M. Anscombe and G. H. von Wright (Oxford).

Wittgenstein, Ludwig: 1967, *Philosophical Investigations* (Oxford).

Wittgenstein, Ludwig: 1967, *Zettel* (eds. G. E. M. Anscombe and G. H. von Wright).

von Wright, Georg Henrik: 1968, 'An Essay in Deontic Logic and the General Theory of Action', *Acta Philosophica Fennica.*

von Wright, Georg Henrik: 1985, 'Is and Ought', in: *Man, Law and Modern Forms of Life*, Law and Philosophy Library, pp. 263 ff.

von Wright, Georg Henrik: 1971, *Explanation and Understanding* (London).

von Wright, Georg Henrik: 1985, 'Is and Ought', in: *Man, Law and Modern Forms of Life* (eds. E. Bulygin, J.-L. Gardles, and J. Nüniluoto), pp. 263 ff.

von Wright, Georg Henrik: 1981, *Humanismi elämänasenteena* (Keuruu).

von Wright, Georg Henrik: 1958, *Logiikka, filosofia ja kieli* (Keuruu).

von Wright, Georg Henrik: 1963, *Norm and Action* (London).

von Wright, Georg Henrik: 1968, *Normien eksistenssi*, Lecture (Mimeograph) (Helsinki).

von Wright, Georg Henrik: 1963, 'Normit ja logiikka', *Ajatus*, pp. 255 ff.

von Wright, Georg Henrik: 1982, 'Wittgenstein in Relation to His Times', in: *Wittgenstein and His Times* (ed. Brian McGuinness) (Oxford), pp. 117 ff.

von Wright, Georg Henrik: 1972, 'Wittgenstein on Certainty', in: *Problems in the Theory of Knowledge* (ed. G. H. von Wright) (Den Haag).

von Wright, Georg Henrik: 1982, *Wittgenstein* (Oxford).

Wróblewski, Jerzy: 1984, 'Dilemmas of the Normativistic Concept of Legal System', *Rechtstheorie, Beiheft* **5**, 319 ff.

Wróblewski, Jerzy: 1983, 'Fuzziness of Legal System', in: *Essays in Legal Theory in Honor of Kaarle Makkonen* (Vammala), pp. 311 ff.

Wróblewski, Jerzy: 1979, 'Justification of Legal Decisions. Revue Internale de Philosophie', *La Nouvelle Rhetorique. Essais en hommage a Chaim Perelman* **127–128**, pp. 277 ff.

Wróblewski, Jerzy: 1971, *Legal Decision and Its Justification*, Proceeding of the World Congress for Legal and Social Philosophy (Brussels) (ed. H. Hubien), pp. 233 ff.

Wróblewski, Jerzy: 1983, *Meaning and Truth in Judicial Decision*, 2nd edition (ed. Aulis Aarnio).

Wróblewski, Jerzy: 1974, 'Legal Syllogism and Rationality of Judicial Decision', *Rechtstheorie* **5**, pp. 33 ff.

Wróblewski, Jerzy: 1984, 'Paradigms of Justifying Legal Decisions', in: *Theory of Legal Science* (eds. A. Peczenik *et al.*) (Dordrecht), pp. 253 ff.

Wróblewski, Jerzy: 1972, 'System of Norms and Legal System', *Rivista Internationale di filosofia del Diritto* **2**, pp. 281 ff.

Wróblewski, Jerzy: 1979, 'Verification and Justification in the Legal Sciences', *Rechtstheorie, Beiheft* **1**, 195 ff.

Zippelius, Reinhold: 1982, *Rechtsphilosophie* (München).

Zitting, Simo: 1952, 'Omistajan oikeuksista ja velvollisuuksista I–II', *LM*, pp. 378 ff and 501 ff.

Zitting, Simo: 1951, *Omistajanvaihdoksesta silmälläpitäen erityisesti lainhuudatuksen vaikutuksia* (Vammala).

Zuleta Puceiro, Enrique: 1981, *Paradigma Dogmatico y Ciencia del Derecho* (Madrid).

Zuleta Puceiro, Enrique: 1983, 'Scientific Paradigms and Legal Change', in: *Essays in Legal Theory in Honor of Kaarle Makkonen* (Vammala), pp. 331 ff.

Zuleta Puceiro, Enrique: 1981, 'System and Function in Legal Dogmatics', *Rechtstheorie, Beiheft* **2**, 349 ff.

INDEX

Only the authors who are referred to in the text are mentioned in the index.